Mechanics 2
for AQA

CAMBRIDGE
UNIVERSITY PRESS

The School Mathematics Project

SMP AS/A2 Mathematics writing team Spencer Instone, John Ling, Paul Scruton, Susan Shilton, Heather West

SMP design and administration Melanie Bull, Pam Keetch, Nicky Lake, Cathy Syred, Ann White

The authors thank Sue Glover for the technical advice she gave when this AS/A2 project began and for her detailed editorial contribution to this book. The authors are also very grateful to those teachers who advised on the book at the planning stage and commented in detail on draft chapters.

CAMBRIDGE UNIVERSITY PRESS
Cambridge, New York, Melbourne, Madrid, Cape Town, Singapore, São Paulo, Delhi, Dubai, Tokyo, Mexico City

Cambridge University Press
The Edinburgh Building, Cambridge CB2 8RU, UK

www.cambridge.org
Information on this title: www.cambridge.org/9780521605328

© The School Mathematics Project 2005

First published 2005
Reprinted 2008, 2010

Printed in the United Kingdom by Short Run Press, Exeter

A catalogue record for this publication is available from the British Library

ISBN 978-0-521-60532-8 Paperback

Typesetting and technical illustrations by The School Mathematics Project
Illustrations on pages 10, 24, 84 and 92 by Chris Evans

The authors and publisher are grateful to the Assessment and Qualifications Alliance for permission to reproduce questions from past examination papers. Individual questions are marked AQA.

Using this book

Each chapter begins with a **summary** of what the student is expected to learn.

The chapter then has sections lettered A, B, C, ... (see the contents overleaf). In most cases a section consists of development material, worked examples and an exercise.

The **development material** interweaves explanation with questions that involve the student in making sense of ideas and techniques. Development questions are labelled according to their section letter (A1, A2, ..., B1, B2, ...) and answers to them are provided.

D Some development questions are particularly suitable for discussion – either by the whole class or by smaller groups – because they have the potential to bring out a key issue or clarify a technique. Such **discussion questions** are marked with a bar, as here.

K **Key points** established in the development material are marked with a bar as here, so the student may readily refer to them during later work or revision. Each chapter's key points are also gathered together in a panel after the last lettered section.

The **worked examples** have been chosen to clarify ideas and techniques, and as models for students to follow in setting out their own work. Guidance for the student is in italic.

The **exercise** at the end of each lettered section is designed to consolidate the skills and understanding acquired earlier in the section. Unlike those in the development material, questions in the exercise are denoted by a number only.

Starred questions are more demanding.

After the lettered sections and the key points panel there may be a set of **mixed questions**, combining ideas from several sections in the chapter; these may also involve topics from earlier chapters.

Every chapter ends with a selection of **questions for self-assessment** ('Test yourself').

Included in the mixed questions and 'Test yourself' are **past AQA exam questions**, to give the student an idea of the style and standard that may be expected, and to build confidence.

Contents

1 Moments

In this chapter you will learn
• what is meant by the moment of a force
• about the conditions for equilibrium of a rigid body

Key points from Mechanics 1

• A particle is an object that can be treated as if it were a point, so that all forces acting on it act at the same point.

• A set of forces acting at a point is said to be in equilibrium if the resultant is zero. If the forces are in equilibrium, the total component in any direction is zero.

• The normal reaction, of magnitude R, is the force at right angles to a surface which the surface exerts on an object in contact with it.

• A rough surface can offer a friction force parallel to the surface. This friction force has a maximum magnitude given by $F_{max} = \mu R$, where μ is the coefficient of friction.

• When the magnitude F of the friction force on an object is at its maximum, so that the object is about to move, the object is said to be in limiting equilibrium. If the object is in equilibrium but not limiting equilibrium, then $F < \mu R$.

• An object of mass m kg has a weight of mg newtons ($g = 9.8 \, \text{m s}^{-2}$).

A Moment of a force (answers p 146)

In the situations studied in Mechanics 1, we looked at forces acting on a particle. In this case all the forces act at the same point.

If the object is not a particle, it is possible for the forces acting on it to be applied at different points.

For example, imagine that a ruler is placed on a smooth horizontal table and you are looking down on it.
In the first diagram below, two forces that are equal and opposite act on the ruler at the same point.
In the second diagram, the same two forces act at different points.

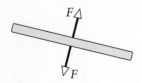

(D)   **A1** Describe what happens to the ruler in each case.

In the second case the two forces are equal and opposite but are not in equilibrium. Because their **lines of action** are different (in fact parallel), the effect on the ruler is different – it will turn.

The ruler is an example of a **rigid body**: this means an object that is not distorted by the forces acting on it – it stays the same shape and size.

D   **A2** A spanner is used to loosen a nut. A force is applied to the spanner as shown. Describe the effect of the force in each case shown.

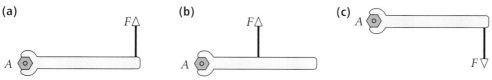

The turning effect of a force depends not only on the magnitude of the force but also on its point of application. If the magnitude stays the same but the line of action is moved further away from the point A about which the spanner turns, the turning effect is increased. The turning effect will be either clockwise or anticlockwise, depending on the direction of the force.

The turning effect about A is measured by the product of the magnitude of the force and the distance of the line of action from A. This quantity is called the **moment** of the force about A.

Moment of force F about point A = magnitude of F × distance of line of action from A

K   The moment of a force about a point is the product of the magnitude of the force and the perpendicular distance from the point to the line of action of the force.

Moment of F about O = Fd

The **sense** of a moment is either clockwise or anticlockwise. Anticlockwise moments are taken as positive and clockwise moments as negative.

The units of a moment are newton metres ($N\,m$).

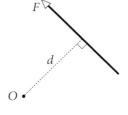

A3 Find the moment of each force about point O.

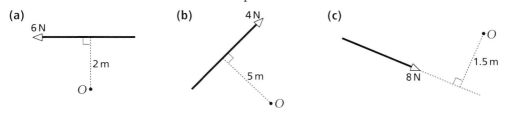

A4 A force F is applied as shown to the same spanner as in A2.

    (a) Will the turning effect be more, less or the same as in A2 (a)?

    (b) What is the perpendicular distance, d, from the point A to the line of action of F?

    (c) Given that the magnitude of F is $8\,N$, find the moment of F about A.

A5 Find the moment of each force about O.

(a) 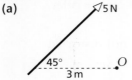 **(b)** 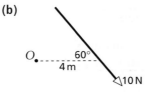 **(c)**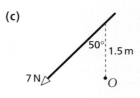

A **lamina** is an object which can be modelled as a plane area with mass but negligible thickness.

ABCD is a square lamina of side 2 m.
A force of 10 N acts at vertex *A* as shown.
If the lamina were fixed at vertex *B*, the force would cause a turning effect about *B*. This is the moment of the force about *B*.
The moment of the force about *B* is $10 \times 2 = 20$ N m clockwise, or -20 N m.

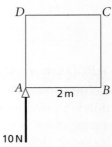

A6 Calculate the moment of the 10 N force about

    (a) *C*   **(b)** *D*   **(c)** *A*

A7 The force is moved so that it acts as shown.
Calculate the moment of the 10 N force about

    (a) *A*   **(b)** *B*

    (c) *C*   **(d)** *D*

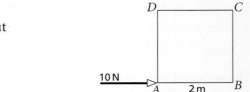

 If the line of action of a force acts through a point, then the moment of the force about that point is zero.

Example 1

Forces of 4 N and 6 N act on the lamina *ABCD* as shown.

Find the total moment of these forces about *O*.

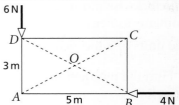

Solution

If O were fixed, the 4 N force would cause the lamina to move clockwise and the 6 N force would cause it to move anticlockwise.
The line of action of the 4 N force is 1.5 m from O and the line of action of the 6 N force is 2.5 m from O.

Moment of 4 N force about $O = 4 \times 1.5 = 6$ N m clockwise

Moment of 6 N force about $O = 6 \times 2.5 = 15$ N m anticlockwise

The total moment is the sum of the moments of the individual forces.
Remember that anticlockwise moments are positive and clockwise moments are negative.

Total moment $= 15 - 6 = 9$ N m

---

1 Find the moment of each force about O.

(a)

(b)

(c)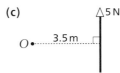

(d)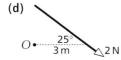

(e)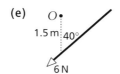

(f)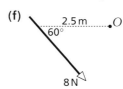

2 *ABCD* is a rectangular lamina.
A force of 8 N acts at *D* as shown.
Find the moment of this force about

(a) *A*   **(b)** *B*

(c) *C*   **(d)** *D*

3 *PQRS* is a square lamina of side 5 m with centre *O*.
Forces of 3 N and 5 N act as shown.
Find the total moment of these forces about

(a) *P*   **(b)** *S*   **(c)** *O*

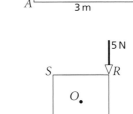

4 *AB* is a light rod of length 6 m.
Forces act on the rod as shown.
Find the total moment of these forces about

(a) *A*   **(b)** *B*

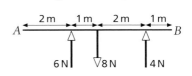

5 *ABC* is a light rigid equilateral triangular framework of side 2 m.
Forces act on the framework as shown.
Find the total moment of these forces about

(a) *A*   **(b)** *B*   **(c)** *C*

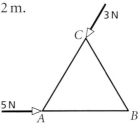

6 *ABCD* is a square lamina of side 3 m.
Forces of magnitude *F* N and 2*F* N act on the lamina as shown.
The total moment of these forces about the centre *O* is 27 N m.
Find the value of *F*.

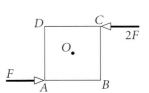

B Equilibrium of a rigid body (answers p 146)

Sasha 25 kg

Kieran 20 kg

Imagine these two children playing on a seesaw
of length 4 m and mass 30 kg, pivoted at its mid-point.
They want to get the seesaw to balance.

D **B1** **(a)** Describe what happens to the seesaw if they sit at equal distances
on either side of the central pivot.

(b) Who do you think should move to try to get the seesaw to balance?

The seesaw can be modelled as a **uniform rod**, that is a body which can be
modelled as a straight line with its mass concentrated at its mid-point.
The point on a body at which its mass can be considered to be concentrated
is called the **centre of mass** of the body.
The centre of mass of a uniform rod is at its mid-point.

The pivot, P, of the seesaw is at its mid-point.

Suppose that Kieran sits at one end of the seesaw, that is 2 m from P,
and that Sasha's distance from P is x m.

Taking the seesaw and children as one composite object, the forces in newtons
acting on the object are

the weight of the seesaw, 30g acting at its centre

Kieran's weight, 20g

Sasha's weight, 25g

the upward reaction R of the pivot

The force diagram for the seesaw is shown.

We need to find the value of x for which the seesaw is in equilibrium.

For equilibrium, the total anticlockwise moment about P must equal the total
clockwise moment about P.

The forces R N and 30g N go through P, so they have zero moment about P.

So $\quad 25g \times x = 20g \times 2$

$\Rightarrow \quad x = \dfrac{40g}{25g} = 1.6$

So Sasha must sit 1.6 m from the pivot.

Additionally, for equilibrium, the resultant of the forces on the seesaw must be zero.

B2 Use the fact that the resultant force on the seesaw is zero to find R.

When a particle is in equilibrium, the resultant of the forces acting on it is zero.
This condition is not sufficient for a rigid body to be in equilibrium.
A rigid body is in equilibrium if the resultant force is zero and the total
moment is zero.

As the seesaw is in equilibrium, if the pivot is replaced by a force with the same magnitude as the reaction R N the seesaw will remain in equilibrium.

The force diagram for the seesaw is unchanged.

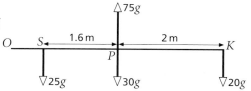

B3 (a) Find the total moment of the forces about S.

(b) Find the total moment of the forces about K.

(c) Find the total moment of the forces about O.

(d) Comment on your results.

 A rigid body is in equilibrium if the resultant force is zero and the total moment about any point is zero.

Note that all the sets of forces in this chapter are coplanar, that is they act in the same plane.

B4 A uniform rod of weight 50 N rests horizontally in equilibrium on two smooth supports at A and B as shown.

The force diagram for the rod is shown. R_A and R_B are the magnitudes of the reactions at A and B.

The rod is in equilibrium, so the total moment about any point is zero.

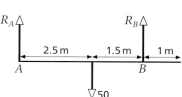

(a) Use the fact that the total moment of all the forces about A is zero to write down an equation involving R_B. Hence find the value of R_B.

(b) Now do the same for the total moment about B, and hence find the value of R_A.

(c) Resolve the forces vertically to check that they are in equilibrium.

Finding the total moment about a point A is usually called 'taking moments about A'. This can be abbreviated to M(A).
If the total moment about A is zero, it follows that the sum of the anticlockwise moments about A is equal to the sum of the clockwise moments about A.

B5 The supports are moved to the positions shown and the rod remains in equilibrium.

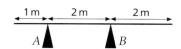

(a) Draw a force diagram for the rod.

(b) By taking moments about B, find the reaction at A.

(c) By taking moments about A, find the reaction at B.

(d) What effect has moving the supports had on the reactions?

B6 A particle of weight 10 N is positioned on the rod, 1 m from B as shown. The rod remains in equilibrium.

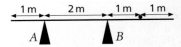

(a) Draw a force diagram for the rod.

(b) Find the reaction at A.

(c) Find the reaction at B.

A **non-uniform rod** is a body which can be modelled as a straight line with its mass concentrated at some point other than its mid-point.
The centre of mass of a non-uniform rod is generally not at its mid-point.

B7 A non-uniform rod PQ of length 6 m and weight 75 N is resting horizontally on supports at P and Q. The centre of mass of the rod is 2 m from P.

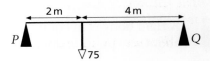

(a) Draw a force diagram for the rod.

(b) Find the reaction at P.

(c) Find the reaction at Q.

B8 A particle of weight 30 N is positioned at the centre of rod PQ.

(a) Find the reaction at P.

(b) Find the reaction at Q.

K A problem about a rigid body in equilibrium can be solved by recognising that the total moment about an appropriate point equals zero and that the forces resolved in any direction equal zero.
Taking moments about a point through which an unknown force acts can eliminate the need to find that force.

Example 2

A uniform rod has weight 30 N and length 4 m. It is suspended by a light string attached at point C. The rod is held in equilibrium by a vertical force applied at the end B as shown.

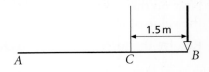

Find the magnitude of the applied force.

Solution

Sketch a force diagram showing all the forces in newtons acting on the rod.

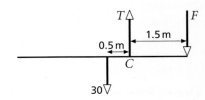

The question does not require the tension to be found, so take moments about C to set up an equation without T.

M(C): $30 \times 0.5 = F \times 1.5$

$\Rightarrow$ $F = 10$

The magnitude of the applied force is 10 N.

Example 3

A uniform rod of weight 40 N rests horizontally in
equilibrium on two smooth supports at A and B as shown.
A particle of weight 60 N is placed on the rod at X.
The reaction on the rod at A is three times the reaction at B.
Find the distance AX.

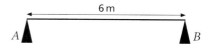

Solution

Sketch a force diagram showing all the forces acting on the rod.
The reaction at A is three times the reaction at B,
so label these forces 3R and R.

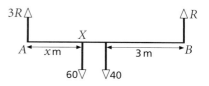

The distance AX, in metres, is labelled x so $XB = 6 - x$.

Take moments about A.

$M(A)$: $60x + 40 \times 3 = 6R$

$\Rightarrow$ $60x + 120 = 6R$ (1)

Take moments about B.

$M(B)$: $3R \times 6 = 60(6 - x) + 40 \times 3$

$\Rightarrow$ $18R = 480 - 60x$ (2)

Multiply (1) by 3. $18R = 180x + 360$ (3)

Subtract (2) from (3). $0 = 240x - 120$

$x = 0.5$

The distance AX is 0.5 m.

Exercise B (answers p 147)

1 Each diagram below shows a light rod in equilibrium under the action of
coplanar parallel forces in newtons. Find the values of the lettered forces.

(a)

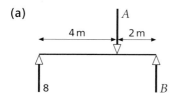

(b)

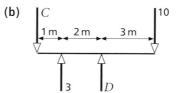

(c)

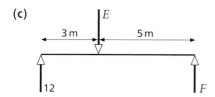

(d)

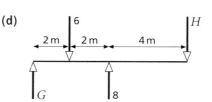

2 A seesaw of length 6 m is pivoted at its mid-point P.
Khyle sits on one side of the seesaw, 3 m from the pivot, and Jack sits on the other side, 2.4 m from the pivot. The seesaw is in equilibrium.
Given that Khyle has mass 32 kg, find the mass of Jack.

3 A uniform rod of weight 12 N and length 6 m hangs in equilibrium in a horizontal position.
It is held in position by two light vertical cables attached at A and B as shown.

(a) Draw a force diagram for the rod.

(b) Find the tension in the cable at A.

(c) Find the tension in the cable at B.

4 A uniform rod of weight 14 N rests in equilibrium on supports at X and Y as shown.

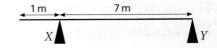

(a) Find the reaction at X.

(b) Find the reaction at Y.

5 A non-uniform rod AB of length 5 m and weight 100 N rests horizontally in equilibrium on supports at X and Y as shown.
The centre of mass is 2 m from B.

(a) Draw a force diagram for the rod.

(b) Find the reaction at X.

(c) Find the reaction at Y.

6 A non-uniform rod AD of length 2 m and weight 25 N hangs in equilibrium in a horizontal position.
It is held in position by two light vertical cables attached at B and C as shown.
The centre of mass of the rod is 0.6 m from A.

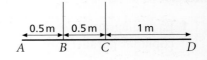

(a) Find the tension in the cable at B.

(b) Find the tension in the cable at C.

7 A non-uniform rod of weight 60 N rests horizontally in equilibrium on supports at P and Q as shown.
The reaction at P is four times the reaction at Q.
Find the position of the centre of mass of the rod.

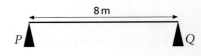

8 A uniform plank AC of mass 55 kg and length 10 m rests horizontally in equilibrium on supports at B and C as shown.

A child of mass 20 kg stands on the plank at A. The plank remains in equilibrium.
The reaction on the plank at B is now twice the reaction at C.
Find the distance AB.

C Tilting (answers p 147)

C1 A uniform beam rests horizontally in equilibrium on two smooth supports as shown. Tim stands on the beam.
Describe what might happen to the beam if Tim stands between

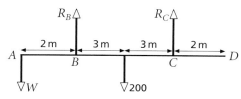

(a) A and B (b) B and C (c) C and D

The beam may or may not remain in equilibrium depending on several factors including Tim's weight, the weight of the beam, the length of the beam and where the supports are placed.

The beam AD is of length $10\,\text{m}$ and weight $200\,\text{N}$. The supports at B and C are positioned symmetrically $2\,\text{m}$ from A and D respectively.
Tim stands on the beam at A.

The force diagram for the beam is shown.

The reactions at the supports B and C will vary depending on Tim's weight, $W\,\text{N}$.

C2 (a) By taking moments about B, find an equation that links W and R_C.

(b) Describe what happens to R_C as W increases.

(c) What is the maximum value of W for the beam to remain in equilibrium?

(d) Describe what happens to R_B as W increases.

(e) Write down the values of R_B and R_C as the beam is about to tilt.

C3 The supports for the beam are moved and it now rests horizontally in equilibrium as shown. Neeta stands on the beam at D and it just remains in equilibrium.

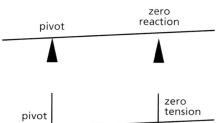

(a) Which of the supports will be the pivot if the beam tilts?

(b) By taking moments about this pivot, find Neeta's weight.

(c) Find the magnitudes of the reactions at B and C.

K

When a rod or beam is about to tilt about one support, the reaction of the other support on the rod is zero.

When a suspended rod is about to tilt about one support, the tension at the other support is zero.

Example 4

A uniform beam AD of mass $30\,\text{kg}$ rests horizontally in equilibrium on supports at B and C as shown. When a block is placed on the beam at A, it just remains in equilibrium. Find the mass of the block.

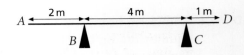

Solution

Draw a force diagram with the block at A.
The beam is about to tilt about B, so the reaction at C is zero.
The mass of the block is labelled m.

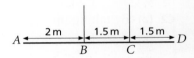

The reaction at B is not required   M(B): $2mg = 30g \times 1.5$
so take moments about B.

Do not substitute for g as it cancels out. $m = \dfrac{30 \times 1.5}{2}$

$\Rightarrow$ $m = 22.5$

The mass of the block is $22.5\,\text{kg}$.

Example 5

A uniform beam AD of length $5\,\text{m}$ hangs in equilibrium in a horizontal position. It is held in position by two light vertical cables attached at B and C as shown.

When a weight of $300\,\text{N}$ is hung from A the beam is about to tilt.
Find the maximum weight that can be hung from D without the beam tilting.

Solution

Draw a force diagram with the weight acting at A.
The beam is about to tilt, so the tension at C is zero.
The weight of the beam is unknown, so is labelled W.

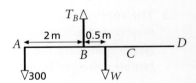

Take moments about B.   M(B): $300 \times 2 = W \times 0.5$

$\Rightarrow$ $W = 1200$

Now draw a force diagram with a weight at D
and the weight of the beam shown.
When the weight at D is a maximum the beam will be
about to tilt, so the tension at B is zero.
The unknown weight at D is labelled F.

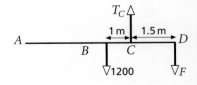

Take moments about C.   M(C): $1200 \times 1 = F \times 1.5$

$\Rightarrow$ $F = 800$

The maximum weight that can be hung from D is $800\,\text{N}$.

Exercise C (answers p 147)

1 A uniform rod of weight 60 N and length 8 m rests horizontally in equilibrium on supports at B and C as shown. A force, F N, is applied at A so that the rod is just about to tilt.

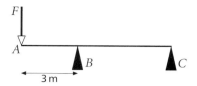

(a) What is the reaction at C?

(b) Find the magnitude of F.

(c) Find the reaction at B.

2 A uniform beam AD of length 8 m and weight 400 N rests in equilibrium on supports at B and C as shown. When Peter stands on the beam 2.2 m from D it just remains in equilibrium.

(a) At which of the supports is the reaction zero?

(b) By taking moments about the pivot, find Peter's weight.

(c) Find the reaction at the pivot.

3 A uniform shelf of length 2 m rests in equilibrium on smooth supports 0.6 m from each end.
A pile of books of weight 25 N is placed on one end of the shelf, such that the shelf just remains in equilibrium.
By modelling the books as a particle, find the weight of the shelf.

4 A non-uniform rod PQ, of length 4 m and weight 20 N, is suspended from light cables attached at A and B as shown.
When a weight of 15 N is hung from P the rod is about to tilt.
Find the distance of the centre of mass of the rod from P.

5 A bench is constructed from a plank of length 5 m and weight 150 N supported on blocks 1 m from each end.
The bench can be modelled as a uniform rod resting on smooth supports.
Find the maximum weight of a person who sits on the end of the bench if the bench is to remain in equilibrium.

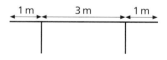

6 A non-uniform rod AB of weight 40 N and length 3 m is suspended in equilibrium from two light cables attached at P and Q as shown.
When a weight of 24 N is hung from A the rod just remains in equilibrium.

(a) Find the distance of the centre of mass from P.

(b) Find the maximum weight that can be hung from B for the rod to remain in equilibrium.

D Non-parallel forces (answers p 148)

In sections B and C we considered problems with parallel forces acting on a rigid body in equilibrium. We will extend this to systems of coplanar forces in equilibrium where the forces are not all parallel.

K For a system of coplanar forces in equilibrium, the total moment about any point equals zero and the total component of the forces in any direction equals zero.

A drawbridge of mass 500 kg and length 6 m is pivoted at point P and is held in a horizontal position by a cable attached at point Q as shown.

Assume that the drawbridge can be modelled as a uniform rod and that the cable is light.

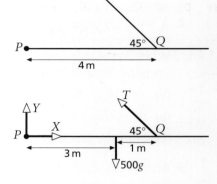

The force diagram for the drawbridge is shown. The reaction at the pivot can no longer be assumed to be vertical, so we represent it by the horizontal and vertical components X and Y newtons. The reaction at the pivot is the resultant of these two components.

The moments of the forces X and Y about P are zero because the lines of action of the forces pass through P. So taking moments about P will allow us to find the tension in the cable, T newtons.

This diagram shows the perpendicular distance d from P to the line of action of T.

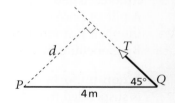

D1 (a) Explain why the moment of T about the point P is $4T\sin 45°$.

(b) By taking moments about P, show that $1500g = 4T\sin 45°$.

(c) Find, to 3 s.f., the value of T.

D2 (a) Resolve the forces vertically to find the value of Y.

(b) Resolve the forces horizontally to find the value of X.

(c) Find the magnitude and direction of the reaction at P.

When a rigid body is freely hinged at a point, a reaction force will act at that point. Since the direction of the reaction is not known, it can be represented by its horizontal and vertical components.

D3 A uniform shelf AB of mass 2 kg is freely hinged at the wall at A, and held in a horizontal position by a force applied at B as shown.

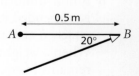

(a) Sketch a force diagram for the shelf.

(b) By taking moments about A, find the magnitude of the force at B in newtons.

(c) Find the magnitude and direction of the reaction at the wall.

Imagine a ladder leaning against a wall as shown.
The wall and the ground are both modelled as smooth
and the ladder is uniform.

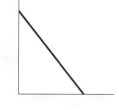

D4 (a) Sketch a diagram showing the forces acting on the ladder.

(b) Describe what happens to the ladder.

This is clearly not a good model for the case where the ladder is stationary.
The model can be improved by treating the ground as rough but the wall as smooth.

D5 (a) Sketch a diagram showing the forces acting on the ladder in this case.

(b) Describe what could happen to the ladder in this case.

A ladder of length 4 m and weight 100 N rests in equilibrium
at 60° to the horizontal with one end against a smooth wall.
The base rests on rough horizontal ground.
The force diagram for the ladder is shown.
We need to find the values of the reaction forces and
the friction force.

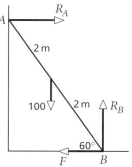

Resolving the forces vertically gives $R_B = 100$.

Resolving the forces horizontally gives $R_A = F$.

We have not been told that the ladder is in limiting equilibrium, so we cannot
use $F = \mu R$ to find the friction force and hence the reaction at the wall.

Taking moments about a point will give a third equation which can be used
to solve the problem.

D6 Explain why taking moments about B will allow you to find R_A directly.

The diagrams below show the perpendicular distance from the point B to
the line of action of the two required forces.

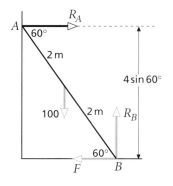
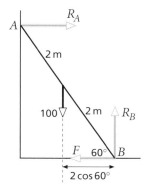

$M(B)$: $R_A \times 4\sin 60° = 100 \times 2\cos 60°$ $\Rightarrow$ $R_A = \dfrac{50\cos 60°}{\sin 60°}$

The forces in newtons on the ladder are, to 3 s.f., $R_A = 28.9$, $R_B = 100$ and $F = 28.9$.

D **D7** A man now climbs up the ladder.
What happens to the forces on the ladder as he does so?

D8 This is the force diagram for the ladder when a man of weight 750 N has climbed a distance of x m up the ladder.

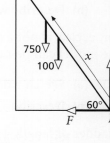

(a) Resolve the forces vertically to find the value of R_B in newtons.

(b) Resolve the forces horizontally to write down an equation relating R_A and F.

(c) By taking moments about B, find an equation relating R_A and x.

(d) Given that the coefficient of friction is 0.4, find the maximum value of the friction force and hence the value of R_A when the ladder is in limiting equilibrium.

(e) Use your equation from (c) to find the value of x when the ladder is in limiting equilibrium.
State the maximum distance the man can climb up the ladder before it slips.

Example 6

A uniform rod AB of length 4 m and weight 20 N rests in equilibrium with the end A on rough horizontal ground. The rod is supported at 60° to the horizontal by a smooth peg at C where $AC = 3$ m.

Show that $\mu \geq \dfrac{\sqrt{3}}{5}$, where μ is the coefficient of friction between the rod and the ground.

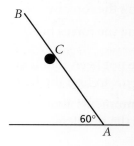

Solution

Sketch a force diagram showing all of the forces acting on the rod. The peg is smooth so the reaction at the peg is normal to the rod at the point of contact.

Take moments about A. $\text{M}(A)$: $20 \times 2 \cos 60° = 3R_C$

$\Rightarrow$ $R_C = \frac{40}{3} \times \frac{1}{2} = \frac{20}{3}$

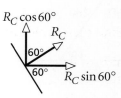

The remaining forces can be found by resolving the forces on the rod vertically and horizontally.
The diagram shows the vertical and horizontal components of R_C.

Resolve forces vertically. $R_A + R_C \cos 60° = 20$

$\Rightarrow$ $R_A = 20 - \frac{20}{3} \times \frac{1}{2} = \frac{50}{3}$

Resolve forces horizontally. $F = R_C \sin 60° = \frac{20}{3} \times \frac{\sqrt{3}}{2} = \frac{10\sqrt{3}}{3}$

For equilibrium $F \le \mu R_A$. $\quad \frac{10\sqrt{3}}{3} \le \frac{50}{3}\mu$

$$\Rightarrow \quad \mu \ge \frac{10\sqrt{3}}{50}$$

$$\Rightarrow \quad \mu \ge \frac{\sqrt{3}}{5}$$

Exercise D (answers p 148)

1 A uniform rod AB of length 4 m and weight 60 N is pivoted at A and held in a horizontal position by a light cable attached at C as shown.

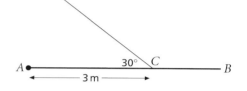

(a) Draw a force diagram for the rod.

(b) Show that the moment about A of the tension T newtons in the cable is $3T\sin 30°$.

(c) Find the magnitude of T.

2 A uniform rod AB of length 2 m and weight W N is hinged at A and held at an angle of 60° to the horizontal by a smooth support at C as shown.
Find, in terms of W, the magnitude of the reaction at C.

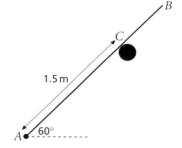

3 A uniform ladder of length 5 m and mass 12 kg leans against a smooth wall with its base on rough ground as shown. The ladder is in limiting equilibrium.

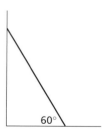

(a) Draw a force diagram for the ladder.

(b) Taking g as 9.8 m s^{-2}, find the magnitude of the reaction at the wall.

(c) Find the magnitude of the friction force.

(d) Find the coefficient of friction between the ladder and the ground.

4 A uniform flagpole is attached to a wall by a hinge, and is held in position by a light horizontal cable attached at its mid-point as shown. The length of the flagpole is 1.5 m and its weight is 2 kg.

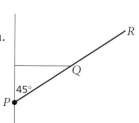

(a) Draw a force diagram for the flagpole.

(b) Find the tension in the cable.

(c) Find the magnitude and direction of the reaction at the hinge.

5 A uniform rod AB of length $2l$ and weight W is freely hinged at B to a fixed support. A horizontal force of magnitude $4W$ is applied at A to keep the rod in equilibrium at an angle θ to the vertical as shown.

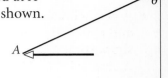

    (a) Draw a force diagram for the rod.

    (b) Write down the horizontal and vertical components of the reaction of the hinge on the rod at B.

    (c) Find the magnitude and direction of the reaction at the hinge.

    (d) Find the value of θ.

6 A uniform ladder of length 6 m and weight 150 N is leaning at an angle of 20° to the vertical against a smooth wall with its base resting on rough horizontal ground. A man of weight 800 N climbs up the ladder.

Given that the coefficient of friction is 0.3, find the maximum distance that the man can climb up the ladder before it slips.

7 A scaffold pole of length 3 m and mass 10 kg leans against a smooth fence of height 1.6 m.
One end of the pole rests on rough ground at 60° to the horizontal as shown.
The coefficient of friction between the pole and the ground is μ.

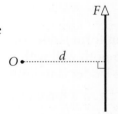

    (a) Draw a diagram to show the forces acting on the pole.

    (b) Calculate the magnitude of the frictional force acting on the base of the pole.

    (c) Find the minimum value of μ for the pole to remain at rest.

Key points

- The moment of a force about a point is the product of the magnitude of the force and the perpendicular distance from the point to the line of action of the force.

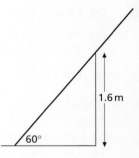

  Moment of F about $O = Fd$

  Anticlockwise moments are taken as positive and clockwise moments as negative.

  The units of a moment are newton metres (N m).   (p 7)

- If the line of action of a force acts through a point, then the moment of the force about that point is zero.   (p 8)

- If a rigid body is in equilibrium the resultant force is zero and the total moment about any point is zero.   (pp 11, 12, 18)

- When a rod resting on two supports is about to pivot about one of the supports, the reaction at the other support is zero (and similarly for tension when a rod is suspended by two light cables.).   (p 15)

1 A bench is constructed from a beam AB of length 6 m and mass 20 kg resting horizontally in equilibrium on supports at X and Y as shown.

A child of mass 25 kg sits on the bench, 2 m from the end A.
The child is modelled as a particle and the bench as a uniform rod.
The bench and child are in equilibrium.

(a) Calculate the magnitude of the reaction force exerted by the support on the beam at X.

(b) Calculate the magnitude of the reaction force exerted by the support on the beam at Y.

(c) A woman now sits on the bench at the end B. The child is still on the bench. The bench just remains in equilibrium.
Calculate the mass of the woman.

2 A uniform beam AB has length 5 metres and mass 10 kg. It is freely pivoted at the point P which is 2 metres from A. A rope is attached to the beam at A and exerts a vertical force on the beam at A.

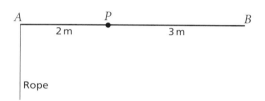

The beam and rope are shown in the diagram.

(a) The beam is in equilibrium and at rest in a horizontal position.

   (i) Show that the tension in the rope is 24.5 N.

   (ii) A particle of mass 40 kg is then fixed to the beam at B. The tension in the rope is increased, so that the beam remains horizontal. Find the tension in the rope in this case.

(b) How would your answer to part (a)(ii) change if the beam had been in equilibrium at an angle to the horizontal, but with the rope still vertical? Explain why.

AQA 2004

3 A uniform rod has length 2 m. It rests horizontally in equilibrium on two supports at X and Y as shown. A particle of weight 20 N is attached to the rod at A and the rod remains in equilibrium.
The reaction on the rod at X has magnitude 40 N.

(a) Find the weight of the rod.

(b) Find the magnitude of the reaction at Y.

(c) The support at Y is now moved to a point Z on the rod and the rod remains in equilibrium with the particle at A.
Given that the reaction at X is now three times the reaction at Z, find the distance AZ.

4 A uniform rod AB of length $2a$ and mass m is freely hinged at A to a fixed support.

A horizontal force is applied at B to keep the rod in equilibrium at 30° to the vertical.

Find the magnitude of the force applied at B.

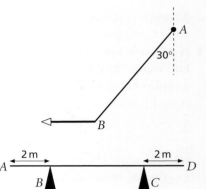

5 A non-uniform rod AD of length 10 m and weight 50 N rests horizontally in equilibrium on supports at B and C as shown.

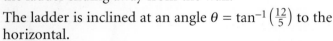

The centre of mass of the rod is 4 m from A.

A particle of weight W newtons is attached to the rod at a point E, where E is x metres from A.

The rod remains in equilibrium and the magnitude of the reaction at B is now three times the magnitude of the reaction at C.

(a) Show that $W = \dfrac{50}{7 - 2x}$.

(b) Hence deduce the possible range of values of x.

6 A uniform ladder AB, of weight W and length $4a$, is resting with A against a smooth vertical wall and B on rough horizontal ground.

A man of weight $4W$ is standing at a point C on the ladder, where $BC = 3a$. The force exerted by the man's hands on the ladder is negligible and the centre of mass of the man is vertically above C.

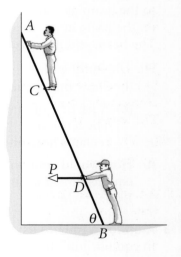

Another man stands on the ground near the bottom of the ladder and pushes on the ladder at the point D, where $BD = a$. The force applied at D is horizontal, of magnitude P and is just sufficient to prevent the ladder sliding away from the wall.

The ladder is inclined at an angle $\theta = \tan^{-1}\left(\frac{12}{5}\right)$ to the horizontal.

The coefficient of friction between the base of the ladder and the ground is $\frac{1}{4}$.

(a) Show that the horizontal frictional force at B is of magnitude $\dfrac{5W}{4}$.

(b) Find the value of P in terms of W.

AQA 2004

Test yourself (answers p 149)

1 A uniform metal bar, of mass 30 kg and length 3 m, rests in a horizontal position, on two supports at A and B, as shown in the diagram.

Find the magnitude of each of the reaction forces acting on the bar at the supports at A and B.

AQA 2001

2 A uniform plank, *AB*, rests horizontally on two fixed
vertical supports at *C* and *D*.
The plank has mass 10 kg and length 2.5 m.
The supports at *C* and *D* are 0.25 m from
A and *B* respectively, as shown in the diagram.

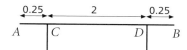

Steve has mass 60 kg and stands on the plank at a point 0.75 m from *A*.

(a) Draw a diagram showing all the forces acting on the plank.

(b) Find the reaction of the supports on the plank.

AQA 2002

3 A uniform metal beam has length 5 metres and mass 250 kg.
It rests horizontally on two supports, *A* and *B*,
which are 3 metres apart. Support *A* is at one end
of the beam, as shown in the diagram.

(a) Find the magnitudes of the forces exerted on the beam by the supports.

(b) A man, of mass 80 kg, walks along the beam from *A* towards the
other end of the beam.
Find the distance he can walk past *B*, before the beam starts to tip.

AQA 2002

4 The diagram shows a vertical section *AC* through
the centre of gravity of a uniform trapdoor.
The trapdoor is a square of side 1.5 m and mass 12 kg.
It is smoothly hinged along the horizontal edge through *A*.

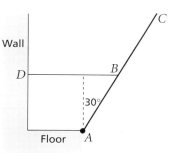

The trapdoor is held open at 30° to the vertical
by a horizontal, light bar *BD*. The bar is smoothly
connected to the trapdoor at *B* and to the wall at *D*.
The length *AB* = 0.5 m.

(a) On a diagram, show clearly all the forces acting on the trapdoor.

(b) By taking moments about *A*, find the tension in *BD*.

AQA 2002

5 A uniform ladder *AB*, of mass 20 kg and length 5 metres,
rests with *B* on a rough horizontal floor and with
A against a smooth vertical wall.
The ladder is at an angle of 60° to the horizontal and the
coefficient of friction between the ladder and the floor is 0.4.
A man of mass 80 kg is standing on the ladder at the point *C*,
x metres from *B*.

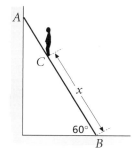

(a) Draw a diagram showing the forces acting on the ladder.

(b) Given that the ladder is in limiting equilibrium

   (i) show that the force on the ladder at *A* is of magnitude 392 N

   (ii) find the value of *x*

AQA 2003

2 Centre of mass

In this chapter you will learn how to find
• the centre of mass of a system of particles
• the centre of mass of a composite body
• the position of a suspended body

A Centre of mass of a system of particles (answers p 150)

In the previous chapter we saw that the point on a body at which its mass can be considered to be concentrated is called the centre of mass of the body.

Consider a light rod of length 2 m with a particle of mass 1 kg attached at each end.
Remember that if an object is modelled as light, its mass can be ignored.

The mass of the system of rod and particles can be considered to be concentrated at its centre of mass.

The resultant of the weights of the particles
• has a magnitude equal to the sum of the two separate weights
• acts through the centre of mass of the system

The system of rod and particles can be supported at the halfway point, which is the centre of mass, and it will remain in equilibrium.

A1 (a) Draw a force diagram for the system of rod and particles.

(b) By taking moments about the support, show that the system is in equilibrium.

If one of the 1 kg particles is replaced by a 2 kg particle, the centre of mass of the system will no longer be in the centre of the rod. The support will need to be moved for the system to remain in equilibrium.

A2 By taking moments about the support, find the distance, x m, of the centre of mass of the system from A.

The system of rod and particles can be replaced by an equivalent single particle of the same total mass acting at the centre of mass of the system.

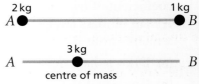

A3 (a) Find the total moment about A of the weights of the two particles.

(b) Find the total moment about A of the weight of the equivalent particle acting at the centre of mass.

A4 (a) Find the total moment about B of the weights of the two particles.

(b) Find the total moment about B of the weight of the equivalent particle acting at the centre of mass.

A5 **(a)** Find the total moment about the mid-point of the rod of the weights of the two particles.

(b) Find the total moment about the mid-point of the rod of the weight of the equivalent particle acting at the centre of mass.

In fact, the total moment of the forces for the system of rod and particles about **any** point is equal to the moment of the force on the equivalent particle at the centre of mass of the system.

 When calculating moments about a given point, a set of particles can be replaced by a single particle of the same total mass concentrated at the centre of mass.

Consider a system of particles arranged in a horizontal straight line as shown.

This is the force diagram for the system.

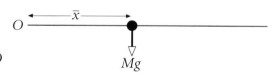

The total moment about O is $m_1gx_1 + m_2gx_2 + m_3gx_3$.

The system of particles can be replaced with a single particle of the same total mass positioned at the centre of mass of the system with force diagram as shown, where $\bar{x}$ is the distance of the centre of mass from O and M is the total mass of the individual particles.

The total moment about O is $Mg\bar{x}$.

The two systems are equivalent, so the total moment is equal to the sum of the individual moments.

$$Mg\bar{x} = m_1gx_1 + m_2gx_2 + m_3gx_3$$
$$\Rightarrow \quad M\bar{x} = m_1x_1 + m_2x_2 + m_3x_3$$
$$\Rightarrow \quad M\bar{x} = \sum mx$$

This method can be applied to any number of particles where $\sum mx$ is the sum of all the individual products, mass × distance from O.

 The centre of mass of a system of particles arranged in a straight line can be found using

> total mass × distance of centre of mass from O
> = the sum of all the products mass × distance from O

that is,

$$M\bar{x} = \sum mx$$

where M is the total mass and $\bar{x}$ is the distance of the centre of mass from O.

Example 1

Four particles of masses 4 kg, 4 kg, 2 kg and 5 kg are positioned in a straight line as shown. Find the distance of the centre of mass from O.

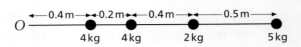

Solution

Use $M\bar{x} = \sum mx$.

$$(4 + 4 + 2 + 5)\bar{x} = 4 \times 0.4 + 4 \times 0.6 + 2 \times 1.0 + 5 \times 1.5$$

$$\Rightarrow \qquad 15\bar{x} = 13.5$$

$$\Rightarrow \qquad \bar{x} = 0.9$$

The centre of mass is 0.9 m from O.

Exercise A (answers p 150)

1 Find the distance from O of the centre of mass of each system of particles.

(a)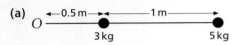

(b)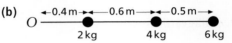

(c)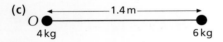

(d)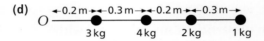

2 A light rod of length 5 m has a particle of mass 3 kg attached at one end and a particle of mass 9 kg attached at the other end.
Find the distance of the centre of mass from the 3 kg particle.

3 A light rod AB has particles attached as shown.

(a) Find the distance of the centre of mass from A.

(b) The 2 kg particle is removed.
Find the new position of the centre of mass.

4 A light rod AB of length 2 m has a particle of mass 10 kg attached at A and a particle of mass m kg attached at B.
Given that the centre of mass is 1.5 m from A, find the value of m.

5 Particles of masses 2 kg, m kg and 4 kg are attached to a light rod AB as shown.
The centre of mass is 2.5 m from A.
Find the value of m.

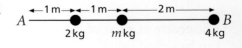

6 A light rod XY of length 6 m has a particle of mass 5 kg attached at X and a particle of mass 6 kg attached at Y.
A particle of mass 4 kg is attached to the rod so that the centre of mass of the system of rod and particles is at the mid-point of the rod.
Find the distance of the 4 kg mass from X.

7 A light rod PQ of length 5 m has particles of mass p kg and $2p$ kg attached.
The centre of mass of the system of rod and particles is 3 m from P.
If the p kg particle is 0.5 m from P, find the distance of the $2p$ kg particle from P.

B A system of particles in a plane

Consider a system of particles arranged with respect to the origin O as shown.

With the y-axis vertical, the total moment of the particles about O is

$$m_1 g x_1 + m_2 g x_2 + m_3 g x_3$$

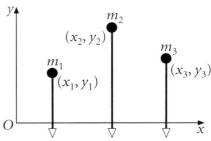

The system can be replaced by a single particle of mass M, where $M = (m_1 + m_2 + m_3)$, acting at the centre of mass of the system $(\bar{x}, \bar{y})$.
The moment of this particle about O is

$$Mg\bar{x}$$

The two systems are equivalent, so the total moment is equal to the sum of the individual moments.

$$Mg\bar{x} = m_1 g x_1 + m_2 g x_2 + m_3 g x_3$$
$$\Rightarrow \quad M\bar{x} = m_1 x_1 + m_2 x_2 + m_3 x_3$$
$$\Rightarrow \quad M\bar{x} = \sum mx$$

If the system is now turned over, so that the x-axis is vertical, the total moment about O is

$$m_1 g y_1 + m_2 g y_2 + m_3 g y_3$$

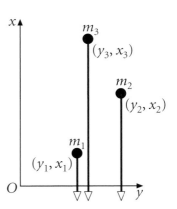

The moment of the equivalent single particle about O is

$$Mg\bar{y}$$

So $\quad Mg\bar{y} = m_1 g y_1 + m_2 g y_2 + m_3 g y_3$
$$\Rightarrow \quad M\bar{y} = m_1 y_1 + m_2 y_2 + m_3 y_3$$
$$\Rightarrow \quad M\bar{y} = \sum my$$

The coordinates, $(\bar{x}, \bar{y})$, of the centre of mass of a system of particles in a plane are given by

$$M\bar{x} = \sum mx, \quad M\bar{y} = \sum my$$

Example 2

A light rectangular framework has particles attached to the corners as shown.

Find the coordinates of its centre of mass with respect to the position of the 2 kg mass.

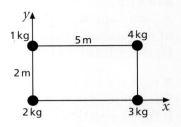

Solution

The framework is light, so its weight can be ignored.

Use $M\bar{x} = \sum mx$.

$$(2 + 3 + 4 + 1)\bar{x} = 2\times0 + 3\times5 + 4\times5 + 1\times0$$

$$\Rightarrow \qquad 10\bar{x} = 35$$

$$\Rightarrow \qquad \bar{x} = 3.5$$

Use $M\bar{y} = \sum my$.

$$(2 + 3 + 4 + 1)\bar{y} = 2\times0 + 3\times0 + 4\times2 + 1\times2$$

$$\Rightarrow \qquad 10\bar{y} = 10$$

$$\Rightarrow \qquad \bar{y} = 1$$

The coordinates of the centre of mass are (3.5, 1).

Exercise B (answers p 150)

1 Find the coordinates of the centre of mass of each system of particles.

(a)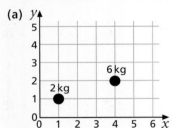

(b)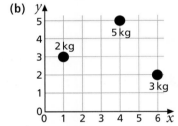

(c)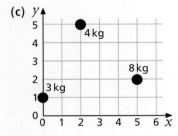

(d)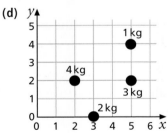

2 A light rectangular framework has particles attached to the corners as shown.
Find the coordinates of the centre of mass with respect to the axes shown.

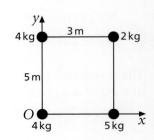

3 A light rectangular framework ABCD has particles attached as shown.

(a) Find the distance of the centre of mass from AD.

(b) Find the distance of the centre of mass from AB.

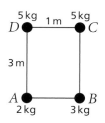

4 Particles are attached to the corners of a light square framework ABCD, of side 3 m, as shown.

(a) Find the coordinates of the centre of mass of the framework with respect to the axes shown.

(b) A particle of mass $3p$ is attached to the mid-point of AB. Find the centre of mass of the new system.

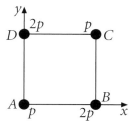

5 A light framework ABC with particles of mass 3 kg, m kg and 5 kg attached as shown has centre of mass at the point with coordinates $(\bar{x}, \bar{y})$.

(a) Given that $\bar{x} = 2$, find the value of m.

(b) Find the y-coordinate of the centre of mass.

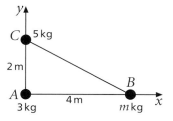

6 A light rectangular framework PQRS has particles attached as shown.

(a) Find the distance of the centre of mass from PQ.

(b) Find the distance of the centre of mass from PS.

(c) The 2 kg particle is removed. Find the position of the new centre of mass.

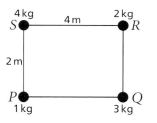

7 A light framework ABCD has particles of mass p kg, 1 kg, q kg and 2 kg attached as shown. The centre of mass of the framework has coordinates $(1, 2)$ with respect to the axes shown. Find the values of p and q.

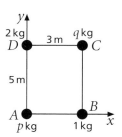

C Centre of mass by symmetry (answers p 150)

C1 A system of particles is attached to a light rectangular
framework as shown.

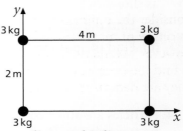

    (a) Calculate the coordinates of the centre of mass
of the system.

    (b) Use the symmetry of the system to explain
your answer to (a).

K   If a system of particles has a line of symmetry, the centre of mass lies on this line.

A lamina can be modelled as a plane area with mass but negligible thickness.
If the lamina is uniform, its mass is distributed evenly throughout its area.

C2 State the position of the centres of mass of the following uniform laminae.

    (a) A circular disc of radius 1 m   (b) A square lamina of side 2 m

    (c) A rectangular lamina of length 3 m and width 2 m

K   If a uniform lamina has a line of symmetry, the centre of mass lies on this line.
If the lamina has more than one line of symmetry, the centre of mass lies on their
point of intersection.

Exercise C (answers p 150)

1 Find, using symmetry or otherwise, the coordinates of the centre of mass of
each of the following systems of particles.

(a)
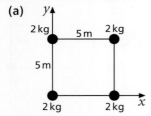

(b)
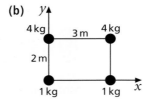

2 Write down the coordinates of the centre of mass of each uniform lamina.

(a)
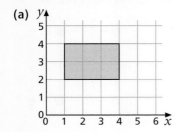

(b)
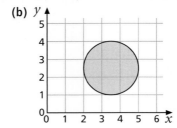

(c)
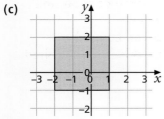

(d)
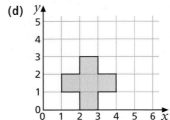

D Centre of mass of a composite body (answers p 150)

Consider the uniform L-shaped lamina shown.
Its centre of mass cannot be found by symmetry.
However, several different methods can be used
to find the centre of mass of a composite body.
They are demonstrated in the following questions.

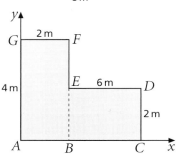

The lamina can be divided into two rectangles
whose centres of mass can be found.

D1 Find the coordinates of the centre of mass
of rectangle

    (a) *ABFG*   **(b)** *BCDE*

The lamina is uniform, so its mass is distributed evenly throughout its area.
Suppose its mass per unit area is $a\,\mathrm{kg\,m^{-2}}$.

D2 Write down an expression for the mass of rectangle

    (a) *ABFG*   **(b)** *BCDE*

Each rectangle can be replaced by a particle of the same mass positioned
at the centre of mass of the rectangle.
The centre of mass of the composite lamina can then be found by replacing
the lamina by these two particles and finding their centre of mass.

D3 Find the coordinates of the centre of mass of the composite lamina.

When using the above approach, you may find it helpful to complete a table like the
one shown below to summarise the known values for the lamina and its components.

	Area	Mass	Distance of centre of mass from *AG*	Distance of centre of mass from *AC*
Rectangle *ABFG*	$8\,\mathrm{m^2}$	$8a\,\mathrm{kg}$	$1\,\mathrm{m}$	$2\,\mathrm{m}$
Rectangle *BCDE*	$12\,\mathrm{m^2}$	$12a\,\mathrm{kg}$	$5\,\mathrm{m}$	$1\,\mathrm{m}$
Lamina	$20\,\mathrm{m^2}$	$20a\,\mathrm{kg}$	$\bar{x}\,\mathrm{m}$	$\bar{y}\,\mathrm{m}$

In the expressions for the coordinates of the centre of mass of the composite lamina
the mass per unit area, a, cancelled out and hence was not required.
The mass of a uniform lamina is proportional to its area, so areas can be used
instead of masses in the calculations, and the mass column in the table is not required.

D4 *ABCDEFGH* is a uniform lamina.

(a) Find the coordinates of the centre of mass of *ABCH*.

(b) Find the coordinates of the centre of mass of *DEFG*.

(c) Find the coordinates of the centre of mass of the lamina.

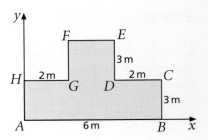

Now consider the uniform lamina shown.
It can be thought of as a large rectangle *ABCD*
with a small rectangle *EFGH* removed.

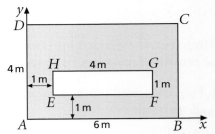

D5 (a) Complete this table showing the areas and centres of mass of
the rectangles and lamina.
Let the coordinates of the centre of mass of the lamina be (x_L, y_L).

	Area	Distance of centre of mass from *AD*	Distance of centre of mass from *AB*
Rectangle *ABCD*	24 m²		
Rectangle *EFGH* before removal	4 m²		
Lamina	20 m²	x_L m	y_L m

(b) Now consider rectangle *ABCD* to be a composite body consisting of
the lamina and rectangle *EFGH*. The centre of mass of *ABCD* is at $(\bar{x}, \bar{y})$.

(i) Use values from the table and $M\bar{x} = \sum mx$ to show that $72 = 12 + 20x_L$.

(ii) Use values from the table and $M\bar{y} = \sum my$ to show that $48 = 6 + 20y_L$.

(iii) Hence find the coordinates of the centre of mass of the lamina.

> The centre of mass of a composite body can be found by replacing each
> component part by a particle positioned at its centre of mass, then finding
> the centre of mass of this system of particles.
> The mass of each component of a uniform lamina is proportional to its area.

Example 3

A uniform rod, *AB*, of mass 0.6 kg is rigidly attached to a uniform plate,
CDEF, of mass 0.9 kg. *B* is the mid-point of *CF*.
Find the distance from *A* of the centre of mass of the composite body.

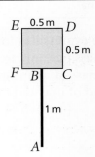

Solution

First find the centre of mass of each of the components of the body.
Each component is symmetrical, so these centres of mass can be found easily.
Take A as the origin.

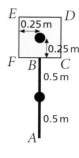

The centres of mass of the rod and the plate are shown on the diagram.
AB is a line of symmetry, so the centre of mass of the composite body
lies on the line *AB*.

Use $M\bar{y} = \Sigma my$.

$$(0.6 + 0.9)\bar{y} = 0.6 \times 0.5 + 0.9 \times 1.25$$
$$\Rightarrow \qquad 1.5\bar{y} = 1.425$$
$$\Rightarrow \qquad \bar{y} = 0.95$$

The centre of mass is 0.95 m from *A*, on the line *AB*.

Example 4

The diagram shows a uniform lamina which has
a rectangle cut out.

Find the coordinates of the centre of mass
of the lamina.

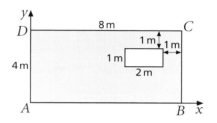

Solution

The lamina consists of a large rectangle with a small rectangle cut out.
Tabulate the areas and centres of mass of the rectangles and lamina.
By symmetry, the centre of mass of each rectangle is at its centre.

	Area	Distance of centre of mass from *AD*	Distance of centre of mass from *AB*
Rectangle *ABCD*	$32\,\text{m}^2$	4 m	2 m
Cut-out rectangle	$2\,\text{m}^2$	6 m	2.5 m
Lamina	$30\,\text{m}^2$	x_L m	y_L m

Consider the rectangle ABCD to be a composite body consisting of the lamina and
the small rectangle.

Distance of centre of mass of rectangle *ABCD* from *AD* is given by

$$32 \times 4 = 2 \times 6 + 30 \times x_L$$
$$\Rightarrow \quad 128 = 12 + 30 x_L$$
$$\Rightarrow \quad x_L = 3.87 \text{ to 3 s.f.}$$

Distance of centre of mass of rectangle *ABCD* from *AB* is given by

$$32 \times 2 = 2 \times 2.5 + 30 \times y_L$$
$$\Rightarrow \quad 64 = 5 + 30 y_L$$
$$\Rightarrow \quad y_L = 1.97 \text{ to 3 s.f.}$$

The centre of mass of the lamina is at (3.87, 1.97).

1 The uniform lamina shown consists of two rectangles.

    (a) Write down the coordinates of the centre of mass of the rectangle *ABCG*.

    (b) Write down the coordinates of the centre of mass of the rectangle *CDEF*.

    (c) Find the coordinates of the centre of mass of the lamina.

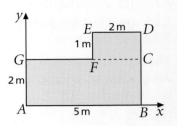

2 Find the coordinates of the centre of mass of each of the following uniform laminae.

    (a)

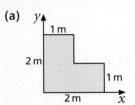

    (b)

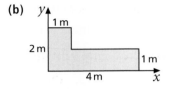

    (c)

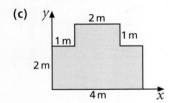

    (d)

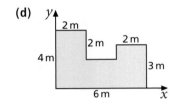

3 The diagram shows a uniform lamina *ABCDEF*.

    (a) Explain why the centre of mass of the lamina must lie on the line that goes through *A* and *D*.

    (b) Find the coordinates of the centre of mass of the lamina.

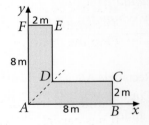

4 A uniform wire is bent to form the triangle shown.

    (a) Complete this table showing the lengths and centres of mass for the components of the triangle.

	Length	Distance of centre of mass from *AC*	Distance of centre of mass from *AB*
Side *AB*	0.3 m	0.15 m	0 m
Side *BC*	0.5 m		
Side *AC*	0.4 m		
Triangle *ABC*		$\bar{x}$ m	$\bar{y}$ m

    (b) Find the distance of the centre of mass of the triangle from *AC*.

    (c) Find the distance of the centre of mass of the triangle from *AB*.

5 A letter C is formed by bending a uniform wire into the shape shown.

   (a) Find the distance of the centre of mass from QR.

   (b) Find the distance of the centre of mass from QP.

6 A uniform rectangular lamina $ABCD$ has a circle of radius 0.5 m cut out as shown.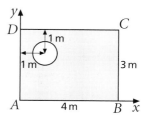

   (a) Find the coordinates of the centre of mass of the rectangle.

   (b) Find the coordinates of the centre of mass of the circle.

   (c) Find, to 2 d.p., the coordinates of the centre of mass of the lamina.

7 Find the coordinates of the centre of mass of each of the following laminae.

   (a) 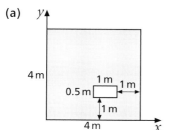   **(b)**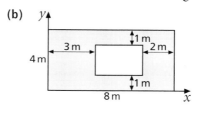

8 A pendulum consists of a disc of mass 0.2 kg and radius 5 cm attached to a uniform rod, AB, of mass 0.1 kg and length 0.9 m. The centre of the disc is fixed at B.
Find the distance of the centre of mass of the pendulum from A.

9 A uniform wire of mass 1.5 kg is bent to form a rectangle. It has particles attached as shown.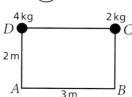

   (a) Show that the distance of the centre of mass of the composite body is 1.8 m from AB.

   (b) Find the distance of the centre of mass from AD.

10 A shop sign is made from a uniform rod, AB, of mass 0.5 kg and length 1.2 m with a uniform plate of mass 1.5 kg attached as shown.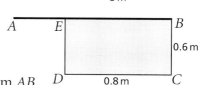

   (a) Find the distance of the centre of mass of the sign from AB.

   (b) Find the distance of the centre of mass of the sign from BC.

11 An earring is made from a uniform metal disc of radius 1.5 cm with a disc of radius 0.5 cm removed as shown.
Find the distance of the centre of mass from A.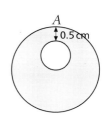

E Suspended objects (answers p 151)

E1 (a) A uniform rectangular lamina *ABCD* is suspended
   by a string attached at *A*.
   It is held in position with the longer side *AB*
   horizontal, as shown.
   If released, do you think it would stay in this position?
   Why not?

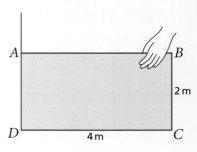

(b) The lamina is now turned and held in
   the position shown.
   Will it stay in this position if released?
   Why not?

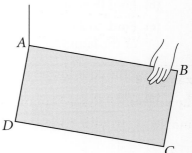

(c) Sketch the position you think it would stay in when released, explaining
   your reason.

(d) Use trigonometry to find the angle between *AB* and the vertical
   when the released lamina is in equilibrium.

E2 (a) Find the distance of the centre of mass of the uniform
   rectangular lamina *PQRS* from the side

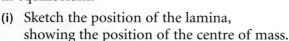

   (i) *PQ*   **(ii)** *PS*

(b) The lamina is suspended from *P* and hangs
   in equilibrium.

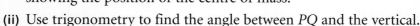

   (i) Sketch the position of the lamina,
       showing the position of the centre of mass.

   (ii) Use trigonometry to find the angle between *PQ* and the vertical.

(c) The lamina is now suspended from *S* and hangs in equilibrium.

   (i) Sketch the position of the lamina, showing the position of the centre of mass.

   (ii) Find the angle between *SP* and the vertical.

E3 The uniform rectangular lamina *KLMN* is suspended
   from *K* and hangs in equilibrium.
   Find the angle between *KL* and the vertical.

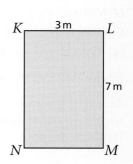

A body freely suspended from one point will hang in equilibrium with its centre of mass vertically below the point of suspension.

E4 (a) Show that the centre of mass of the lamina *ABCDEFG* is 2.25 m from *AG*.

(b) Show that the centre of mass of the lamina *ABCDEFG* is 1.75 m from *AB*.

(c) The lamina is now freely suspended from *A* and hangs in equilibrium.

   (i) Sketch the suspended lamina, showing the position of the centre of mass.

   (ii) Show that the angle between *AB* and the vertical is 38° to the nearest degree.

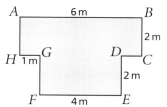

Example 5

The uniform T-shaped lamina shown is freely suspended from *A*. Find, to the nearest degree, the angle *AB* makes with the vertical.

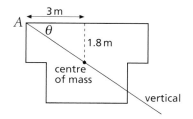

Solution

First find the centre of mass of the composite lamina.

By symmetry, the centre of mass of the lamina is 3 m from *AH*.

Tabulate the area and distance of the centre of mass from AB for each component.

	Area	Distance of centre of mass from *AB*
Rectangle *ABCH*	12 m²	1 m
Rectangle *DEFG*	8 m²	3 m
Lamina	20 m²	$\bar{y}$ m

Hence $20\bar{y} = 12 \times 1 + 8 \times 3 \implies \bar{y} = 1.8$

Now sketch the lamina with the centre of mass marked. Draw a line through A and the centre of mass to indicate the vertical and indicate the angle to be found. You do not need to reorientate the diagram. Use trigonometry to find the angle.

$\tan \theta = \frac{1.8}{3}$

So $\theta = 31°$ to the nearest degree

AB makes an angle of 31° to the vertical.

Example 6

A uniform rectangular lamina $ABCD$ of mass $2\,\text{kg}$ has a particle of mass $p\,\text{kg}$ attached at the mid-point of AD.

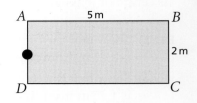

(a) Find, in terms of p, the position of the centre of mass.

(b) The lamina is freely suspended from A.
Given that it hangs in equilibrium with AB at an angle of 45° to the vertical, find the value of p.

Solution

(a) *Tabulate the mass and position of the centre of mass for each component.*

	Mass	Distance of centre of mass from AD	Distance of centre of mass from DC
Rectangle $ABCD$	$2\,\text{kg}$	$2.5\,\text{m}$	$1\,\text{m}$
Particle	$p\,\text{kg}$	$0\,\text{m}$	$1\,\text{m}$
Composite body	$(p+2)\,\text{kg}$	$\bar{x}\,\text{m}$	$\bar{y}\,\text{m}$

Find the centre of mass of the composite body.

$$M\bar{x} = \sum mx \implies (p+2)\bar{x} = 2\times 2.5 + p\times 0 \implies \bar{x} = \frac{5}{p+2}$$

The composite body has a line of symmetry through the mid-point of AD, so $\bar{y} = 1$.

The centre of mass is $\dfrac{5}{p+2}$ m from AD and 1 m from AB.

(b) *The centre of mass is shown on the diagram.*
When the lamina is suspended, the line through A
and the centre of mass is vertical, so this line is drawn
and labelled as vertical.

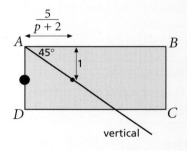

$$\tan 45° = \frac{1}{\dfrac{5}{p+2}}$$

$$\implies \quad \frac{5}{p+2} = 1$$

$$\implies \quad p = 3$$

Exercise E (answers p 152)

1 A uniform wire is bent to form a rectangular framework $PQRS$ as shown, where G is the point of intersection of the diagonals of the rectangle.

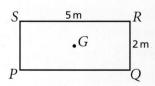

(a) Explain why the centre of mass of the framework is at point G.

(b) The framework is suspended from Q and hangs in equilibrium. Show that the angle QR makes with the vertical is 68° to the nearest degree.

2 *ABCD* is a uniform rectangular lamina as shown.

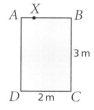

  (a) State the distance of the centre of mass from

   (i) *AB*   (ii) *AD*

  (b) The lamina is suspended from *A* and hangs in equilibrium.
      Find the angle that *AB* makes with the vertical.

  (c) The lamina is now suspended from point *X*, where $AX = 0.5$ m.
      Find the angle that *XB* makes with the vertical.

3 *ABCDEFG* is a uniform lamina as shown.

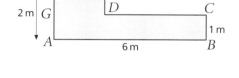

  (a) Show that the distance of the centre of mass
      from *AB* is 0.75 m.

  (b) Find the distance of the centre of mass from *AF*.

  (c) The lamina is freely suspended from *B*.
      Find the angle *BC* makes with the vertical.

4 *PQRS* is a uniform rectangular lamina with
   a rectangle cut out as shown.

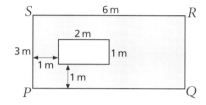

  (a) Find the distance of the centre of mass from

   (i) *PQ*   (ii) *PS*

  (b) The lamina is freely suspended from *S*.
      Find the angle *SP* makes with the vertical.

5 A mobile is made from a light rectangular framework
   with particles attached to the corners as shown.

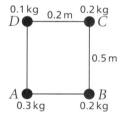

  (a) Find the distance of the centre of mass of the mobile from

   (i) *AB*   (ii) *AD*

  (b) The mobile is freely suspended from the mid-point of *AD*.
      Find the angle that *AD* makes with the vertical.

6 A light rectangular framework has particles attached as shown.

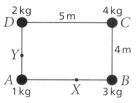

  (a) The framework is freely suspended from *X*
      and hangs with *AB* horizontal.
      Find the distance *AX*.

  (b) It is now suspended from *Y* and hangs with *AD* at
      an angle of 10° to the horizontal, with *A* higher than *D*.
      Find the distance *AY*.

7 A uniform wire of length 5 m and mass 2 kg is bent
   into the shape shown.
   A particle of mass *p* kg is attached to the wire 0.8 m from *A*.
   The framework is freely suspended from *B* and hangs
   with *AB* horizontal.
   Find the value of *p*.

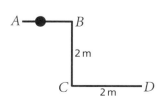

Key points

- The total moment of the weights of a system of particles about a given point is equal to the moment of the weight of a single particle of the same total mass acting at the centre of mass of the system. (p 27)

- The centre of mass of a system of particles arranged in a straight line can be found using

    total mass × distance of centre of mass from O
        = the sum of all the products mass × distance from O

    that is,
    $M\bar{x} = \sum mx$, where M is the total mass and $\bar{x}$ is the distance of the centre of mass from O. (p 27)

- The coordinates, $(\bar{x}, \bar{y})$, of the centre of mass of a system of particles in a plane are given by
    $$M\bar{x} = \sum mx, \quad M\bar{y} = \sum my$$ (p 29)

- If a system of particles or a uniform lamina has a line of symmetry, the centre of mass lies on this line.
    If it has more than one line of symmetry, the centre of mass lies on their point of intersection. (p 32)

- The centre of mass of a composite body can be found by replacing each component part by a particle positioned at its centre of mass, then finding the centre of mass of this system of particles. (p 34)

- The mass of each component of a uniform lamina is proportional to its area. (p 34)

- A body freely suspended from one point will hang in equilibrium with its centre of mass vertically below the point of suspension. (p 39)

Mixed questions (answers p 152)

1 A uniform rod AB has length 4 metres, and C is the mid-point of AB.
    Three particles are attached to the rod:

        one of mass 7 kg at A;

        one of mass 12 kg at C;

        and one of mass 11 kg at B.

    The mass of the uniform rod AB is 10 kg.

    (a) Find the distance of the centre of mass of the system of rod and particles from A.

    (b) The rod rests in a horizontal position supported at A and B.
        Find the magnitudes of the vertical forces exerted by the supports on the rod at A and B.
        AQA 2003

2 A uniform rectangular plate *PQRS* has mass 1 kg.
Particles of mass *m* kilograms are attached to the plate at *Q* and *R*.
The plate is shown in the diagram.
The dimensions of the plate are *PQ* = *SR* = 6 cm
and *PS* = *QR* = 10 cm.

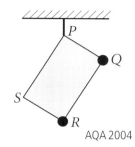

(a) State the distance of the centre of mass of the system from *PQ*.

(b) Show that the distance, in centimetres, of the centre of mass
of the system from *PS* is $\dfrac{12m+3}{2m+1}$.

(c) The plate is freely suspended from *P*, as shown in the diagram.
When the plate hangs in equilibrium, *PS* makes an angle of 45°
with the downward vertical. Find the value of *m*.

AQA 2004

Test yourself (answers p 152)

1 Three particles of masses 1 kg, 3 kg and *m* kg are placed in the *x*–*y* plane
at the points (2, 3), (4, 1) and (8, 6) respectively. The centre of mass of this
system of particles is at the point $(\bar{x}, 3)$. All distances are measured in metres.

(a) Show that *m* = 2.

(b) Find the value of $\bar{x}$.

2 The diagram shows a uniform lamina, which consists
of two rectangles *ABCD* and *DPQR*.
The dimensions are such that:
DR = *PQ* = *CP* = 12 cm;
BC = *QR* = 8 cm;
AB = *AR* = 20 cm.

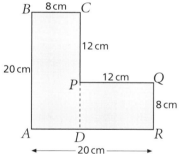

(a) Explain why the centre of mass of the lamina must
lie on the line *AP*.

(b) Find the distance of the centre of mass of the lamina
from *AB*.

(c) The lamina is freely suspended from *B*. Find, to the nearest degree,
the angle that *AB* makes with the vertical through *B*.

AQA 2003

3 A letter *P* is formed by bending a uniform steel rod into
the shape shown, in which *ABCD* is a rectangle.

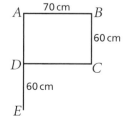

(a) Find the distance of the centre of mass of the letter from the side

(i) *AE*   (ii) *AB*

The letter is to be suspended from a point *F* on the side *AB*.
The point *F* is a distance *x* cm from *A*.

(b) State the value of *x* if the side *AB* is to be horizontal.

(c) Find the value of *x* if the side *AB* is to be at an angle of 5° to the horizontal,
with *A* higher than *B*.

AQA 2001

3 Variable acceleration

In this chapter you will learn how to
- work with position, velocity and acceleration vectors given as functions of time
- use Newton's second law of motion to find a force or an acceleration in one, two or three dimensions

A Motion in one dimension

A small object moves along a straight line. O is a fixed point on the line.

Suppose the displacement, x m, of the object from O at time t s is given by

$$x = t + 0.1t^3$$

The position of the object at $t = 0, 1, 2, 3, 4$ is shown below.

The velocity, v m s^{-1}, of the object is the rate of change of displacement with respect to time.

$$v = \frac{dx}{dt} = 1 + 0.3t^2$$

For example, when $t = 3$, $v = 1 + 0.3 \times 3^2 = 3.7$.

The velocity of the object at $t = 0, 1, 2, 3, 4$ is shown below.

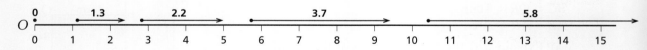

The acceleration, a m s^{-2}, of the object is the rate of change of velocity with respect to time.

$$a = \frac{dv}{dt} = 0.6t$$

The acceleration of the object at $t = 0, 1, 2, 3, 4$ is shown below.

Notice that the acceleration a varies in this example. So you cannot make use of the constant acceleration equations $v = u + at$ and so on. This will be the case throughout this chapter.

The velocity v at time t is obtained by differentiating the displacement x: $v = \dfrac{\mathrm{d}x}{\mathrm{d}t}$

The acceleration a at time t is obtained by differentiating v: $a = \dfrac{\mathrm{d}v}{\mathrm{d}t}$

So a is the second derivative of x with respect to t: $a = \dfrac{\mathrm{d}^2x}{\mathrm{d}t^2}$

The reverse of differentiation is integration.

If a is given as a function of t, by integration we get v: $v = \int a\,\mathrm{d}t$

By integrating v we get x: $x = \int v\,\mathrm{d}t$

Each time we integrate, a constant term has to be added. To find the value of this constant we need some extra information, as in example 1 below.

Calculus requirements

For the work in this chapter, you need to be familiar with the calculus (differentiation and integration) covered in Core 1 to Core 3.
The results you will need most frequently are as follows.

$$\frac{\mathrm{d}}{\mathrm{d}t}\left(t^n\right) = nt^{n-1} \quad\bigg|\quad \frac{\mathrm{d}}{\mathrm{d}t}\left(e^{at}\right) = ae^{at} \quad\bigg|\quad \frac{\mathrm{d}}{\mathrm{d}t}(\sin at) = a\cos at \quad\bigg|\quad \frac{\mathrm{d}}{\mathrm{d}t}(\cos at) = -a\sin at$$

$$\int t^n\,\mathrm{d}t = \frac{1}{n+1}t^{n+1} + c \quad\bigg|\quad \int e^{at}\,\mathrm{d}t = \frac{1}{a}e^{at} + c \quad\bigg|\quad \int \cos at\,\mathrm{d}t = \frac{1}{a}\sin at + c \quad\bigg|\quad \int \sin at\,\mathrm{d}t = -\frac{1}{a}\cos at + c$$

Remember that in the results for $\sin at$ and $\cos at$ the angle at is measured in radians.

Example 1

The velocity $v\,\mathrm{m\,s}^{-1}$ at time t s of an object moving on a straight line is given by the equation $v = 2t^3 - 5\sin t$.
At time $t = 0$ the displacement of the object from the origin is $3\,\mathrm{m}$.

Find an expression for

(a) the acceleration, $a\,\mathrm{m\,s}^{-2}$, of the object in terms of t

(b) the displacement, $x\,\mathrm{m}$, of the object in terms of t

Solution

(a) $a = \dfrac{\mathrm{d}v}{\mathrm{d}t} = 6t^2 - 5\cos t$

(b) $x = \int v\,\mathrm{d}t = \int (2t^3 - 5\sin t)\,\mathrm{d}t = \frac{1}{2}t^4 + 5\cos t + c$, where c is a constant

We are told that the displacement $x = 3$ when $t = 0$, so $3 = 0 + 5 + c$, from which $c = -2$.
So $x = \frac{1}{2}t^4 + 5\cos t - 2$

Exercise A (answers p 153)

In each of these questions, an object is assumed to be moving on a straight line. At time t seconds, the displacement of the object from a fixed point O on the line is x metres, its velocity is $v\,\text{m}\,\text{s}^{-1}$ and its acceleration is $a\,\text{m}\,\text{s}^{-2}$, where x, v and a are functions of t.

1 Given that $x = 3t^4 - t^2$, find v and a in terms of t

2 Find v and a in terms of t given that

    (a) $x = e^{3t} + e^{2t}$
                              (b) $x = \sin 3t + \cos 2t$

3 You are given that $v = 0.5t + 1.5t^2$.

    (a) Find an expression for x in terms of t, including a constant of integration.

    (b) Given that $x = 1$ when $t = 0$,

        (i) find the value of the constant and hence express x in terms of t

        (ii) find the value of x when $t = 2$

4 You are given that $v = \sin 2t + 3e^{\frac{1}{2}t}$.

    (a) Find an expression for a in terms of t.

    (b) **(i)** Find an expression for x in terms of t, including a constant of integration.

        (ii) Given that $x = 0$ when $t = 0$, find the value of the constant and hence express x in terms of t.

5 In each of the following cases, find an expression in terms of t for

    (i) the acceleration a

    (ii) the displacement x, given that $x = 0$ when $t = 0$

    (iii) the value of x when $t = 3$

        (a) $v = 2t^3 - 6t$
                (b) $v = t^4 - 3t^2$
                (c) $v = 4e^{-3t}$

        (d) $v = 3\cos 2t$
                (e) $v = \sin \dfrac{\pi t}{2}$
                (f) $v = 4\cos \dfrac{\pi t}{4}$

6 The position of an object moving on a straight line is given by

$$x = t^2 + 2\sin 3t$$

    (a) Find an expression for

        (i) the velocity of the object

        (ii) the acceleration of the object

    (b) When $t = 0$, the acceleration is $2\,\text{m}\,\text{s}^{-2}$.

        Find, to three significant figures, the first value of t for which the acceleration is 0.

    (c) Show that the first value of t for which the acceleration is $11\,\text{m}\,\text{s}^{-2}$ is $\dfrac{7\pi}{18}$.

7 The acceleration, $a\,\mathrm{m\,s^{-2}}$, of an object moving on a straight line is given by

$$a = 3 + 2\sqrt{t} \quad (t \ge 0)$$

At time $t = 0$, the object passes through the origin $x = 0$ with velocity $4\,\mathrm{m\,s^{-1}}$.

(a) Find an expression in terms of t for

    (i) the velocity of the object

    (ii) the position of the object

(b) Find the speed of the object and its distance from the origin when $t = 2$.

8 The position of a point P moving on a straight line is given by

$$x = 5\sin\frac{\pi t}{6}$$

The positions of P at times $t = 0, 1, 2$ are shown in the diagram below.

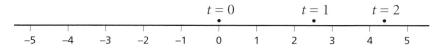

(a) Copy the diagram and add to it the positions of P when $t = 3, 4, 5, \ldots, 12$.

(b) What is the interval between times when $x = 0$?

(c) Find v in terms of t.

(d) What is the value of v when

    (i) $t = 0$ (ii) $t = 3$ (iii) $t = 6$

(e) Describe in words the motion of the point P.

9 The velocity, $v\,\mathrm{m\,s^{-1}}$, of an object moving on a straight line is given by

$$v = pt^2 + qt$$

where p and q are constants.

When $t = 2$, $v = 4$ and $a = -3$.

(a) Find the values of p and q.

(b) Given that $x = 5$ when $t = 2$, find the value of x when $t = 4$.

10 The velocity, $v\,\mathrm{m\,s^{-1}}$, of an object moving on a straight line is given by

$$v = p\sin\pi t + q\sin 2\pi t$$

where p and q are constants.

When $t = \frac{1}{2}$, $v = 5$ and $a = 6$.

(a) Find the values of p and q.

(b) Given that $x = 0$ when $t = 0$, find the value of x when $t = 1$.

B Motion in two dimensions 1 (answers p 153)

Position vector

In two dimensions, the position vector, **r**, of a point is expressed as the sum of two components x and y in the directions of two perpendicular unit vectors **i** and **j**.

$$\mathbf{r} = x\mathbf{i} + y\mathbf{j}$$

For a moving object, each component x, y is a function of t, for example

$$\mathbf{r} = \tfrac{1}{2}t^2\mathbf{i} + 10\sin\tfrac{1}{2}t\mathbf{j}$$

We can find the position vector of the object for each value of t.

When $t = 0$, $\mathbf{r} = 0\mathbf{i} + 0\mathbf{j}$, so the object starts at the origin.

B1 Verify that, when $t = 1$, $\mathbf{r} = 0.5\mathbf{i} + 4.79\mathbf{j}$, and find **r** when $t = 2, 3, 4, 5$.

B2 Plot on a grid the five positions for $t = 0, 1, 2, 3, 4$ and label them '$t = 0$', '$t = 1$' and so on.
Draw a smooth curve through the points to show the path of the moving object.

Velocity vector

Suppose that in a short time interval δt, the change in the position vector is $\delta\mathbf{r} = \delta x\mathbf{i} + \delta y\mathbf{j}$, as shown in this diagram.

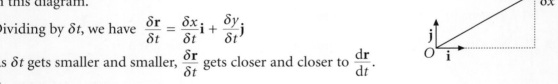

Dividing by δt, we have $\dfrac{\delta\mathbf{r}}{\delta t} = \dfrac{\delta x}{\delta t}\mathbf{i} + \dfrac{\delta y}{\delta t}\mathbf{j}$

As δt gets smaller and smaller, $\dfrac{\delta\mathbf{r}}{\delta t}$ gets closer and closer to $\dfrac{d\mathbf{r}}{dt}$.

$\dfrac{d\mathbf{r}}{dt}$ is the rate of change of position with time, which is the velocity, **v**.

Similarly, $\dfrac{\delta x}{\delta t}$ and $\dfrac{\delta y}{\delta t}$ get closer and closer to $\dfrac{dx}{dt}$ and $\dfrac{dy}{dt}$.

So $\mathbf{v} = \dfrac{dx}{dt}\mathbf{i} + \dfrac{dy}{dt}\mathbf{j}$

This means that **v** is obtained from **r** by differentiating each component separately.

For example, if $\mathbf{r} = \tfrac{1}{2}t^2\mathbf{i} + 10\sin\tfrac{1}{2}t\mathbf{j}$

then $\mathbf{v} = \dfrac{d\mathbf{r}}{dt} = t\mathbf{i} + 5\cos\tfrac{1}{2}t\mathbf{j}$

B3 Verify that, when $t = 0$, $\mathbf{v} = 5\mathbf{j}$, and find **v** when $t = 1, 2, 3, 4, 5$.

Acceleration vector

The acceleration **a** is the rate of change of velocity, or $\dfrac{\mathrm{d}\mathbf{v}}{\mathrm{d}t}$.

This is obtained by differentiating each component of **v** separately:

$$\mathbf{v} = t\mathbf{i} + 5\cos\tfrac{1}{2}t\mathbf{j}$$
$$\mathbf{a} = \frac{\mathrm{d}\mathbf{v}}{\mathrm{d}t} = \mathbf{i} - 2.5\sin\tfrac{1}{2}t\mathbf{j}$$

B4 Find **a** when $t = 0, 1, 2, 3, 4, 5$.

Position, velocity and acceleration vectors

The diagram below shows the path of the object, together with the velocity and acceleration vectors at each of the points where $t = 1, 2, 3, 4, 5$.

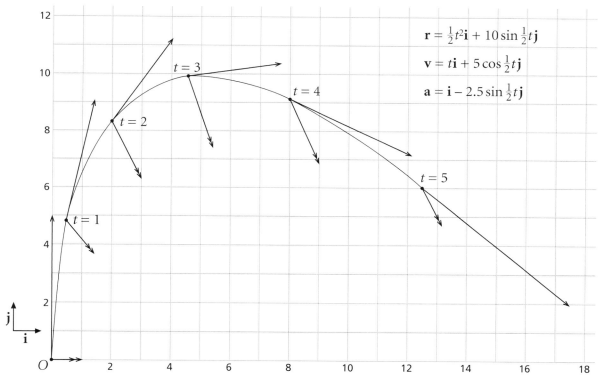

$$\mathbf{r} = \tfrac{1}{2}t^2\mathbf{i} + 10\sin\tfrac{1}{2}t\mathbf{j}$$
$$\mathbf{v} = t\mathbf{i} + 5\cos\tfrac{1}{2}t\mathbf{j}$$
$$\mathbf{a} = \mathbf{i} - 2.5\sin\tfrac{1}{2}t\mathbf{j}$$

Notice that

- the velocity is always in the direction of the tangent to the path of the object
- the acceleration is always directed towards the 'inside' of the curve of the path

B5 Between $t = 3$ and $t = 4$, there is a point where the velocity of the object is, at that instant, in the **i**-direction. At this point, the **j**-component of **v** is 0, so $5\cos\tfrac{1}{2}t = 0$. Find the value of t at this instant, correct to two decimal places.

The direction in which an object is moving at an instant is the direction of its velocity.

If the component of velocity in the **i**-direction is 0, then at that instant the object is moving in the **j**-direction, and vice versa.

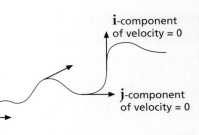

The diagram below shows the path of an object whose position is given by

$$\mathbf{r} = t^2\mathbf{i} + 4\left(1 + \cos \tfrac{1}{3}\pi t\right)\mathbf{j}$$

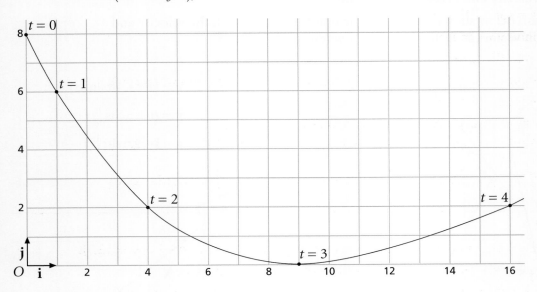

B6 (a) Verify that the positions at $t = 0, 1, 2, 3, 4$ shown in the diagram are correct.

(b) By differentiating **r** with respect to t, find an expression for the velocity **v**.

(c) Find the value of **v** when $t = 0, 1, 2, 3, 4$, and check from the diagram that the results you get are reasonable.

(d) What is special about the velocity when $t = 3$?

(e) By differentiating **v** with respect to t, find an expression for the acceleration **a**.

(f) Find the value of **a** when $t = 0, 1, 2, 3, 4$, and check from the diagram that the results you get are reasonable.

B7 Find expressions for **v** and **a** for each of the following paths.

(a) $\mathbf{r} = 5t^2\mathbf{i} + 4t\mathbf{j}$

(b) $\mathbf{r} = (2t^2 - 3t)\mathbf{i} + 4t^3\mathbf{j}$

(c) $\mathbf{r} = 5e^t\mathbf{i} + t^2\mathbf{j}$

(d) $\mathbf{r} = e^{2t}\mathbf{i} + e^{3t}\mathbf{j}$

(e) $\mathbf{r} = \sin t\mathbf{i} + \sin 2t\mathbf{j}$

(f) $\mathbf{r} = \cos \tfrac{1}{2}\pi t\mathbf{i} + \sin \tfrac{1}{3}\pi t\mathbf{j}$

The magnitude of **r** is denoted by $|\mathbf{r}|$ or r.
Similarly for $|\mathbf{v}|$ and $|\mathbf{a}|$.

The magnitude of a vector is found by using Pythagoras's theorem. The angle the vector makes with the **i**-direction can be found using trigonometry.

$|\mathbf{r}|$ is the distance from the origin.

$|\mathbf{v}|$ is the speed.

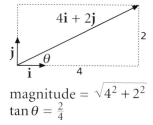

magnitude $= \sqrt{4^2 + 2^2}$
$\tan\theta = \frac{2}{4}$

B8 The velocity, $\mathbf{v}\,\mathrm{m\,s}^{-1}$, of an object at time t s is given by

$$\mathbf{v} = (3t + 2)\mathbf{i} + (t^2 - 1)\mathbf{j}$$

(a) Find **v** when $t = 2$.

(b) Find the speed of the object when $t = 2$.

(c) Find the angle that the velocity makes with the **i**-direction when $t = 2$.

(d) Find the acceleration $\mathbf{a}\,\mathrm{m\,s}^{-2}$ at time t.

(e) Find the magnitude of the acceleration when $t = 2$.

(f) Find the angle that the acceleration makes with the **i**-direction when $t = 2$.

If $\mathbf{r} = \mathrm{f}(t)\mathbf{i} + \mathrm{g}(t)\mathbf{j}$, then $\mathbf{v} = \dfrac{\mathrm{d}\mathbf{r}}{\mathrm{d}t} = \mathrm{f}'(t)\mathbf{i} + \mathrm{g}'(t)\mathbf{j}$ and $\mathbf{a} = \dfrac{\mathrm{d}\mathbf{v}}{\mathrm{d}t} = \mathrm{f}''(t)\mathbf{i} + \mathrm{g}''(t)\mathbf{j}$

Example 2

The position vector, $\mathbf{r}$ m, of a particle at time t s is given by $\mathbf{r} = \sin 2t\,\mathbf{i} + (t + \cos 2t)\mathbf{j}$.

(a) Find an expression for the velocity $\mathbf{v}\,\mathrm{m\,s}^{-1}$ of the particle at time t.

(b) Find the first value of t after $t = 0$ for which the particle is moving in the direction of **i**.

(c) Show that the magnitude of the acceleration of the particle is constant.

Solution

(a) $\mathbf{v} = \dfrac{\mathrm{d}\mathbf{r}}{\mathrm{d}t} = 2\cos 2t\,\mathbf{i} + (1 - 2\sin 2t)\mathbf{j}$

(b) If the particle is moving in the direction of **i**, the **j**-component of its velocity is 0.

$$1 - 2\sin 2t = 0 \implies \sin 2t = \tfrac{1}{2}$$
$$\implies \quad 2t = \tfrac{1}{6}\pi \ \left(\text{or } \tfrac{5}{6}\pi, \ldots, \text{but only the first value is required}\right)$$
$$\implies \quad t = \tfrac{1}{12}\pi$$

(c) $\mathbf{a} = \dfrac{\mathrm{d}\mathbf{v}}{\mathrm{d}t} = -4\sin 2t\,\mathbf{i} - 4\cos 2t\,\mathbf{j}$

$$|\mathbf{a}| = \sqrt{\left(-4\sin 2t\right)^2 + \left(-4\cos 2t\right)^2} = \sqrt{16\left(\sin^2 2t + \cos^2 2t\right)}$$
$$= \sqrt{16} = 4 \ (\text{because } \sin^2\theta + \cos^2\theta = 1 \text{ for all } \theta)$$

Note: Although the magnitude of the acceleration is constant, the acceleration itself is not constant because its direction is changing.

Example 3

The position vector, $\mathbf{r}$ km, at time t hours, of a boat relative to a point O on the edge of a lake is given by

$$\mathbf{r} = (1 - \cos 3t)\mathbf{i} - 2t\mathbf{j} \quad (t \geq 0)$$

where $\mathbf{i}$ and $\mathbf{j}$ are unit vectors in the directions east and north respectively. Find the value of t for which the boat is first moving south-east.

Solution

The direction of the boat is the direction of its velocity $\mathbf{v}$.

$$\mathbf{v} = \frac{\mathrm{d}\mathbf{r}}{\mathrm{d}t} = 3\sin 3t\,\mathbf{i} - 2\mathbf{j}$$

South-east is the direction of the vector $\mathbf{i} - \mathbf{j}$. (See diagram.)

When $\mathbf{v}$ is in the direction south-east, $\mathbf{v}$ must be a multiple of $\mathbf{i} - \mathbf{j}$.
So $\mathbf{v}$ must be of the form $A(\mathbf{i} - \mathbf{j}) = A\mathbf{i} - A\mathbf{j}$.
In other words, ($\mathbf{j}$-component of $\mathbf{v}$) = $-$($\mathbf{i}$-component of $\mathbf{v}$).

So $-2 = -3\sin 3t \Rightarrow \sin 3t = \frac{2}{3} \Rightarrow 3t = \sin^{-1}\frac{2}{3}$ (the first value whose sine is $\frac{2}{3}$)

$$= 0.7297\ldots, \text{ from which } t = 0.243 \text{ (to 3 s.f.)}$$

Exercise B (answers p 154)

Give answers to three significant figures where appropriate.

1 The position vector, $\mathbf{r}$ m, of a particle at time t s is given by
$$\mathbf{r} = (5t - t^2)\mathbf{i} + t^3\mathbf{j}$$
(a) Find an expression for the velocity of the particle at time t.
(b) Find the speed of the particle when $t = 2$.
(c) Find an expression for the acceleration of the particle at time t.
(d) Find the magnitude of the acceleration when $t = 2$.

2 The velocity, $\mathbf{v}$ m s^{-1}, of a particle at time t s is given by
$$\mathbf{v} = (t + t^3)\mathbf{i} - 4t^2\mathbf{j}$$
(a) Find an expression for the acceleration of the particle at time t.
(b) Find the magnitude of the acceleration when $t = 3$.

3 The position vector, $\mathbf{r}$ m, of a particle at time t s is given by
$$\mathbf{r} = 16t^2\mathbf{i} + (t^3 - 48t)\mathbf{j} \quad (t \geq 0)$$
(a) Find an expression for the velocity of the particle at time t.
(b) Find the time at which the particle is moving in the $\mathbf{i}$-direction.
(c) Find the time at which the particle is moving in the direction of the vector $\mathbf{i} - \mathbf{j}$.

4 The position vector, $\mathbf{r}$ m, of a particle at time t s is given by
$$\mathbf{r} = (t^3 - 7t^2 + 8)\mathbf{i} + (t^2 - 6t)\mathbf{j}$$
   (a) Find an expression for the velocity of the particle at time t.
   (b) Find the value of t when the particle is moving in the direction of $\mathbf{i}$.
   (c) Find the speed of the particle at this time.
   (d) Show that there are two values of t for which the particle is moving in the direction of $\mathbf{j}$ and find these values.
   (e) Find the speed of the particle at each of these times.

5 The position vector, $\mathbf{r}$ cm, of a point moving on a screen, is given by
$$\mathbf{r} = \left(\tfrac{1}{4}e^t - t\right)\mathbf{i} + \left(e^{\frac{1}{2}t} - 3t\right)\mathbf{j}$$
where $\mathbf{i}$ is a horizontal unit vector and $\mathbf{j}$ is a vertical unit vector.

   (a) Find an expression for the velocity of the moving point at time t.
   (b) Show that when $t = \ln 4$ the velocity of the point is vertical.
   (c) Find the value of t for which the velocity is horizontal.

6 The position vector, $\mathbf{r}$ m, of a particle at time t s is given by
$$\mathbf{r} = \sin 5t\,\mathbf{i} + 4t\,\mathbf{j}$$
   (a) Find an expression for the velocity of the particle at time t.
   (b) Show that the velocity of the particle is in the direction of $\mathbf{i} + \mathbf{j}$ whenever $\cos 5t = 0.8$.
   (c) (i) Find the first value of t after $t = 0$ for which the velocity is in the direction of $\mathbf{i} + \mathbf{j}$.
   (ii) Find the magnitude of the acceleration of the particle at this time.

7 The unit vectors $\mathbf{i}$ and $\mathbf{j}$ are directed east and north respectively.
The position vector, $\mathbf{r}$ m, of a boat at time t s is given by
$$\mathbf{r} = 10\sin\frac{t}{30}\,\mathbf{i} + 15\sin\frac{t}{45}\,\mathbf{j}$$
   (a) Find an expression for the velocity of the boat at time t.
   (b) Find, to 3 s.f., the speed of the boat when $t = 15$.
   (c) (i) Find, to the nearest second, the time when the boat is first travelling due north.
   (ii) Find the speed of the boat at this time.
   (iii) Find the distance of the boat from its starting point at this time.
   (iv) Find the magnitude of the acceleration of the particle at this time.

8 The position vector, $\mathbf{r}$ m, of a particle at time t s is given by

$$\mathbf{r} = 3\cos \pi t \mathbf{i} + 4\sin \pi t \mathbf{j}$$

(a) Find the distance of the particle from the origin at time $t = \frac{1}{4}$.

(b) Find an expression for the velocity of the particle at time t.

(c) Find the speed of the particle at time $t = \frac{1}{4}$.

(d) Find the magnitude of the acceleration of the particle at time

    (i) $t = \frac{1}{4}$ (ii) $t = \frac{1}{2}$ (iii) $t = 1$

9 The velocity, $\mathbf{v}$ m s^{-1}, of a particle at time t s is given by

$$\mathbf{v} = 4e^{-t}\mathbf{i} - 3e^{-2t}\mathbf{j}$$

(a) Find the speed of the particle when $t = 0$.

(b) Find the magnitude of the acceleration of the particle when $t = 0$.

10 The position vector, $\mathbf{r}$ m, of a particle at time t s is given by

$$\mathbf{r} = 4e^{0.5t}\mathbf{i} + 24e^{0.2t}\mathbf{j}$$

(a) Find an expression for the velocity of the particle at time t.

(b) At time T the particle is moving in the direction of the vector $\mathbf{i} + \mathbf{j}$.

Show that $e^{0.3T} = 2.4$, and hence find the value of T.

11 The position vector, $\mathbf{r}$ m, of a particle at time t s relative to an origin O is given by

$$\mathbf{r} = Ae^{2t}\mathbf{i} + Be^{3t}\mathbf{j}, \text{ where } A \text{ and } B \text{ are positive constants}$$

(a) Find the values of A and B given the following information:

- The speed of the particle at time $t = 0$ is $20\,\text{m s}^{-1}$.
- The magnitude of the acceleration of the particle at time $t = 0$ is $50\,\text{m s}^{-2}$.

(b) Find the distance of the particle from the origin at time $t = 0$.

12 A wheel of radius 1 metre rolls along a horizontal straight track, making one complete revolution per second. At time $t = 0$, a point P on the circumference of the wheel is in contact with the track. This starting position of P is taken as the origin.

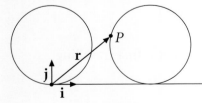

It can be shown that the position vector, $\mathbf{r}$ metres, of P at time t is given by

$$\mathbf{r} = (2\pi t - \sin 2\pi t)\mathbf{i} + (1 - \cos 2\pi t)\mathbf{j}$$

where $\mathbf{i}$ and $\mathbf{j}$ are horizontal and vertical unit vectors respectively.

(a) Show that the speed of the point P at time t is $4\pi \sin \pi t$ m s^{-1}.

(b) What is the speed of P each time it passes through its highest position?

C Motion in two dimensions 2 (answers p 155)

Because $\mathbf{v} = \dfrac{d\mathbf{r}}{dt}$, it follows that $\mathbf{r} = \int \mathbf{v} \, dt$.

For example, suppose $\mathbf{v} = t^2 \mathbf{i} + e^{4t}\mathbf{j}$.

Then $\mathbf{r} = \int \mathbf{v} \, dt = \int (t^2 \mathbf{i} + e^{4t}\mathbf{j}) \, dt$

$\qquad\qquad = \left(\int t^2 \, dt\right)\mathbf{i} + \left(\int e^{4t} \, dt\right)\mathbf{j}$ separating into components

$\qquad\qquad = \left(\tfrac{1}{3}t^3 + c_1\right)\mathbf{i} + \left(\tfrac{1}{4}e^{4t} + c_2\right)\mathbf{j}$ integrating each component and including a constant of integration for each

$\qquad\qquad = \tfrac{1}{3}t^3\mathbf{i} + \tfrac{1}{4}e^{4t}\mathbf{j} + (c_1\mathbf{i} + c_2\mathbf{j})$ collecting the constants of integration

The two constants of integration can be written as a single constant vector $\mathbf{c}$:

$\qquad \mathbf{r} = \tfrac{1}{3}t^3\mathbf{i} + \tfrac{1}{4}e^{4t}\mathbf{j} + \mathbf{c}$

All that has happened here is that each component of $\mathbf{v}$ has been integrated and a constant of integration has been added. But as we are working in two dimensions, the constant of integration is a vector $\mathbf{c}$.

To find the value of $\mathbf{c}$, we need more information.

For example, suppose that $\mathbf{r} = \mathbf{0}$ $(= 0\mathbf{i} + 0\mathbf{j})$ when $t = 0$.

Then $\tfrac{1}{3}0^3\mathbf{i} + \tfrac{1}{4}e^0\mathbf{j} + \mathbf{c} = \mathbf{0}$

$\Rightarrow \qquad\qquad\qquad \tfrac{1}{4}\mathbf{j} + \mathbf{c} = \mathbf{0}$

$\Rightarrow \qquad\qquad\qquad\qquad \mathbf{c} = -\tfrac{1}{4}\mathbf{j}$

So $\mathbf{r} = \tfrac{1}{3}t^3\mathbf{i} + \tfrac{1}{4}e^{4t}\mathbf{j} - \tfrac{1}{4}\mathbf{j}$

$\qquad = \tfrac{1}{3}t^3\mathbf{i} + \tfrac{1}{4}(e^{4t} - 1)\mathbf{j}$ (collecting terms in $\mathbf{i}$ and $\mathbf{j}$)

C1 Given that

$\qquad \mathbf{v} = 6t^2\mathbf{i} + (4t - 3)\mathbf{j}$

and that $\mathbf{r} = \mathbf{i} + \mathbf{j}$ when $t = 0$, find $\mathbf{r}$ in terms of t.

C2 Given that

$\qquad \mathbf{v} = e^{3t}\mathbf{i} + \sin 2t \, \mathbf{j}$,

and that $\mathbf{r} = \mathbf{0}$ when $t = 0$, show that

$\qquad \mathbf{r} = \tfrac{1}{3}(e^{3t} - 1)\mathbf{i} - \tfrac{1}{2}(\cos 2t - 1)\mathbf{j}$

The process of finding $\mathbf{v}$ from $\mathbf{a}$ by integration is similar: $\mathbf{v} = \int \mathbf{a} \, dt$.

C3 Given that

$\qquad \mathbf{a} = 3(t^2 - 4)\mathbf{i} + (t + 2)\mathbf{j}$

and that $\mathbf{v} = 2\mathbf{i} - \mathbf{j}$ when $t = 0$, find $\mathbf{v}$ in terms of t.

🅚 $\mathbf{v} = \int \mathbf{a} \, dt \qquad \mathbf{r} = \int \mathbf{v} \, dt$ Include a constant of integration $\mathbf{c}$.

Example 4

A particle passes the origin $\mathbf{r} = \mathbf{0}$ at time $t = 0$. The velocity, $\mathbf{v}\,\mathrm{m\,s^{-1}}$, of the particle at time $t\,\mathrm{s}$ is given by $\mathbf{v} = e^{\frac{1}{2}t}\mathbf{i} + (1 + e^{2t})\mathbf{j}$.

Find an expression for the position vector of the particle in terms of t in the form $a\mathbf{i} + b\mathbf{j}$.

Solution

$\mathbf{r} = \int \mathbf{v}\,\mathrm{d}t = 2e^{\frac{1}{2}t}\mathbf{i} + \left(t + \frac{1}{2}e^{2t}\right)\mathbf{j} + \mathbf{c}$

When $t = 0$, $\mathbf{r} = \mathbf{0}$. So $2e^0\mathbf{i} + \left(0 + \frac{1}{2}e^0\right)\mathbf{j} + \mathbf{c} = \mathbf{0}$

$\Rightarrow \qquad\qquad 2\mathbf{i} + \frac{1}{2}\mathbf{j} + \mathbf{c} = \mathbf{0}$

$\Rightarrow \qquad\qquad\qquad\qquad \mathbf{c} = -2\mathbf{i} - \frac{1}{2}\mathbf{j}$

So $\mathbf{r} = 2e^{\frac{1}{2}t}\mathbf{i} + \left(t + \frac{1}{2}e^{2t}\right)\mathbf{j} - 2\mathbf{i} - \frac{1}{2}\mathbf{j}$

$\qquad = (2e^{\frac{1}{2}t} - 2)\mathbf{i} + (t + \frac{1}{2}e^{2t} - \frac{1}{2})\mathbf{j}$

Exercise C (answers p 156)

1 The velocity, $\mathbf{v}\,\mathrm{m\,s^{-1}}$, of a particle at time $t\,\mathrm{s}$ is given by $\mathbf{v} = (8t - 6t^2)\mathbf{i} + (4t + 3t^2)\mathbf{j}$. Given that $\mathbf{r} = \mathbf{0}$ when $t = 0$, find an expression for $\mathbf{r}$ in terms of t.

2 The acceleration, $\mathbf{a}\,\mathrm{m\,s^{-2}}$, of a particle at time $t\,\mathrm{s}$ is given by $\mathbf{a} = (2 + 5t)\mathbf{i} + (4t + t^2)\mathbf{j}$. Given that the velocity $\mathbf{v} = 2\mathbf{i}$ when $t = 0$, find an expression for $\mathbf{v}$ in terms of t.

3 The acceleration, $\mathbf{a}\,\mathrm{m\,s^{-2}}$, of a particle at time $t\,\mathrm{s}$ is given by $\mathbf{a} = (t - 1)\mathbf{i} + (t^3 - t)\mathbf{j}$. At time $t = 0$, the particle passes through the origin with velocity $5\mathbf{j}\,\mathrm{m\,s^{-1}}$.

Find an expression for

(a) $\mathbf{v}$ in terms of t \qquad\qquad\qquad (b) $\mathbf{r}$ in terms of t

4 Given that $\mathbf{v} = 3\cos\frac{1}{2}t\mathbf{i} + 2\sin\frac{1}{2}t\mathbf{j}$, and that $\mathbf{r} = \mathbf{0}$ when $t = 0$, find $\mathbf{r}$ in terms of t.

5 In each case below, find expressions for $\mathbf{v}$ and for $\mathbf{r}$ in terms of t, given the velocity and the position of the particle at time $t = 0$.
Give each answer in the form $a\mathbf{i} + b\mathbf{j}$.

(a) $\mathbf{a} = (9t^2 + 2)\mathbf{i} + (12t^2 - 1)\mathbf{j}$ \qquad $\mathbf{v} = \mathbf{i} + \mathbf{j}$ and $\mathbf{r} = \mathbf{0}$ when $t = 0$

(b) $\mathbf{a} = 3\cos 4t\mathbf{i} + 2\sin 2t\mathbf{j}$ \qquad\qquad $\mathbf{v} = 6\mathbf{j}$ and $\mathbf{r} = \mathbf{0}$ when $t = 0$

(c) $\mathbf{a} = (e^{-t})\mathbf{i} + (1 - e^{-2t})\mathbf{j}$ \qquad\quad $\mathbf{v} = \mathbf{0}$ and $\mathbf{r} = \mathbf{0}$ when $t = 0$

(d) $\mathbf{a} = 2\cos\frac{1}{6}t\mathbf{i} + 2\sin\frac{1}{6}t\mathbf{j}$ \qquad\quad $\mathbf{v} = \mathbf{0}$ and $\mathbf{r} = \mathbf{0}$ when $t = 0$

6 The velocity, $\mathbf{v}\,\mathrm{m\,s^{-1}}$, of a particle at time $t\,\mathrm{s}$ is given by $\mathbf{v} = (3t - t^2)\mathbf{i} + 8t^3\mathbf{j}$. At time $t = 0$, the particle passes through the origin.

(a) Find the values of t for which the particle is moving in the direction of $\mathbf{j}$.

(b) Find an expression for the acceleration of the particle at time t.

(c) Find an expression for the position of the particle at time t.

D Motion in three dimensions (answers p 156)

In three dimensions, positions, velocities and accelerations are specified in terms of three unit vectors $\mathbf{i}, \mathbf{j}, \mathbf{k}$ that are mutually perpendicular (that is, at right angles to each other).

In many applications, $\mathbf{i}$ and $\mathbf{j}$ are both horizontal and $\mathbf{k}$ is vertical.

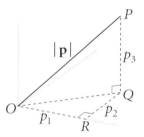

D1 Given that $\mathbf{v} = (4t - 5)\mathbf{i} + (3t^2 + 8t)\mathbf{j} + (7 - 2t)\mathbf{k}$
and that $\mathbf{r} = 5\mathbf{i}$ when $t = 0$,

(a) find $\mathbf{a}$ in terms of t

(b) find $\mathbf{r}$ in terms of t

The magnitude of a three-dimensional vector can be found using Pythagoras's theorem.

The diagram shows a vector $\mathbf{p}$ (which may be a position, velocity, acceleration or force) whose three components are p_1, p_2 and p_3.

$$\mathbf{p} = p_1\mathbf{i} + p_2\mathbf{j} + p_3\mathbf{k}$$

Applying Pythagoras to triangle OQR, we have $OQ^2 = p_1{}^2 + p_2{}^2$.
Applying Pythagoras to triangle OPQ, we have $|\mathbf{p}|^2 = OQ^2 + p_3{}^2$

So $|\mathbf{p}|^2 = p_1{}^2 + p_2{}^2 + p_3{}^2$, from which $|\mathbf{p}| = \sqrt{p_1{}^2 + p_2{}^2 + p_3{}^2}$.

If $\mathbf{r} = \mathrm{f}(t)\mathbf{i} + \mathrm{g}(t)\mathbf{j} + \mathrm{h}(t)\mathbf{k}$,

then $\mathbf{v} = \dfrac{\mathrm{d}\mathbf{r}}{\mathrm{d}t} = \mathrm{f}'(t)\mathbf{i} + \mathrm{g}'(t)\mathbf{j} + \mathrm{h}'(t)\mathbf{k}$ and $\mathbf{a} = \dfrac{\mathrm{d}\mathbf{v}}{\mathrm{d}t} = \mathrm{f}''(t)\mathbf{i} + \mathrm{g}''(t)\mathbf{j} + \mathrm{h}''(t)\mathbf{k}$.

Example 5

The position vector, $\mathbf{r}$ m, of an object at time t s is given by

$$\mathbf{r} = (t^3 - 5t^2 + 3t)\mathbf{i} + (t^3 - 8t^2 + 5t)\mathbf{j} + (e^{2t} - 3t)\mathbf{k}$$

where $\mathbf{i}$ and $\mathbf{j}$ are horizontal unit vectors and $\mathbf{k}$ is a vertical unit vector.

Find the times when the object is moving

(a) horizontally   (b) vertically

Solution

To find the direction of motion we need the velocity $\mathbf{v}$.

$$\mathbf{v} = \frac{\mathrm{d}\mathbf{r}}{\mathrm{d}t} = (3t^2 - 10t + 3)\mathbf{i} + (3t^2 - 16t + 5)\mathbf{j} + (2e^{2t} - 3)\mathbf{k}$$

(a) When the object is moving horizontally, the $\mathbf{k}$-component of $\mathbf{v}$ is 0.

$$2e^{2t} - 3 = 0 \implies e^{2t} = \tfrac{3}{2} \implies 2t = \ln\tfrac{3}{2} \implies t = \tfrac{1}{2}\ln\tfrac{3}{2}$$

(b) When the object is moving vertically, both the $\mathbf{i}$-component and $\mathbf{j}$-components are 0.

So $3t^2 - 10t + 3 = 0$ and $3t^2 - 16t + 5 = 0$

$$\implies (3t - 1)(t - 3) = 0 \quad \text{and} \quad (3t - 1)(t - 5) = 0$$

The only value of t that makes both components zero is $t = \tfrac{1}{3}$.

Exercise D (answers p 156)

1 The position vector, $\mathbf{r}$ m, of a particle at time t s is given by

$$\mathbf{r} = t^2\mathbf{i} + (4t^2 - 2)\mathbf{j} + (t^3 - t^2)\mathbf{k}$$

where $\mathbf{i}$ and $\mathbf{j}$ are horizontal unit vectors and $\mathbf{k}$ is vertically upwards.

(a) Find an expression for the velocity, $\mathbf{v}$ m s^{-1}, of the particle at time t.

(b) Find the times at which the particle is moving horizontally.

(c) Find the speed of the particle when $t = 2$.

(d) Find an expression for the acceleration, $\mathbf{a}$ m s^{-2}, of the particle at time t.

(e) Find the time at which the acceleration is horizontal.

(f) Find the magnitude of the acceleration when $t = 0$.

2 The velocity, $\mathbf{v}$ m s^{-1}, of a particle at time t s is given by

$$\mathbf{v} = 4t\mathbf{i} + 3t\mathbf{j} + \cos\tfrac{1}{4}\pi t\,\mathbf{k}$$

where $\mathbf{i}$ and $\mathbf{j}$ are horizontal unit vectors and $\mathbf{k}$ is vertically upwards.

(a) Find the time at which the particle is first moving horizontally.

(b) Find the speed of the particle when it is first moving horizontally.

(c) Find the speed of the particle when it is moving horizontally for the second time.

(d) Find an expression for the acceleration, $\mathbf{a}$ m s^{-2}, of the particle at time t.

(e) Find an expression for the position vector, $\mathbf{r}$ m, of the particle at time t, given that $\mathbf{r} = \mathbf{0}$ when $t = 0$.

3 The position vector, $\mathbf{r}$ m, of a radio-controlled model aircraft at time t s is given by

$$\mathbf{r} = 50\cos 0.1t\,\mathbf{i} + 50\sin 0.1t\,\mathbf{j} + 10(2 - e^{-0.5t})\mathbf{k}$$

where $\mathbf{i}$ and $\mathbf{j}$ are in the directions east and north respectively, $\mathbf{k}$ is vertically upwards and the origin is at ground level.

(a) What happens to the height of the aircraft as time increases?

(b) Show that the **horizontal** distance of the aircraft from the origin is constant. What does this tell you about the path of the aircraft?

(c) Find an expression for the velocity, $\mathbf{v}$ m s^{-1}, of the aircraft at time t.

(d) Show that the speed of the aircraft at time t is $5\sqrt{1 + e^{-t}}$ m s^{-1}.

(e) What happens to the speed as time increases?

(f) Find an expression for the acceleration, $\mathbf{a}$ m s^{-2}, of the aircraft at time t.

(g) Find the magnitude of the acceleration at time $t = 0$.

(h) Show that as time increases, the magnitude of the acceleration becomes closer and closer to 0.5 m s^{-2}.

E Using Newton's laws in one dimension (answers p 156)

Newton's second law of motion, in the form $F = ma$, applies to the motion of a particle in a straight line.

If the resultant force F newtons acting on a particle varies with time, so does the acceleration a (and vice versa).

For example, suppose the resultant force F newtons acting on a particle of mass 5 kg is given by

$$F = 4t - 3t^2$$

Substituting for F and m in $F = ma$, we get: $4t - 3t^2 = 5a$

$$\Rightarrow \quad a = 0.8t - 0.6t^2$$

Once an expression for a has been found, it can be integrated to get an expression for v, and so on.

If, on the other hand, an expression for a is given, using $F = ma$ gives an expression for F.

E1 The displacement x m at time t s of a particle of mass 2.5 kg moving on a straight line is given by

$$x = 3t^2 - 2t^3$$

(a) By differentiation, find an expression for the velocity v m s^{-1} at time t.

(b) Find an expression for the acceleration a m s^{-1} at time t.

(c) Use Newton's second law to find an expression for the resultant force, F newtons, acting on the particle at time t.

(d) Find the magnitude of the resultant force when $t = 2$.

(e) Find the time at which the force is instantaneously zero.

E2 A particle of mass 0.4 kg moves in a straight line. At time t s a force $F = 6\sqrt{t} - 2$ newtons acts on the particle and is the only force acting.

(a) Find an expression for the acceleration, a m s^{-2}, of the particle at time t.

(b) Find the value of t for which the acceleration is zero.

The particle is instantaneously at rest at the origin at time $t = 0$.

(c) Find an expression for the velocity of the particle at time t.

(d) Find an expression for the displacement of the particle from the origin at time t.

(e) Show that there is a value of t other than $t = 0$ for which the particle is instantaneously at rest, and find this value.

(f) Find the force acting on the particle at each of the times when it is instantaneously at rest.

K Newton's second law $F = ma$ applies when F and a are functions of time.

If F is given as a function of t, then an expression for a in terms of t can be derived, and vice versa.

Example 6

A particle of mass 0.5 kg moves on a straight line. At time t s a force $F = 2\cos\frac{1}{6}t$ newtons acts on the particle. At time $t = 0$ the particle passes the origin with velocity $-8\,\mathrm{m\,s^{-1}}$.

(a) Find an expression for the acceleration of the particle at time t.

(b) Find an expression for the velocity of the particle at time t.

(c) Find the value of t for which the particle is first instantaneously at rest. Give your answer correct to 3 s.f.

Solution

(a) Use N2L (Newton's 2nd law). $\qquad F = ma$

$$2\cos\tfrac{1}{6}t = 0.5a$$

$$\Rightarrow \qquad a = 4\cos\tfrac{1}{6}t$$

(b) Integrate a to get v. $\qquad v = 24\sin\tfrac{1}{6}t + c$

When $t = 0$, $v = -8$, so $-8 = 0 + c \Rightarrow c = -8$

So $\qquad\qquad\qquad\qquad v = 24\sin\tfrac{1}{6}t - 8$

(c) When $v = 0$, $24\sin\tfrac{1}{6}t - 8 = 0 \Rightarrow \sin\tfrac{1}{6}t = \tfrac{1}{3}$

$$\Rightarrow \qquad \tfrac{1}{6}t = \sin^{-1}\tfrac{1}{3} = 0.3398\ldots \;(radians)$$

$$\Rightarrow \qquad t = 6\times 0.3398\ldots = 2.04 \;(\text{to 3 s.f.})$$

Exercise E (answers p 157)

1 A particle of mass 0.5 kg moves on a straight line. At time t s a force $F = t^2 - 3t$ newtons acts on the particle. At time $t = 0$ the particle is instantaneously at rest at the origin.

   (a) Find an expression for the acceleration of the particle at time t.

   (b) Find an expression for the velocity of the particle at time t.

   (c) The particle is instantaneously at rest when $t = 0$. When is it next instantaneously at rest?

   (d) Find an expression for the displacement of the particle at time t.

   (e) Find the time at which the particle returns to the origin.

   (f) Find the velocity of the particle as it passes through the origin at this time.

2 A particle of mass 0.3 kg moves on a straight line. The particle's displacement x m at time t s is given by $x = 5(1 - \cos 0.2t)$.

   (a) Find an expression for the velocity of the particle at time t.

   (b) Find an expression for the acceleration of the particle at time t.

   (c) Find an expression for the resultant force acting on the particle at time t.

   (d) Find, correct to 3 s.f., the time at which the force is first instantaneously zero.

3 A particle of mass $0.2\,\text{kg}$ moves on a straight line. A force of $(6 - kt)$ newtons, where k is a positive constant, acts at time $t\,\text{s}$ on the particle.

(a) Find an expression for the acceleration, $a\,\text{m}\,\text{s}^{-2}$, of the particle at time t.

At time $t = 0$, the particle is instantaneously at rest at the origin $x = 0$.

(b) Find an expression for the velocity, $v\,\text{m}\,\text{s}^{-1}$, of the particle at time t.

(c) Find an expression for the displacement, $x\,\text{m}$, of the particle at time t.

(d) Given that the particle passes the origin at time $t = 4$, find

    (i) the value of k

    (ii) the velocity with which the particle passes the origin at time $t = 4$

4 The displacement $x\,\text{m}$ at time $t\,\text{s}$ of a particle of mass $1.2\,\text{kg}$ moving on a straight line is given by

$$x = 3t^2 + 3t + 6e^{-2t}$$

(a) Find an expression for the velocity, $v\,\text{m}\,\text{s}^{-1}$, of the particle at time t.

(b) Find an expression for the acceleration, $a\,\text{m}\,\text{s}^{-2}$, of the particle at time t.

(c) Find the magnitude of the resultant force acting on the particle at time $t = 0$.

(d) What happens to the magnitude of the force as t gets larger and larger?

5 A particle of mass $0.05\,\text{kg}$ moves on a straight line. A force of $1.5\sqrt{t}$ newtons acts at time $t\,\text{s}$ on the particle, where $t \geq 0$.

(a) Find an expression for the acceleration of the particle at time t.

At time $t = 0$, the particle is at the origin $x = 0$ and moving with velocity $2\,\text{m}\,\text{s}^{-1}$.

(b) Find an expression for the velocity of the particle at time t.

(c) Find the time when the particle is moving with speed $69.5\,\text{m}\,\text{s}^{-1}$.

(d) Find an expression for the displacement $x\,\text{m}$ at time t.

(e) Find the distance of the particle from the origin when the speed is $69.5\,\text{m}\,\text{s}^{-1}$.

6 The motion of a vehicle on a straight horizontal test track is modelled by the equation

$$v = 20 + 0.1t - 0.5e^{0.1t}$$

where $v\,\text{m}\,\text{s}^{-1}$ is the velocity of the vehicle at time $t\,\text{s}$. The mass of the vehicle is $40\,\text{kg}$.

(a) Find an expression for the acceleration, $a\,\text{m}\,\text{s}^{-2}$, of the vehicle at time t.

(b) Find an expression for the resultant horizontal force F newtons acting on the vehicle at time t.

(c) Find the value of t for which the force F is instantaneously zero.

7 A small sphere of mass $0.05\,\text{kg}$ rolls along a straight horizontal groove. Its displacement $x\,\text{m}$ from the origin at time t seconds is given by

$$x = 20t - 3t^2 - \tfrac{1}{2}t^3$$

Find an expression for the magnitude of the horizontal force on the sphere at time t.

F Using Newton's laws in two or three dimensions (answers p 157)

Newton's second law of motion in vector form is $\mathbf{F} = m\mathbf{a}$.

This equation may be used either to find $\mathbf{F}$ from $\mathbf{a}$, or to find $\mathbf{a}$ from $\mathbf{F}$.

If $\mathbf{a}$ is a function of time, then so is $\mathbf{F}$ (and vice versa).

F1 The velocity $\mathbf{v}\,\mathrm{m\,s}^{-1}$ at time $t\,\mathrm{s}$ of a particle of mass $3\,\mathrm{kg}$ is given by

$$\mathbf{v} = (5t^2 - 2t)\mathbf{i} + 2t^3\mathbf{j} + 10t\mathbf{k}$$

(a) Find the acceleration $\mathbf{a}\,\mathrm{m\,s}^{-2}$ in terms of t.

(b) Use Newton's second law to show that the resultant force $\mathbf{F}$ newtons acting on the particle at time $t\,\mathrm{s}$ is given by

$$\mathbf{F} = 6(5t - 1)\mathbf{i} + 18t^2\mathbf{j} + 30\mathbf{k}$$

(c) Show that at time $t = 1$ the magnitude of the force is $30\sqrt{2}$ newtons.

F2 A particle of mass $2.5\,\mathrm{kg}$ is at the origin at time $t = 0$ and moving with velocity $(3\mathbf{i} - 2\mathbf{j})\,\mathrm{m\,s}^{-1}$. It is acted on by a force $\mathbf{F}$ newtons, where $\mathbf{F} = 15t^2\mathbf{i}$.

(a) Use Newton's second law to find an expression for the acceleration, $\mathbf{a}\,\mathrm{m\,s}^{-2}$, of the particle in terms of t.

(b) By integration find an expression for the velocity, $\mathbf{v}\,\mathrm{m\,s}^{-1}$, of the particle in terms of t, including a constant of integration.

(c) Use the information about the velocity when $t = 0$ to show that

$$\mathbf{v} = (2t^3 + 3)\mathbf{i} - 2\mathbf{j}$$

(d) By integrating again and using the information about the position of the particle when $t = 0$, find $\mathbf{r}$ in terms of t.

(e) Find the distance of the particle from the origin when $t = 2$, correct to three significant figures.

In two or three dimensions, Newton's second law of motion is $\mathbf{F} = m\mathbf{a}$.

If $\mathbf{F}$ is a function of time t, then so is $\mathbf{a}$ (and vice versa).

Example 7

A particle of mass $4\,\mathrm{kg}$ is acted on by a force $\mathbf{F}$ newtons at time t seconds, where

$$\mathbf{F} = 4t\mathbf{i} - 6t^2\mathbf{j} + 2\mathbf{k}$$

No other force acts on the particle.

(a) Find an expression for the acceleration of the particle.

(b) At time $t = 0$, the velocity of the particle is $(6\mathbf{i} - 8\mathbf{k})\,\mathrm{m\,s}^{-1}$. Find an expression for the velocity $\mathbf{v}\,\mathrm{m\,s}^{-1}$ at time t.

(c) The particle is initially at the origin. Find an expression for the position vector, $\mathbf{r}$ metres, of the particle at time t.

Solution

(a) Use N2L: $\mathbf{F} = m\mathbf{a}$

$4t\mathbf{i} - 6t^2\mathbf{j} + 2\mathbf{k} = 4\mathbf{a}$, so $\mathbf{a} = t\mathbf{i} - \frac{3}{2}t^2\mathbf{j} + \frac{1}{2}\mathbf{k}$

(b) Integrate $\mathbf{a}$: $\mathbf{v} = \frac{1}{2}t^2\mathbf{i} - \frac{1}{2}t^3\mathbf{j} + \frac{1}{2}t\mathbf{k} + \mathbf{c}$

When $t = 0$, $\mathbf{v} = 6\mathbf{i} - 8\mathbf{k}$

So $6\mathbf{i} - 8\mathbf{k} = 0\mathbf{i} - 0\mathbf{j} + 0\mathbf{k} + \mathbf{c} \implies \mathbf{c} = 6\mathbf{i} - 8\mathbf{k}$

So $\mathbf{v} = \frac{1}{2}t^2\mathbf{i} - \frac{1}{2}t^3\mathbf{j} + \frac{1}{2}t\mathbf{k} + 6\mathbf{i} - 8\mathbf{k}$

$\qquad = \left(\frac{1}{2}t^2 + 6\right)\mathbf{i} - \frac{1}{2}t^3\mathbf{j} + \left(\frac{1}{2}t - 8\right)\mathbf{k}$

(c) Integrate $\mathbf{v}$: $\mathbf{r} = \left(\frac{1}{6}t^3 + 6t\right)\mathbf{i} - \frac{1}{8}t^4\mathbf{j} + \left(\frac{1}{4}t^2 - 8t\right)\mathbf{k} + \mathbf{c}$

When $t = 0$, $\mathbf{r} = \mathbf{0}$

So $\mathbf{0} = 0\mathbf{i} - 0\mathbf{j} + 0\mathbf{k} + \mathbf{c} \implies \mathbf{c} = \mathbf{0}$

So $\mathbf{r} = \left(\frac{1}{6}t^3 + 6t\right)\mathbf{i} - \frac{1}{8}t^4\mathbf{j} + \left(\frac{1}{4}t^2 - 8t\right)\mathbf{k}$

Exercise F (answers p 157)

1 The acceleration, $\mathbf{a}\,\mathrm{m\,s^{-2}}$, of a particle at time $t\,\mathrm{s}$ is given by $\mathbf{a} = (4 - 5t)\mathbf{i} + (t - t^2)\mathbf{j}$.
The mass of the particle is $0.4\,\mathrm{kg}$. Find an expression for the resultant force on
the particle at time t.

2 The velocity, $\mathbf{v}\,\mathrm{m\,s^{-1}}$, of a particle at time $t\,\mathrm{s}$ is given by $\mathbf{v} = (10t - t^2)\mathbf{i} + (7t + 3)\mathbf{j}$.
The mass of the particle is $0.2\,\mathrm{kg}$. Find an expression for

(a) the acceleration of the particle at time t

(b) the resultant force on the particle at time t

3 The resultant force $\mathbf{F}$ newtons acting on a particle of mass $0.5\,\mathrm{kg}$ at time $t\,\mathrm{s}$
is given by

$\qquad \mathbf{F} = (t^2 - 2)\mathbf{i} + (2t + 3)\mathbf{j}$

(a) Find an expression for the acceleration of the particle at time t.

(b) Given that the velocity of the particle at time $t = 0$ is $4\mathbf{i}\,\mathrm{m\,s^{-1}}$, find an
expression for the velocity at time t.

4 The position vector, $\mathbf{r}\,\mathrm{m}$, of a particle of mass $2\,\mathrm{kg}$ at time $t\,\mathrm{s}$ is given by

$\qquad \mathbf{r} = t^3\mathbf{i} + (t^2 - 2t)\mathbf{j} + t^2\mathbf{k}$

(a) Find an expression for the velocity $\mathbf{v}\,\mathrm{m\,s^{-1}}$ at time t.

(b) Find an expression for the acceleration $\mathbf{a}\,\mathrm{m\,s^{-2}}$ at time t.

(c) Find an expression for the resultant force $\mathbf{F}$ newtons acting on the particle
at time t.

(d) Find the magnitude of the force when $t = 2$.

5 The velocity, $\mathbf{v}\,\text{m}\,\text{s}^{-1}$, of a particle of mass 0.1 kg at time $t\,\text{s}$ is given by

$$\mathbf{v} = 5t\mathbf{i} - 2t\mathbf{j} + 20\sin\tfrac{1}{8}\pi t\,\mathbf{k}$$

(a) Find an expression for the acceleration $\mathbf{a}\,\text{m}\,\text{s}^{-2}$ at time t.

(b) Find an expression for the resultant force $\mathbf{F}$ newtons acting on the particle at time t.

(c) Find the magnitude of the force when $t = 4$.

6 A particle of mass 0.2 kg moves under the action of a single force $\mathbf{F}$ newtons that varies with time. The velocity, $\mathbf{v}\,\text{m}\,\text{s}^{-1}$, of the particle at time $t\,\text{s}$ is given by

$$\mathbf{v} = 8\mathbf{i} + 3\sin 2t\mathbf{j} + 3\cos 2t\mathbf{k}$$

(a) Find an expression for $\mathbf{F}$ in terms of t.

(b) Show that $|\mathbf{F}|$ is constant, and find its value.

7 A particle of mass 2.5 kg passes through the origin at time $t = 0$ with a velocity of $4\mathbf{k}\,\text{m}\,\text{s}^{-1}$. The resultant force $\mathbf{F}$ newtons on the particle at time $t\,\text{s}$ is given by

$$\mathbf{F} = 10\mathbf{i} + 30t\mathbf{j} - 2e^{0.2t}\mathbf{k}$$

where $\mathbf{i}$ and $\mathbf{j}$ are horizontal and $\mathbf{k}$ is vertically upwards.

(a) Find an expression for the velocity $\mathbf{v}\,\text{m}\,\text{s}^{-1}$ at time t.

(b) Find the value of t when the particle is moving horizontally.

(c) Find the speed of the particle when it is moving horizontally.

Key points

- If $x = f(t)$, then $v = \dfrac{\mathrm{d}x}{\mathrm{d}t} = f'(t)$ and $a = \dfrac{\mathrm{d}v}{\mathrm{d}t} = f''(t)$ (p 45)

- If $\mathbf{r} = f(t)\mathbf{i} + g(t)\mathbf{j}$, then

$$\mathbf{v} = \dfrac{\mathrm{d}\mathbf{r}}{\mathrm{d}t} = f'(t)\mathbf{i} + g'(t)\mathbf{j} \qquad\qquad \mathbf{a} = \dfrac{\mathrm{d}\mathbf{v}}{\mathrm{d}t} = f''(t)\mathbf{i} + g''(t)\mathbf{j}$$ (p 51)

- If $\mathbf{r} = f(t)\mathbf{i} + g(t)\mathbf{j} + h(t)\mathbf{k}$, then

$$\mathbf{v} = \dfrac{\mathrm{d}\mathbf{r}}{\mathrm{d}t} = f'(t)\mathbf{i} + g'(t)\mathbf{j} + h'(t)\mathbf{k} \qquad \mathbf{a} = \dfrac{\mathrm{d}\mathbf{v}}{\mathrm{d}t} = f''(t)\mathbf{i} + g''(t)\mathbf{j} + h''(t)\mathbf{k}$$ (p 57)

- $\mathbf{v} = \int \mathbf{a}\,\mathrm{d}t \quad \mathbf{r} = \int \mathbf{v}\,\mathrm{d}t$ 　　　Include a constant of integration, whose value can be found from information given. (p 55)

Mixed questions (answers p 158)

1 A particle moves along a straight line. At time t the displacement of the particle from its initial position is x, where

$$x = 4t + 2e^{-t} - 2$$

(a) Find the velocity of the particle at time t.

(b) Find the acceleration of the particle at time t.

(c) Describe what happens to the acceleration of the particle as t increases. 　　AQA 2003

2 A particle moves so that at time t seconds its position **r** metres is given by

$$\mathbf{r} = (t^3 - 3t^2)\mathbf{i} + (4t + 2t^2)\mathbf{j}$$

where **i** and **j** are perpendicular unit vectors.

(a) By differentiating, find the velocity of the particle at time t.

(b) Find, but do not simplify, an expression for the magnitude of the acceleration of the particle.

(c) Find the time when the magnitude of the acceleration is a minimum and find its magnitude at this time.

3 A particle moves so that its acceleration at time t is given by

$$\mathbf{a} = -4\cos t\,\mathbf{i} + 3\sin t\,\mathbf{j} + \tfrac{1}{2}\mathbf{k}$$

where the unit vectors **i**, **j** and **k** are mutually perpendicular.
The initial position of the particle is $4\mathbf{i}$ and its initial velocity is $\tfrac{1}{2}\mathbf{j}$.

(a) Find an expression for the velocity of the particle at time t.

(b) Find the position vector of the particle at time t.

(c) Find the distance of the particle from the origin when $t = \dfrac{\pi}{2}$.

AQA 2001

4 A possible model for the acceleration, $a\,\mathrm{m\,s^{-2}}$, of a particle at time t seconds is

$$a = 8 - ht$$

where h is a positive constant.

(a) The acceleration is zero when $t = 4$.

  (i) Find h.

  (ii) Write down an expression for a in terms of t.

(b) The velocity of the particle is $2\,\mathrm{m\,s^{-1}}$ when $t = 4$. Find the velocity of the particle at time t.

AQA 2004

5 A force **F** newtons acts on a particle of mass $5\,\mathrm{kg}$. At time t seconds,

$$\mathbf{F} = 4\mathbf{i} + 8t\mathbf{j} + 5(1 - e^{-0.01t})\mathbf{k}$$

where the unit vectors **i**, **j** and **k** are mutually perpendicular.
At time $t = 0$, the particle is at rest at the origin.

(a) Find an expression for the velocity of the particle at time t.

(b) Find an expression for the position vector of the particle at time t.

6 A boat moves so that its position vector, **r** metres, at time t seconds is

$$\mathbf{r} = 40\cos\left(\frac{t}{20}\right)\mathbf{i} + 80\sin\left(\frac{t}{20}\right)\mathbf{j}$$

The unit vectors **i** and **j** are directed east and north respectively.

(a) Find an expression for the velocity of the boat at time t.

(b) In what direction is the boat travelling when $t = 0$? Justify your answer.

(c) At what time is the boat travelling due south for the first time?

AQA 2003

3 Variable acceleration | **65**

7 A particle moves on a straight line. At time t seconds its acceleration, $a\,\mathrm{m\,s^{-2}}$, is given by

$$a = 20\sin 4t$$

(a) Initially the particle is at rest. Find an expression for the velocity of the particle at time t.

(b) Initially the displacement of the particle from the origin is 0.8 metres. Find an expression for the displacement of the particle at time t.   AQA 2004

8 A cyclist moves from rest along a straight horizontal road. At time t seconds, the displacement of the cyclist from his initial position is s metres.

(a) For $0 \leq t \leq 10$,

$$s = \frac{t^4}{400} - \frac{t^3}{10} + \frac{3t^2}{2}$$

   (i) Find s when $t = 10$.

   (ii) Find the velocity of the cyclist when $t = 10$.

   (iii) Find the acceleration of the cyclist when $t = 10$.

(b) For $t \geq 10$, the cyclist moves with a constant velocity so that

$$s = ht - k$$

where h and k are constants. Find the values of h and k.   AQA 2004

9 A ball is projected from a point on the ground. Taking air resistance into account, the position vector of the ball, $\mathbf{r}$ metres, relative to its starting point is modelled by the equation

$$\mathbf{r} = 15(1 - e^{-2t})\mathbf{i} + (25(1 - e^{-2t}) - 5t)\mathbf{j}$$

where $\mathbf{i}$ and $\mathbf{j}$ are unit vectors in the horizontal and upward vertical directions respectively.

(a) Find an expression for the velocity, $\mathbf{v}\,\mathrm{m\,s^{-1}}$, of the ball at time t.

(b) Find the speed with which the ball was initially projected.

(c) In what direction is the ball moving at the highest point of its path?

(d) Find the time at which the ball reaches its highest point.

(e) Find the speed of the ball at its highest point.

(f) Find the maximum height of the ball.

(g) Find the acceleration, $\mathbf{a}\,\mathrm{m\,s^{-2}}$, of the ball at its highest point.

(h) Show that, if the ball returns to the ground after a time T seconds, then the distance of the ball from its starting point when it returns to the ground is $3T$ metres.

10 A particle of mass $0.2\,\text{kg}$ moves so that its velocity $\mathbf{v}\,\text{m}\,\text{s}^{-1}$ at time t seconds is given by

$$\mathbf{v} = 3\sin\tfrac{1}{2}t\,\mathbf{i} + 3\cos\tfrac{1}{2}t\,\mathbf{j} + 2t\,\mathbf{k}$$

where the unit vectors $\mathbf{i}$, $\mathbf{j}$ and $\mathbf{k}$ are mutually perpendicular.
The initial position of the particle is $6\mathbf{i}$.

(a) Find an expression for the position vector of the particle at time t.

(b) Find an expression for the force $\mathbf{F}$ newtons acting on the particle at time t.

(c) Show that the magnitude of the force is constant and find its value.

Test yourself (answers p 158)

1 A particle moves along a straight line. At time t seconds, the acceleration, $a\,\text{m}\,\text{s}^{-2}$, of the particle is given by

$$a = 2 - 2e^{-t}$$

At time $t = 0$ the particle is at the origin moving with a velocity of $4\,\text{m}\,\text{s}^{-1}$.

(a) Show that the velocity, $v\,\text{m}\,\text{s}^{-1}$, at time t seconds is given by

$$v = 2t + 2e^{-t} + 2$$

(b) Find an expression for the distance of the particle from the origin at time t.   AQA 2003

2 A sky diver jumps at time $t = 0$ from an aeroplane that is travelling horizontally. The velocity, $\mathbf{v}\,\text{m}\,\text{s}^{-1}$, of the sky diver at time t seconds is given by

$$\mathbf{v} = 70e^{-0.1t}\mathbf{i} + 40(e^{-0.1t} - 1)\mathbf{j}$$

where $\mathbf{i}$ and $\mathbf{j}$ are unit vectors in the horizontal and upward vertical directions respectively.

(a) Describe what happens to the velocity of the sky diver as t increases.

(b) Taking the origin to be the initial position of the sky diver, find an expression for his position vector at time t seconds.   AQA 2002

3 A particle has mass $2000\,\text{kg}$. A single force, $\mathbf{F} = 1000t\mathbf{i} - 5000\mathbf{j}$ newtons, acts on the particle at time t seconds. The unit vectors $\mathbf{i}$ and $\mathbf{j}$ are perpendicular. No other forces act on the particle.

(a) Find an expression for the acceleration of the particle.

(b) At time $t = 0$, the velocity of the particle is $6\mathbf{j}\,\text{m}\,\text{s}^{-1}$. Show that at time t the velocity, $\mathbf{v}\,\text{m}\,\text{s}^{-1}$, of the particle is given by

$$\mathbf{v} = \frac{t^2}{4}\mathbf{i} + \left(6 - \frac{5t}{2}\right)\mathbf{j}$$

(c) The particle is initially at the origin. Find an expression for the position vector, $\mathbf{r}$ metres, of the particle at time t seconds.   AQA 2003

4 Differential equations

In this chapter you will learn how to
- form a differential equation by applying Newton's second law of motion
- solve the resulting differential equation by separating variables

A Forming and solving a differential equation (answers p 159)

Situations frequently arise in mechanics where a force acting on an object is a function of the speed of the object.

For example, a force of resistance (such as air resistance) may be modelled as proportional to the speed, or proportional to the square of the speed. Which model is chosen will depend on the results of experiments.

Suppose a particle of mass 0.4 kg is moving in a horizontal straight line and is subject to a resistance force of magnitude $0.1v^2$ newtons, where $v\,\text{m s}^{-1}$ is the speed of the particle at time t s.

The situation is shown in the diagram.

The only force on the particle is the resistance.

The acceleration of the particle is $\dfrac{\mathrm{d}v}{\mathrm{d}t}$.

Applying Newton's second law (N2L), we have $-0.1v^2 = 0.4\dfrac{\mathrm{d}v}{\mathrm{d}t}$

$$\text{so} \quad \frac{\mathrm{d}v}{\mathrm{d}t} = -\tfrac{1}{4}v^2$$

The negative sign shows that the resistance is in the opposite direction to the velocity.

This is an example of a differential equation.

It is very important to note how this equation differs from those you met in the previous chapter. There you were dealing with situations where the acceleration is a function of **time**, so you could go, for example,

from $\quad \dfrac{\mathrm{d}v}{\mathrm{d}t} = 4t - t^2$

to $\quad v = 2t^2 - \tfrac{1}{3}t^3 + c$ by direct integration.

In the example above, the acceleration $\dfrac{\mathrm{d}v}{\mathrm{d}t}$ is a function of v.

The equation $\dfrac{\mathrm{d}v}{\mathrm{d}t} = -\tfrac{1}{4}v^2$ cannot be solved by direct integration.

Note

The method of solving differential equations like the one above is described in Core 4, chapter 6. A brief recap of the method is given on the next page.

The first step in solving the differential equation is to 'separate the variables'. This means rewriting it so that v and dv appear on one side only, and t and dt on the other.

$$\frac{dv}{dt} = -\tfrac{1}{4}v^2$$

This becomes

$$\frac{1}{v^2}\,dv = -\tfrac{1}{4}\,dt$$

Integrate both sides.

$$\int \frac{1}{v^2}\,dv = -\int \tfrac{1}{4}\,dt$$

$$\int v^{-2}\,dv = -\int \tfrac{1}{4}\,dt$$

The constant of integration is added to one side only.

$$-v^{-1} = -\tfrac{1}{4}t + c$$

$$\frac{1}{v} = \tfrac{1}{4}t - c$$

At this stage we have the 'general solution' that contains a constant of integration.

To find the value of c, more information is needed. We need to know the value of v for a given value of t.

Suppose that $v = 5$ when $t = 0$. So $\tfrac{1}{5} = 0 - c$, from which $c = -\tfrac{1}{5}$.

With this value of c inserted, the equation becomes $\quad \dfrac{1}{v} = \tfrac{1}{4}t + \tfrac{1}{5}$

To 'tidy up' fractions, multiply both sides by 20. $\quad \dfrac{20}{v} = 5t + 4 \ $ so $\ v = \dfrac{20}{5t + 4}$

The resulting equation can be used to find v for a given value of t, and vice versa.

A1 **(a)** Re-do the working above, but for the case where the resistance force is of magnitude $0.1v^3$ newtons and, as before, $v = 5$ when $t = 0$. Show that
$$v^2 = \frac{50}{25t + 2}$$
   (b) Find the value of v when $t = 8$.
   (c) Find the value of t for which $v = 2$.

A2 **(a)** Re-do the working above, but for the case where the resistance force is of magnitude $0.1v^4$ newtons and, as before, $v = 5$ when $t = 0$. Show that
$$v^3 = \frac{500}{375t + 4}$$
   (b) Find the value of v when $t = 0.8$.
   (c) Find the value of t for which $v = 2$.

A3 Re-do the working above, but for the case where the resistance force is of magnitude $0.1v^{\frac{1}{2}}$ newtons and, as before, $v = 5$ when $t = 0$.

The case where the resistance is of the form kv leads to a different type of solution.

For example, suppose the same particle as before is subject to a resistance force of magnitude $0.1v$ newtons. As before, $v = 5$ when $t = 0$.

Applying N2L, we have

$$-0.1v = 0.4\frac{dv}{dt}$$

$$\frac{dv}{dt} = -\tfrac{1}{4}v$$

$$\frac{1}{v}\,dv = -\tfrac{1}{4}\,dt$$

$$\int \frac{1}{v}\,dv = -\int \tfrac{1}{4}\,dt$$

$$\ln v = -\tfrac{1}{4}t + c$$

You would now expect to find the value of c by using the fact that $v = 5$ when $t = 0$. It is possible to do that (the working is shown later) but it is better to continue with the general solution to get it into a more useful form, as follows:

'Exponentiate' (e to the power of) each side.

$$e^{\ln v} = e^{-\frac{1}{4}t + c} = e^{-\frac{1}{4}t}e^{c}$$

$$\Rightarrow \quad v = Ae^{-\frac{1}{4}t} \text{ where } A = e^{c}$$
$$(A \text{ is now the unknown constant.})$$

Now use the fact that $v = 5$ when $t = 0$.

$$5 = Ae^{0} = A$$

So $\quad v = 5e^{-\frac{1}{4}t}$

The other method follows. It involves using the fact that $v = 5$ when $t = 0$ before exponentiating. (You may prefer this second method.)

$$\ln v = -\tfrac{1}{4}t + c$$

When $t = 0$, $v = 5$, so $\qquad \ln 5 = 0 + c$ from which $c = \ln 5$

So the solution can be written as $\qquad \ln v = -\tfrac{1}{4}t + \ln 5$

Then 'exponentiate' each side. $\qquad e^{\ln v} = e^{-\frac{1}{4}t + \ln 5} = e^{-\frac{1}{4}t}e^{\ln 5} = e^{\ln 5}e^{-\frac{1}{4}t} = 5e^{-\frac{1}{4}t}$

$$\Rightarrow \quad v = 5e^{-\frac{1}{4}t}$$

A4 From the equation $v = 5e^{-\frac{1}{4}t}$, what can you say about the value of v as t gets larger and larger?

A5 A car of mass m kg is travelling along a straight horizontal road. When its speed is $U\,\mathrm{m\,s^{-1}}$, the engine is switched off. A force of resistance of magnitude kv^4 newtons acts on the car, where $v\,\mathrm{m\,s^{-1}}$ is the speed of the car t seconds after the engine was switched off and k is a constant.

(a) Form a differential equation for the motion of the car after the engine is switched off and show that it may be written in separated form as

$$-\frac{m}{v^4}\,dv = k\,dt$$

(b) Integrate both sides of this equation; include a constant of integration.

(c) Use the fact that $v = U$ when $t = 0$ to find the value of the constant.

(d) Hence show that $v^3 = \dfrac{mU^3}{3ktU^3 + m}$.

When the resultant force acting on an object is of the form $\pm kv^n$, application of Newton's second law leads to a differential equation of the form $\pm kv^n = m\dfrac{dv}{dt}$ that can be solved by separating variables.

Having found v as a function of t, it is then possible to integrate to find the displacement x as a function of t.

For example, the working on the opposite page leads to $\qquad v = 5e^{-\frac{1}{4}t}$

So if x m is the displacement at time t, then $\qquad \dfrac{dx}{dt} = 5e^{-\frac{1}{4}t}$

This equation can be solved by direct integration: $\qquad x = \dfrac{5}{-\frac{1}{4}}e^{-\frac{1}{4}t} + c = -20e^{-\frac{1}{4}t} + c$

From the fact that $x = 0$ when $t = 0$, it follows that $0 = -20 + c$, so $c = 20$.
So $x = 20(1 - e^{-\frac{1}{4}t})$.

A6 What happens to the displacement in this case as t increases?

Example 1

A particle of mass m kg moving in a straight line is acted on by a force of magnitude kmv newtons in the direction of motion, where v m s^{-1} is the speed of the particle at time t s. Its displacement is x m.
At time $t = 0$, $x = 0$ and the speed of the particle is U m s^{-1}.

Show that

(a) $v = Ue^{kt}$

(b) $x = \dfrac{U}{k}(e^{kt} - 1)$

Solution

(a) Apply N2L. $\quad kmv = m\dfrac{dv}{dt}$

$$\frac{1}{v}\,dv = k\,dt$$

$$\int \frac{1}{v}\,dv = \int k\,dt$$

$$\ln v = kt + c$$

$$v = e^{kt + c}$$

$$v = Ae^{kt} \quad \text{where } A = e^c$$

When $t = 0$, $v = U$, so $U = Ae^0$, from which $A = U$.

So $v = Ue^{kt}$

(b) $v = \dfrac{dx}{dt}$, so $\dfrac{dx}{dt} = Ue^{kt}$

Integrate. $\quad x = \dfrac{U}{k}e^{kt} + c$

When $t = 0$, $x = 0$

$$0 = \frac{U}{k} + c \quad \text{so} \quad c = -\frac{U}{k}$$

So $\qquad x = \dfrac{U}{k}e^{kt} - \dfrac{U}{k}$

$$= \dfrac{U}{k}(e^{kt} - 1)$$

Exercise A (answers p 160)

1 A motor boat of mass 750 kg is travelling in a straight line at $8\,\mathrm{m\,s^{-1}}$ when its engine cuts out. After this the boat is subject to a force of resistance of magnitude $60v^2$ newtons, where $v\,\mathrm{m\,s^{-1}}$ is the speed of the boat t seconds after the engine cuts out.

(a) Show that $v = \dfrac{200}{25 + 16t}$.

(b) How long does it take for the boat's speed to be reduced to $4\,\mathrm{m\,s^{-1}}$?

2 A truck of mass 500 kg is travelling on a horizontal track at a speed of $20\,\mathrm{m\,s^{-1}}$. It enters a tunnel and is then subject to air resistance. The magnitude of the resistance force is $40v$ newtons, where $v\,\mathrm{m\,s^{-1}}$ is the speed of the truck t seconds after entering the tunnel. There is no other force on the truck.

(a) Show that $v = 20e^{-0.08t}$.

(b) By integration, show that the displacement, $x\,\mathrm{m}$, of the truck since entering the tunnel is given by
$$x = 250(1 - e^{-0.08t})$$

(c) Describe what happens to the speed and the distance travelled as t increases.

3 A particle of mass $m\,\mathrm{kg}$ is moving in a straight line. A resistance force of magnitude kmv^3 newtons acts on the particle, where $v\,\mathrm{m\,s^{-1}}$ is the speed of the particle at time $t\,\mathrm{s}$. At time $t = 0$ the speed of the particle is $U\,\mathrm{m\,s^{-1}}$.

(a) Show that $t = \dfrac{1}{2k}\left(\dfrac{1}{v^2} - \dfrac{1}{U^2}\right)$.

(b) Given that the particle's speed decreases from $20\,\mathrm{m\,s^{-1}}$ to $10\,\mathrm{m\,s^{-1}}$ in $10\,\mathrm{s}$, find the value of k.

4 A test truck of mass 0.4 kg is catapulted along a horizontal track. It leaves the catapult at a speed of $80\,\mathrm{m\,s^{-1}}$. The only force acting on the truck after it leaves the catapult is a resistance force of magnitude $0.05v$ newtons, where $v\,\mathrm{m\,s^{-1}}$ is the speed of the truck t seconds after being catapulted.

(a) Show that $v = 80e^{-0.125t}$.

(b) Show that if $x\,\mathrm{m}$ is the distance travelled by the truck t seconds after being catapulted, then $x = 640(1 - e^{-0.125t})$.

5 A particle of mass $m\,\mathrm{kg}$ moves in a straight line. It is acted on by a resistance force of magnitude $km\sqrt{v}$ newtons, where $v\,\mathrm{m\,s^{-1}}$ is the speed of the particle at time t seconds and k is a constant. At time $t = 0$, the displacement is 0 and the speed of the particle is $U\,\mathrm{m\,s^{-1}}$.

(a) Show that $v = \left(\sqrt{U} - \tfrac{1}{2}kt\right)^2$.

(b) What happens to the particle at time $t = \dfrac{2\sqrt{U}}{k}$?

(c) Show that the displacement, $x\,\mathrm{m}$, of the particle at time t is given by
$$x = Ut - \tfrac{1}{2}k\sqrt{U}\,t^2 + \tfrac{1}{12}k^2t^3$$

6 The motion of a model car along a straight horizontal track is assisted by pushing until it reaches a speed of $5\,\mathrm{m\,s^{-1}}$. At this point the assistance is withdrawn and the car is driven by its engine, which exerts a driving force of $\dfrac{100}{v}$ newtons, where $v\,\mathrm{m\,s^{-1}}$ is the speed of the car t seconds after the assistance is withdrawn. The mass of the car is $8\,\mathrm{kg}$. There is no resistance force acting on the car.

(a) Show that $v = 5(t + 1)^{\frac{1}{2}}$.

(b) Find the time taken for the car's speed to reach $40\,\mathrm{m\,s^{-1}}$.

(c) Show that the displacement, $x\,\mathrm{m}$, of the car at time t is given by
$$x = \tfrac{10}{3}\left((t + 1)^{\frac{3}{2}} - 1\right)$$

7 A particle of mass $m\,\mathrm{kg}$ moves in a straight line. The resistance force acting on the particle is of magnitude kmv^2 where $v\,\mathrm{m\,s^{-1}}$ is the speed of the particle at time t seconds and k is a constant.

(a) Form a differential equation for the motion of the particle.

(b) Given that the speed of the particle decreases from $20\,\mathrm{m\,s^{-1}}$ to $5\,\mathrm{m\,s^{-1}}$ in 6 seconds, find the value of k.

Test yourself (answers p 162)

1 A particle, of mass m, moves in a straight line on a smooth horizontal surface. As it moves it experiences a resistance force of magnitude kv^2, where k is a constant and v is the speed of the particle, at time t. The particle moves with speed U at time $t = 0$.

Show that $v = \dfrac{mU}{Ukt + m}$.
AQA 2002

2 A particle of mass m is moving along a straight horizontal line. At time t the particle has speed v. Initially the particle is at the origin and has speed U. As it moves the particle is subject to a resistance force of magnitude mkv^3.

(a) Show that $v^2 = \dfrac{U^2}{2kU^2 t + 1}$.

(b) What happens to v as t increases?
AQA 2003

3 A car of mass $m\,\mathrm{kg}$ passes a point on a straight horizontal road with speed $U\,\mathrm{m\,s^{-1}}$. The driving force of the car's engine is of magnitude $\dfrac{P}{v}$ newtons, where $v\,\mathrm{m\,s^{-1}}$ is the car's speed t seconds later and P is a constant.

Show that $v^2 = U^2 + \dfrac{2Pt}{m}$.

5 Uniform circular motion

In this chapter you will learn how to
• convert between different units for angular speed
• relate the speed of an object to its angular speed
• find the acceleration of an object moving in a circle
• solve problems involving circular motion with constant speed

Key points from Core 2

- Angles can be measured in radians, where 2π radians $= 360°$.

- If an arc subtends an angle of θ radians at the centre of a circle of radius r, the length of the arc is $r\theta$.

A Angular speed (answers p 163)

Consider the following situations.
• A child sitting on a roundabout
• A car travelling round a corner
• A satellite orbiting the Earth

All of these are examples of circular motion, which we will study in this chapter. Here we will look only at objects that are travelling with constant speed, but in a later chapter we will consider objects moving in a circle with variable speed.

A particle is placed on a rough horizontal turntable rotating with constant speed. As the turntable rotates, the distance of the particle from the centre of the turntable remains constant and the particle moves in a circle.

D **A1** (a) Explain why the velocity of the particle is not constant.

   (b) What is the direction of the velocity at any instant?

A2 (a) Given that the particle is a distance of 0.1 m from the centre of the turntable, find, in terms of π, the distance travelled by the particle as the turntable makes one complete revolution.

   (b) It takes 2 seconds for the turntable to make one revolution. Find, in terms of π, the speed of the particle.

When motion takes place in a circle it is often useful to describe the motion in terms of the **angular speed** of the particle. This is the rate at which the line from the centre of the circle to the particle is turning.

In question A2 the angular speed of the particle was described by giving the time for one revolution. The angular speed can also be expressed in revolutions per minute (r.p.m.) or radians per second (rad s^{-1}).

In work on circular motion angles are always measured in radians.

A3 Find, in revolutions per minute, the angular speed of a turntable that makes one complete revolution in

(a) 4 seconds   (b) 5 minutes

A4 Find, in terms of π, the angular speed in radians per second of a turntable that makes one complete revolution in

(a) 5 seconds   (b) 3 minutes

A5 A wheel is rotating at 80 r.p.m.

(a) Find, to 3 s.f., its angular speed in radians per second.

(b) How long does it take to complete one revolution?

A6 A roundabout is turning with angular speed $5\,\text{rad}\,\text{s}^{-1}$.

(a) What is its angular speed in r.p.m.?

(b) How long does it take to complete one revolution?

A7 The minute hand on a clock takes one hour to make a complete revolution. Find, to 3 s.f., its angular speed in

(a) r.p.m.   (b) $\text{rad}\,\text{s}^{-1}$

Consider a turntable that rotates at a constant n revolutions per minute.

In 1 second it will perform $\dfrac{n}{60}$ revolutions.

In each revolution it turns through 2π radians.

Hence its angular speed is $\dfrac{2\pi n}{60}$ radians per second.

If it turns through $\dfrac{n}{60}$ revolutions per second, the time for 1 revolution is $\dfrac{60}{n}$ s.

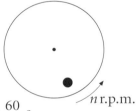

n r.p.m.

K The angular speed of an object moving in a circle is the rate at which the object is rotating.

An angular speed of n r.p.m. is equivalent to $\dfrac{2\pi n}{60}\,\text{rad}\,\text{s}^{-1}$.

The object will complete one revolution in $\dfrac{60}{n}$ s.

A8 A turntable is rotating at a constant angular speed of $4\,\text{rad}\,\text{s}^{-1}$. A penny is placed on the rough surface of the turntable so that its centre is 0.1 m from the centre of the turntable.

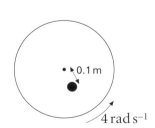

0.1 m

$4\,\text{rad}\,\text{s}^{-1}$

(a) (i) Show that the penny moves 0.1 m when the turntable rotates through 1 radian.

(ii) Find the speed of the penny.

(b) Another penny is placed on the turntable so that its centre is 0.2 m from the centre of the turntable.

(i) Explain why its speed is not the same as that of the first penny.

(ii) Find the speed of this penny.

(c) Where would you place a penny on the turntable so that its speed was half that of the first penny? Explain your answer.

We have seen that although the angular speed of a particle does not depend on the radius of the circle, the speed does depend on the radius.

Consider a particle moving in a circle with centre O and radius r metres, with a constant angular speed ω (omega) radians per second.

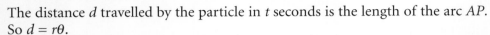

In t seconds, the particle turns through ωt radians, from A to P.
So if θ is the angle turned through, then $\theta = \omega t$.

The distance d travelled by the particle in t seconds is the length of the arc AP.
So $d = r\theta$.
But $\theta = \omega t$, hence $d = r\omega t$.

The speed of the particle, v metres per second, is given by $v = \dfrac{d}{t}$, so $v = \dfrac{r\omega t}{t} = r\omega$.

> **K** A particle moving round a circle of radius r m with angular speed ω rad s^{-1} has a speed of v m s^{-1}, where
>
> $$v = r\omega$$

Example 1

A turntable of radius 15 cm rotates at 45 r.p.m.

(a) Find its angular speed in rad s^{-1}.

(b) Find the speed of the edge of the turntable in m s^{-1}.

Solution

(a) *Convert the speed in r.p.m. to rad s^{-1}.*
$$45 \text{ r.p.m.} = \frac{2\pi \times 45}{60} \text{ rad s}^{-1}$$
$$= 1.5\pi \text{ rad s}^{-1}$$
$$= 4.71 \text{ rad s}^{-1} \text{ to 3 s.f.}$$

(b) *Use $v = r\omega$. Convert the radius to metres and use the exact value for ω.*
$$v = 0.15 \times 1.5\pi = 0.707 \text{ m s}^{-1} \text{ to 3 s.f.}$$

Exercise A (answers p 163)

1 A wheel is rotating at 100 r.p.m.

   (a) Find its angular speed in radians per second.

   (b) How long does it take to complete one revolution?

2 A turntable rotates at 8 rad s^{-1}.

   (a) Find its angular speed in r.p.m.

   (b) How long does it take to complete one revolution?

3 The beam of light from a lighthouse rotates at a constant speed.
It shines in my direction once every 5 seconds.
Find its angular speed in rad s^{-1}.

4 The second hand on a clock is 9 cm long.

  (a) How long does it take to complete one revolution?

  (b) Find its angular speed in rad s^{-1}.

  (c) Find the speed of the tip of hand in m s^{-1}.

5 A helicopter's rotor blade is rotating at 50 r.p.m.

  (a) Find the angular speed of the blade in rad s^{-1}.

  (b) The blade is 4 m long. Find the speed of the tip of the blade.

6 A child's mobile consists of a circular frame of radius 0.2 m with four balls hanging from it.
The mobile completes one revolution in 40 seconds.

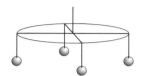

  (a) Find the angular speed of the mobile in rad s^{-1}.

  (b) Find the speed of one of the balls.

7 A funfair roundabout is rotating with an angular velocity of $2.5\,\text{rad s}^{-1}$.

  (a) How many revolutions will take place in a 30 second ride?

  (b) Will is sitting in a car that is 4 m from the centre of the roundabout. What is his speed?

  (c) Karen is sitting in a car that is 3 m from the centre of the roundabout. What is her speed?

8 The drum of a washing machine rotates at 800 r.p.m. on the spin cycle.
The diameter of the drum is 45 cm.
Find the speed, in m s^{-1}, of a point on the drum.

9 The London Eye takes 30 minutes to complete one revolution.
The diameter of the rim is 122 metres.
Find the speed, in m s^{-1}, of a point on the rim.

10 The Earth has radius 6.38×10^6 metres. It spins about its axis through the poles approximately once every 24 hours.

  (a) What is the approximate speed of an object on the Earth's equator due to this rotation?

  (b) What is the approximate speed of an object at the north pole due to this rotation?

11 The largest moon of the planet Jupiter is Ganymede. Its orbit can be modelled as circular and it takes 7.15 Earth days for Ganymede to orbit Jupiter.

  (a) Find the angular speed, in rad s^{-1}, of Ganymede about Jupiter.

  (b) Given that Ganymede orbits Jupiter at a mean distance of 1.07×10^9 m, find the speed of rotation in m s^{-1}.

B Velocity and acceleration (answers p 163)

A particle moving in a circle with a constant angular speed has a constant speed.
But its velocity is not constant, because its direction is changing.

The first diagram shows a particle moving in a circle with constant
angular speed. At any time, its direction of motion is along a
tangent to the circle.

At the point A the particle's velocity is the vector $\mathbf{u}$.
A short time later, at the point B, its velocity is $\mathbf{v}$.
Because the speed is constant, the magnitudes of $\mathbf{u}$ and $\mathbf{v}$ are equal.

The change in velocity is shown in the second diagram.

When A and B are very close together, the change in velocity is directed at
right angles to the velocity vectors and thus towards the centre of the circle.

This can be shown more rigorously by differentiation, as follows.

A particle P moves in a circle of radius r about centre O
with angular speed ω. It starts from A and is at P at time t.

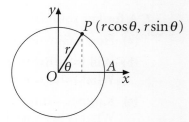

The displacement $\mathbf{r}$ of the particle at time t is given by

$$\mathbf{r} = r\cos\theta\,\mathbf{i} + r\sin\theta\,\mathbf{j}$$

We have seen that $\theta = \omega t$, so $\mathbf{r} = r\cos\omega t\,\mathbf{i} + r\sin\omega t\,\mathbf{j}$.

B1 (a) Show by differentiation that the velocity $\mathbf{v}$ of the particle
is given by $\mathbf{v} = \omega r(-\sin\omega t\,\mathbf{i} + \cos\omega t\,\mathbf{j})$.

   (b) Find the magnitude of $\mathbf{v}$.

   (c) By differentiating $\mathbf{v}$, find an expression for the acceleration $\mathbf{a}$ of the particle.

   (d) Find the magnitude of $\mathbf{a}$.

   (e) Show that $\mathbf{a} = -\omega^2\mathbf{r}$, and hence explain why the acceleration is towards
the centre of the circle.

B2 Given that $v = r\omega$, show that $a = \dfrac{v^2}{r}$.

K

A particle moving round a circle of radius $r\,\mathrm{m}$ with angular speed $\omega\,\mathrm{rad\,s^{-1}}$

and speed $v\,\mathrm{m\,s^{-1}}$ has an acceleration $a\,\mathrm{m\,s^{-2}}$, where $a = r\omega^2 = \dfrac{v^2}{r}$.

The velocity of the particle is directed along a tangent to the circle and
the acceleration is directed towards the centre of the circle.

Note that when you are asked to find the 'acceleration' of an object, it is
usually taken to mean the 'magnitude of the acceleration'.

B3 A particle is 0.2 m from the centre of a turntable rotating at $5\,\mathrm{rad\,s^{-1}}$.
Find the acceleration of the particle.

B4 A car is travelling at a constant speed of $9\,\mathrm{m\,s^{-1}}$ around a bend of radius 20 m.
Find the acceleration of the car.

Example 2

A children's roundabout rotates at a constant rate of 10 r.p.m.
A boy sits on the roundabout 1.5 m from its centre.
Find the acceleration of the boy.

Solution

Convert the speed in r.p.m. to rad s^{-1}. $\quad$ 10 r.p.m. $= \dfrac{2\pi \times 10}{60}$ rad s^{-1}

$\Rightarrow \qquad$ angular speed, $\omega = \dfrac{\pi}{3}$ rad s^{-1}

The boy is moving at constant speed, but he is accelerating because the direction of the velocity is changing. The acceleration is directed towards the centre of the circle.

Use $a = r\omega^2$.
$$a = 1.5 \times \left(\frac{\pi}{3}\right)^2$$
The boy's acceleration is 1.64 m s^{-2} to 3 s.f.

Exercise B (answers p 163)

1 A turntable rotates at 8 rad s^{-1}.

(a) Find the acceleration of an object 0.1 m from the centre of the turntable.

(b) Find the acceleration of an object 0.2 m from the centre of the turntable.

2 A wheel of radius 0.4 m rotates at 10 rad s^{-1}.

(a) (i) Find the magnitude of the velocity of a point on the circumference of the wheel.

$\quad$ (ii) What is the direction of this velocity?

(b) (i) Find the magnitude of the acceleration of a point on the circumference of the wheel.

$\quad$ (ii) What is the direction of this acceleration?

3 A turntable rotates with a constant angular speed of 0.5 rad s^{-1}.
A coin is placed on the turntable, 15 cm from its axis of rotation.
Find the acceleration of the coin.

4 A racing car is travelling at a constant speed of 120 km h^{-1} around a bend that is part of a circle.

(a) Find the speed of the car in m s^{-1}.

(b) The magnitude of the acceleration is 30 m s^{-2}.
Find the radius of the bend.

5 In a device for simulating the accelerations produced in rocket flights,
a horizontal arm of length 7 m is rotated about a vertical axis.
It is required to produce an acceleration of 120 m s^{-2} (about 12 times the acceleration due to gravity).
Find the angular velocity of the arm.

6 A roundabout in a children's playground takes 10 seconds to complete one revolution. The radius of the roundabout is 2 m.

    (a) A child sits 1 m from the centre. Find

        (i) her speed   **(ii)** her acceleration

    (b) She moves so that she is 1.5 m from the centre. Find

        (i) her speed   **(ii)** her acceleration

7 The minute hand on a clock is 5 cm long.
Find the acceleration of the tip of the hand.

8 The Moon takes 27.3 days to orbit the Earth.

    (a) Find the angular speed, in rad s^{-1}, of the Moon about the Earth.

    (b) The radius of the Moon's orbit is 3.84×10^8 m.
Find the acceleration of the Moon.

9 A turntable rotates at 45 r.p.m. An object is placed on the turntable so that it moves at a constant speed of 8 m s^{-1}.
Find the magnitude of the acceleration of the object.

C Forces in circular motion (answers p 164)

We have seen that an object moving in a circle with constant speed experiences an acceleration directed towards the centre of the circle.
Newton's second law (N2L) tells us that the resultant force on the object must also act towards the centre of the circle. This is not saying that an extra force is acting, but tells us about the direction of the resultant of the forces already acting on the object.

C1 For each of the following situations, describe the force that is acting towards the centre of the circle to cause the circular motion.

    (a) A conker, on a piece of string, rotating in a circle on a horizontal table

    (b) A satellite orbiting the Earth

    (c) A car driving round a roundabout

C2 An object of mass m kg is moving round a circle of radius r m with angular speed ω rad s^{-1}.

    (a) Use Newton's second law to show that the resultant force acting towards the centre of the circle is given by $F = mr\omega^2$.

    (b) Show that the resultant force can also be written as $F = \dfrac{mv^2}{r}$, where $v \text{ m s}^{-1}$ is the speed of the object.

For an object moving in a circle with constant speed the magnitude of the resultant force, F N, acting towards the centre of the circle is given by

$$F = mr\omega^2 = \frac{mv^2}{r}$$

D

C3 A particle of mass m kg is attached to one end of a light inextensible string of length r m. The other end of the string is fixed to a point O on a smooth horizontal surface. The particle moves in a circle on the surface with a constant angular speed, ω rad s^{-1}.

(a) Draw a force diagram for the particle.

(b) Use Newton's second law to find an expression for the tension in the string.

(c) Describe what happens to the tension if the angular speed of the particle is doubled.

(d) Describe the motion of the particle if the string breaks.

C4 A particle of mass 2 kg is attached to one end of a light inextensible string of length 0.4 m. The other end of the string is fixed to a point O on a smooth horizontal surface. The particle moves in a circle, centre O, on the surface with a constant speed of 1.2 m s^{-1}.

(a) Find the acceleration of the particle.

(b) Find the tension in the string.

(c) The maximum possible tension in the string is 20 N.
Find the maximum possible speed of the particle.

(d) What is the particle's maximum angular speed?

C5 A turntable is rotating at a constant angular speed of 6 rad s^{-1}. A particle of mass 0.2 kg is placed on the turntable 0.05 m from its centre and does not slip.

(a) Draw a force diagram for the particle.

(b) Find the magnitude of the friction force on the particle.

(c) Another particle of mass 0.2 kg is placed on the turntable, a distance of 0.1 m from its centre.
Assuming that the particle does not slip, find the magnitude of the friction force on the particle.

When the force towards the centre of the circle is a friction force, this force must be less than or equal to the limiting value of the friction force.
If the resultant force required to keep the object moving in a circle is greater than the limiting value, then the object will slip and no longer move in a circle.

C6 A turntable is rotating at a constant 30 revolutions per minute.
A particle of mass 0.4 kg is placed on the turntable, 0.2 m from its centre, and does not slip.

(a) Find the angular speed, in rad s^{-1}, of the turntable.

(b) Find the acceleration of the particle.

(c) Find the magnitude of the friction force acting on the particle.

(d) Find the magnitude of the normal reaction of the turntable on the particle.

(e) Given that the particle is in limiting equilibrium, find the coefficient of friction between the particle and the plane.

Example 3

A satellite of mass $300\,\text{kg}$ is travelling in a circular orbit $830\,\text{km}$ above the surface of the Earth. The satellite takes 102 minutes to complete each orbit. Given that the radius of the Earth is $6380\,\text{km}$, find the magnitude of the gravitational force between the satellite and the Earth.

Solution

Find the angular speed in $\text{rad}\,\text{s}^{-1}$.
$$\omega = \tfrac{1}{102}\ \text{r.p.m.} = \tfrac{1}{102} \times \frac{2\pi}{60}\ \text{rad}\,\text{s}^{-1}$$
$$= \frac{\pi}{3060}\ \text{rad}\,\text{s}^{-1}$$

Find the radius of the orbit in metres. $\quad r = (830 + 6380) \times 1000 = 7.21 \times 10^6$

The resultant force towards the centre of the circle is the gravitational force.

Use N2L.
$$F = mr\omega^2 = 300 \times 7.21 \times 10^6 \times \left(\frac{\pi}{3060}\right)^2$$
$$= 2279.8\ldots$$

The gravitational force between the satellite and the Earth is $2280\,\text{N}$ to 3 s.f.

Example 4

A counter of mass $0.02\,\text{kg}$ is placed $0.3\,\text{m}$ from the centre of a turntable rotating at a constant angular speed of $\omega\ \text{rad}\,\text{s}^{-1}$.
The coefficient of friction between the counter and the turntable is 0.6.
Find the maximum value of ω if the counter does not slip.

Solution

Draw a force diagram for the counter.
Show the acceleration using a double-headed arrow.

Resolve vertically. $\qquad\qquad\qquad\qquad R = 0.02g$

The maximum value of ω is when the counter is in limiting equilibrium.

Use $F = \mu R$. $\qquad\qquad\qquad\qquad F = 0.6 \times 0.02g = 0.012g$

Apply N2L horizontally. $\qquad\qquad F = mr\omega^2$
$$0.012g = 0.02 \times 0.3\omega^2$$
$$\Rightarrow \omega^2 = \frac{0.012g}{0.006} = 19.6$$
$$\Rightarrow \omega = 4.43 \text{ to 3 s.f.}$$

The maximum angular speed of the turntable is $4.43\,\text{rad}\,\text{s}^{-1}$ to 3 s.f.

Exercise C (answers p 164)

1 An object of mass $2\,kg$ moves at a constant speed of $5\,m\,s^{-1}$ in a circle of radius $0.25\,m$.
Find the magnitude and direction of the resultant force on the object.

2 A particle of mass $0.3\,kg$ moves with a constant angular speed of $4\,rad\,s^{-1}$ in a circle of radius $0.1\,m$.
Find the magnitude of the resultant force on the particle.

3 A car travelling at $15\,m\,s^{-1}$ is going round a bend, which is part of a circle of radius $150\,m$.

Given that the mass of the car is $1500\,kg$, find the frictional force towards the centre of the circle on the tyres of the car.

4 A satellite of mass $500\,kg$ is travelling in a circular orbit $35\,800\,km$ above the equator. The satellite completes one orbit every 24 hours.

Given that the radius of the Earth is $6380\,km$, find the magnitude of the gravitational force between the Earth and the satellite.

5 A particle of mass $3\,kg$ is attached to one end of a light inextensible string of length $0.5\,m$. The other end of the string is fixed to a point O on a smooth horizontal surface. The particle moves in a circle, centre O, on the surface with a constant angular speed of $4\,rad\,s^{-1}$.

(a) (i) Find the magnitude of the velocity of the particle.

(ii) What is the direction of the velocity?

(b) (i) Find the magnitude of the acceleration of the particle.

(ii) What is the direction of the acceleration?

(c) Find the tension in the string.

(d) The string breaks. Describe the subsequent motion of the particle.

6 A turntable is rotating at a constant angular speed of $4\,rad\,s^{-1}$.
An object of mass $0.1\,kg$ is placed on the turntable $0.2\,m$ from its centre and does not slip.

(a) Draw a force diagram for the object.

(b) Find the magnitude of the friction force on the object.

(c) Another object of mass $0.1\,kg$ is placed on the turntable $0.25\,m$ from its centre. Given that this particle is about to slip, find the coefficient of friction between the object and the turntable.

7 A car of mass $1400\,kg$ travels round a horizontal bend of radius $120\,m$ at $24\,m\,s^{-1}$.

(a) Show that the magnitude of the friction force towards the centre of the bend is $6720\,N$.

(b) Find the least possible value of the coefficient of friction between the tyres and the ground.

8 A bead of mass 0.08 kg is attached to one end of a string of length 0.9 m. The other end of the string is fixed to a point O on a smooth horizontal surface. The bead is made to rotate in a horizontal circle, centre O, with the string taut.

Given that the maximum tension in the string is 25 N, find the maximum angular velocity of the bead.

9 A fairground ride consists of a large hollow cylinder of internal radius 5 metres. This can be made to rotate about its axis and a floor can be raised or lowered. People stand with their backs against the wall. The cylinder starts to rotate faster and faster and then the floor is lowered.

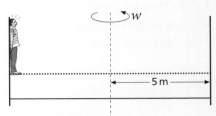

(a) Draw a force diagram for a person when the floor has been lowered.

(b) Describe how the forces change as the speed of the cylinder increases.

(c) Given that the coefficient of friction between a person's body and the cylinder is 0.4, find the angular speed of the cylinder when the floor can first drop, if the people are not to slip down the wall.

10 A particle is placed a distance r m from the centre of a rough turntable. The coefficient of friction between the particle and the turntable is μ. The turntable starts to rotate and its angular speed, ω rad s^{-1}, increases.

Show that, if the particle does not slip, $\omega \leq \sqrt{\dfrac{\mu g}{r}}$.

D Problems needing resolving of forces (answers p 165)

A small mass is hanging on one end of a piece of string. The other end of the string is fixed, and the mass is set moving in a horizontal circle. The string traces out the surface of a cone. This is a **conical pendulum**. We will be looking at motion of this type in this section.

D1 Imagine you are holding a conker on the end of a piece of string. You set the conker rotating in a horizontal circle.

(a) What do you think will happen to the radius of the circle traced out by the conker as you increase its angular speed?

(b) What do you think will happen to the radius if you increase the length of the string and keep the angular speed constant?

We can model this situation by treating the conker as a particle and the string as light and inextensible, and assuming that the effect of air resistance is negligible.

Consider a particle P of mass m kg attached to one end of a light, inextensible string of length l m. The other end, O, of the string is held fixed and the particle moves with constant speed in a horizontal circle with its centre vertically below O. The string makes an angle θ with the vertical.

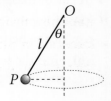

The force diagram for the particle is shown.

The tension can be resolved vertically and horizontally to give

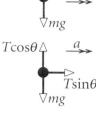

- a vertical component $T\cos\theta$ which balances the weight of the particle
- a horizontal component $T\sin\theta$ which causes the inward acceleration of the particle

D2 (a) Explain why the radius of the circle traced out by the particle is $l\sin\theta$.

(b) Resolve the forces vertically to show that $T = \dfrac{mg}{\cos\theta}$.

(c) By applying Newton's second law horizontally show that $\omega^2 = \dfrac{g}{l\cos\theta}$.

The result obtained in D2 shows that the angular speed of the particle depends on the length of the string and its angle to the vertical, but not on the mass of the particle.

D **D3 (a)** Given that the length of the string is fixed, what happens to the angle θ as the angular speed ω increases?

(b) Explain why the string cannot become horizontal.

(c) If the angular speed of the particle is kept constant and the length of the string is increased, how does the angle θ change?

D4 A conker of mass 0.01 kg is attached to one end of a string of length 0.4 m. The other end is held fixed and the conker moves in a horizontal circle, with the string making an angle of 30° with the vertical.

(a) Draw a force diagram for the conker.

(b) Find the tension in the string.

(c) Show that the acceleration of the conker is 5.66 m s⁻² to 3 s.f.

(d) Find the speed of the conker.

D5 A ball of mass 0.3 kg moves in a horizontal circle of radius 0.4 m on the inside surface of a smooth hemispherical bowl of radius 0.5 m.

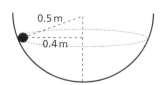

(a) Draw a force diagram for the ball.

(b) What force causes the acceleration of the ball?

(c) By resolving vertically, show that the magnitude of the normal reaction of the bowl on the ball is 4.9 N.

(d) By applying Newton's second law horizontally, find the angular speed of the ball.

K If a body is moving in a horizontal circle

- forces are in equilibrium vertically
- the resultant force acting towards the centre of the circle is given by $F = mr\omega^2 = \dfrac{mv^2}{r}$

Example 5

A particle of mass 2 kg moves in a horizontal circle at $5\,\text{m}\,\text{s}^{-1}$
on the inside surface of a smooth cone as shown.
The semi-vertical angle of the cone is 30°.
Find the radius of the circle.

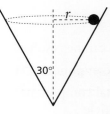

Solution

Draw a force diagram for the particle.

Resolve vertically.

$$R\sin 30° = 2g$$

$$\Rightarrow \qquad R = 39.2$$

Apply N2L horizontally.

$$F = \frac{mv^2}{r}$$

$$\Rightarrow \quad R\cos 30° = \frac{2\times 5^2}{r}$$

$$\Rightarrow \qquad r = \frac{50}{39.2\cos 30°} = 1.47$$

The radius of the circle is 1.47 m to 3 s.f.

Example 6

A particle P of mass 0.5 kg is attached to two strings of length 0.5 m
and 0.3 m. The strings are fixed at points A and B as shown, with A
vertically above B. The particle moves in a horizontal circle, centre B,
of radius 0.3 m at an angular speed of $8\,\text{rad}\,\text{s}^{-1}$.
Find the tension in each string.

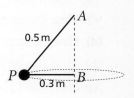

Solution

Draw a force diagram for the particle.

Find the values of $\sin\theta$ and $\cos\theta$.

$$h^2 = 0.5^2 - 0.3^2$$

$$\Rightarrow \qquad h = 0.4$$

$$\Rightarrow \quad \cos\theta = 0.6,\ \sin\theta = 0.8$$

Resolve vertically.

$$T_A \sin\theta = 0.5g$$

$$\Rightarrow \quad 0.8T_A = 4.9$$

$$\Rightarrow \qquad T_A = 6.125$$

Apply N2L horizontally.

$$F = mr\omega^2$$
$$T_A \cos\theta + T_B = 0.5 \times 0.3 \times 8^2$$
$$\Rightarrow \quad 6.125 \times 0.6 + T_B = 9.6$$
$$\Rightarrow \qquad\qquad T_B = 5.925$$

The tension in AP is 6.125 N and the tension in BP is 5.925 N.

Exercise D (answers p 165)

1 A conical pendulum has length 80 cm and a bob of mass 0.5 kg which is rotating in a horizontal circle of radius 30 cm.

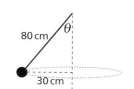

   (a) Draw a force diagram for the bob.

   (b) Find, to the nearest degree, the angle θ between the string and the vertical.

   (c) Find the tension in the string.

   (d) Find the acceleration of the bob.

   (e) Find the speed of the bob.

2 A particle of mass 0.2 kg moves in a horizontal circle of radius 0.4 m on the inside surface of a smooth cone. The semi-vertical angle of the cone is 30°.

   (a) Draw a force diagram for the particle.

   (b) Find the magnitude of the normal reaction of the cone on the particle.

   (c) Find the angular speed, in $\mathrm{rad\,s^{-1}}$, of the particle.

   (d) How long does it take for the particle to complete one revolution?

3 A smooth hemispherical bowl is fixed with its rim horizontal. An object of mass 0.09 kg follows a horizontal circle on the inside surface of the bowl at a constant 140 r.p.m.

   Given that the internal radius of the bowl is 0.2 m, find the depth of this circle below the rim of the bowl.

4 A cyclist is rounding a bend which is an arc of a circle of radius 10 m. The road is banked at an angle of 30° to the horizontal. The total mass of the cyclist and bicycle is 100 kg. The speed of the cyclist is such that there is no friction force acting sideways on the tyres up or down the slope.

   (a) Draw a force diagram for the cyclist.

   (b) Show that the magnitude of the normal reaction of the road on the cyclist is 1130 N to 3 s.f.

   (c) Find the speed of the cyclist.

   (d) What assumptions have you made in answering this question?

5 A particle of mass m moves in a horizontal circle with constant angular velocity ω on the inside surface of a smooth cone with semi-vertical angle θ.

   (a) Show that the radius r of the circle is given by $r = \dfrac{g}{\omega^2 \tan\theta}$.

   (b) The particle is made to rotate with angular velocity 2ω inside the same cone. Find an expression for the radius of this circle.

6 A ball of mass $0.2\,\text{kg}$ moves in a horizontal circle of radius $0.5\,\text{m}$ on the inside surface of a smooth hemispherical bowl of radius $1\,\text{m}$.

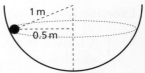

   (a) Find the angular speed of the ball.

   (b) The ball is replaced with a ball of twice the mass of the original. The new ball moves in a horizontal circle with the same radius. What is the angular speed of this ball?

7 A particle P of mass m is attached to one end of a light, inextensible string of length l. The other end of the string is fixed at O and the particle moves with angular speed ω in a horizontal circle of radius r, centre C. The point C is a distance h vertically below O.

   (a) (i) Show that the tension in the string, T, is given by $T = ml\omega^2$.

   (ii) How does T change as the angular speed of the particle is increased?

   (b) (i) Show that $h = \dfrac{g}{\omega^2}$.

   (ii) How does h change as the angular speed of the particle is increased?

8 A particle P of mass $0.4\,\text{kg}$ is attached to one end of a light, inextensible string of length $0.75\,\text{m}$. The other end of the string is fixed at O, and the particle moves in a horizontal circle with centre C at constant speed.

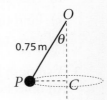

   (a) The string is inclined at an angle θ to the vertical, where $\sin\theta = 0.6$.

   (i) Show that the particle moves in a circle of radius $0.45\,\text{m}$.

   (ii) Find the tension in the string.

   (iii) Find the angular speed, in $\text{rad}\,\text{s}^{-1}$, of the particle.

   (b) The angular speed of the particle is doubled. Find the distance below O of the centre of the circle C.

9 A particle of mass $4\,\text{kg}$ is attached to one end of a string of length $1\,\text{m}$. The other end of the string is fixed at O. The particle is made to rotate in a horizontal circle with centre C, where C is vertically below O. The maximum possible tension in the string is $60\,\text{N}$.

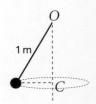

   (a) What happens to the tension in the string as the angular speed of the particle is increased?

   (b) Find the maximum possible angular speed that can be attained.

   (c) Find the angle that the string makes with the vertical in this case.

10 A particle P of mass 2 kg is attached to two light, inextensible strings of lengths 1.5 m and 1.2 m.
The strings are fixed at points A and B, with A vertically above B.
The particle moves in a horizontal circle, centre B.

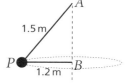

(a) Find the tension in the string AP.

(b) Given that the maximum possible tension in string BP is 50 N, find the maximum possible speed of the particle.

11 A particle P of mass 1 kg is attached to two light, inextensible strings of length 0.8 m.
The other ends of the strings are fixed at A and B, with B 0.8 m vertically below A.
The particle moves in a horizontal circle with angular velocity 6 rad s^{-1} with both strings taut.

Find the tension in each string.

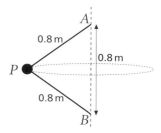

Key points

- The angular speed of an object moving in a circle is the rate at which the object is rotating.

  An angular speed of n r.p.m. is equivalent to $\dfrac{2\pi n}{60}$ rad s^{-1}.

  The object will complete one revolution in $\dfrac{60}{n}$ s. (p 75)

- A particle moving round a circle of radius r m with angular speed ω rad s^{-1} has a speed of v m s^{-1}, where $v = r\omega$. (p 76)

- A particle moving round a circle of radius r m with angular speed ω rad s^{-1} and speed v m s^{-1} has an acceleration a m s^{-2}, where $a = r\omega^2 = \dfrac{v^2}{r}$.

  The velocity of the particle is directed along a tangent to the circle and the acceleration is directed towards the centre of the circle. (p 78)

- For an object moving in a circle with constant speed, the magnitude of the resultant force, F N, acting towards the centre of the circle is given by

  $F = mr\omega^2 = \dfrac{mv^2}{r}$ (p 80)

- If a body is moving in a horizontal circle

  forces are in equilibrium vertically

  the resultant force acting towards the centre of the circle is given by

  $F = mr\omega^2 = \dfrac{mv^2}{r}$ (p 85)

Mixed questions (answers p 166)

1 Two particles are connected by a light, inextensible string. One particle, which has mass 5 kg, follows a circular path of radius 70 cm, on a smooth horizontal table. The string passes through a hole in the table and a second particle, of mass 10 kg, hangs in equilibrium on the other end of the string as shown in the diagram.

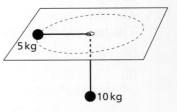

(a) By considering the 10 kg particle, calculate the tension in the string.

(b) Find the speed of the particle on the table.

(c) The string breaks. Describe what happens to the particle on the table.   AQA 2002

2 A car travels round a horizontal bend of radius r m at a constant speed v m s^{-1}. The coefficient of friction between the tyres and the road is μ.

Given that the car doesn't slip, show that $\mu \geq \dfrac{v^2}{rg}$.

3 A particle P, of mass 2 kg, is attached by a light, inextensible string, of length 0.5 metres, to the point O. The particle moves in a circular path on a smooth horizontal table. The centre of the circle is vertically below O. The speed of the particle is 0.3 m s^{-1}, and the string is at an angle of 30° to the vertical.

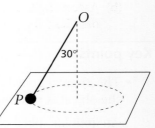

(a) Draw a diagram to show the forces acting on the particle.

(b) Show that the tension in the string is 1.44 N.

(c) Find the magnitude of the normal reaction force on the particle.   AQA 2002

4 A particle of mass m is attached to one end of a light, inextensible string of length l. The other end of the string is fixed at P. The particle moves in a horizontal circle of radius r at a constant speed v, as shown.

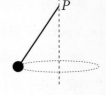

(a) Show that the tension in the string, T, is given by $T = \dfrac{mgl}{\sqrt{l^2 - r^2}}$.

(b) Find v^2 in terms of r, g and l.

(c) A second light, inextensible string, of length l, is then attached to the particle and to Q, a fixed point directly below P, as shown in the diagram. The particle moves in a horizontal circle of radius r at a constant speed V, with both strings taut. Find the tension in the upper string in terms of m, g, l, r and V.

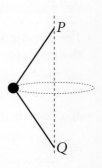

AQA 2002

Test yourself (answers p 166)

1 A coin of mass 0.01 kg is placed on a horizontal turntable. The coin is at a distance of 50 cm from the centre of the turntable. The coefficient of friction between the coin and the turntable is 0.4. The turntable rotates about its centre, so that the coin follows a circular path at a constant speed, without slipping.

    (a) Calculate the maximum magnitude of the friction force acting on the coin.

    (b) Find the maximum angular speed of the turntable in revolutions per minute.

    (c) The angular speed of the turntable is halved. What happens to the magnitude of the friction force acting on the coin?
                                                    AQA 2002

2 The largest moon of the planet Saturn is Titan, whose orbit can be modelled as circular. The time for Titan to complete one orbit of Saturn is approximately 19.5 Earth days and the radius of the circular orbit is approximately 1.22×10^9 m.

    (a) Show that the speed of Titan is approximately $4550\,\mathrm{m\,s^{-1}}$.

    (b) Assuming that the mass of Titan is approximately 1.34×10^{23} kg, find the force on Titan maintaining its circular orbit.

3 A particle of mass 3 kg describes a horizontal circular path on the inside surface of a smooth cone, as shown in the diagram. The radius of the circle is 0.5 metres and the semi-vertical angle of the cone is 30°. The particle moves at a constant speed.

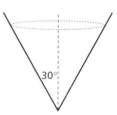

    (a) (i) Show that the magnitude of the normal reaction force on the particle is 58.8 N.

       (ii) Find the speed of the particle.

    (b) The particle moves on the same cone, but in a horizontal circle of greater radius than before.

       (i) What happens to the magnitude of the normal reaction force?

      (ii) What happens to the speed of the particle? Explain your answer.
                                               AQA 2004

4 A particle P of mass m is attached by a light, inextensible thread of length l to a fixed point O. The particle moves with constant angular speed ω in a horizontal circle with centre C. The point C is vertically below O. The thread is inclined to the vertical at an angle θ, as shown in the diagram.

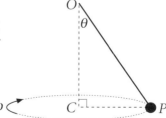

    (a) Find an expression for the tension in the thread. Give your answer in terms of m, l and ω.

    (b) Show that $\cos\theta = \dfrac{g}{l\omega^2}$.

    (c) The greatest tension that the thread can withstand without breaking is 16 N. In the case when $l = 0.4$ metres and $m = 0.1$ kg,

       (i) show that $\omega \leq 20$ radians per second

      (ii) find the greatest possible value of θ, giving your answer to the nearest degree
                                                 AQA 2003

6 Work, energy and power

In this chapter you will
• learn what is meant by the work done by a force
• learn about kinetic energy and gravitational potential energy
• use the work–energy principle and the principle of conservation of energy
• learn what is meant by power

Key points from Mechanics 1

• If a force of F newtons, acting on an object of mass m kg, causes an acceleration a m s^{-2}, then $F = ma$. (Newton's second law)

• If an object is moving with constant velocity, then its acceleration is zero. So the resultant force on the object is zero.

• If an object is moving on a rough surface, the friction force F is equal to μR, where μ is the coefficient of friction and R is the normal reaction.

• The constant acceleration equations for motion in one dimension are

$$v = u + at \qquad\qquad s = ut + \tfrac{1}{2}at^2$$
$$s = \tfrac{1}{2}(u + v)t \qquad\qquad s = vt - \tfrac{1}{2}at^2$$
$$v^2 = u^2 + 2as$$

A Work (answers p 167)

In Mechanics 1 we found that when a force was applied to an object for a period of time it caused a change in momentum of the object. Now we will look at the link between the force applied and the distance moved by the object.

D A1 Imagine a packing case at rest on rough horizontal ground. If you apply a force, F N, to push the packing case along you will do work.

Now you use the same force, F N, to push the case along for twice the distance. What effect will this have on the work you do?

When a force moves an object a given distance, the force does **work**. The further the object is moved, the greater the work done by the force.

K When a constant force F N applied to an object moves it a distance s m in the direction of the force, the work done is defined as the product of the force and the distance.

Work done $= Fs$

The unit of work is the joule (J). This is named after James Prescott Joule (1818–89), an English physicist who established that the various forms of energy are equivalent. 1 joule is the work done when a force of 1 newton acts through a distance of 1 metre.

A2 A truck is pushed along a smooth track by a force of 40 N.
Calculate the work done in moving the truck 10 m.

A3 (a) A packing case is resting on smooth horizontal ground.
It is pulled a distance d m by a horizontal force F N.
State the work done in moving the case.

(b) The force is now inclined at 30° to the horizontal.
The case is again pulled a distance d m.

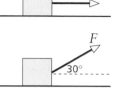

   (i) Draw a force diagram for the packing case.

   (ii) What force is causing the motion of the case?

   (iii) State the work done in moving the case.

When a force is applied at an angle to the direction of motion, only the
component of the force acting in the direction of motion does work.
The component of force that is perpendicular to the direction of motion
does no work, as there is no motion in that direction.

The work done by a constant force moving an object in a straight line,
acting at an angle θ to the direction of motion, is given by

   Work done $= Fs\cos\theta$

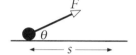

A force acting perpendicular to the direction of motion does no work.

A4 A particle of weight 8 N is pulled 10 m along a smooth horizontal
surface by a force of 25 N inclined at an angle of 40° to the horizontal.

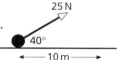

   (a) State the work done by the weight of the particle.

   (b) Find, to 3 s.f., the work done by the 25 N force.

Consider a car driving along a horizontal road. The car's engine provides a
driving force, also known as a **tractive force**, which causes the car to move forwards.
The car's motion may also be subject to resistance forces.

A5 A car moves along a horizontal road at a constant velocity.
The driving force of the car's engine is 2500 N.
Find the work done by the car's engine in moving 50 m.

Example 1

A particle is pulled 5 m along smooth horizontal ground by a force of 80 N.
Calculate the work done by the force when it is

(a) horizontal   **(b)** inclined at 25° to the horizontal

Solution

(a) Work done $= Fs = 80 \times 5 = 400$ J

(b) Work done $= Fs\cos\theta = 80 \times 5 \times \cos 25° = 363$ J to 3 s.f.

Exercise A (answers p 167)

1 An object of mass 2 kg is pushed across a horizontal surface by a
horizontal force of magnitude 15 N.
Find the work done by the force in moving the object 8 m.

2 A car travels at constant speed along a straight horizontal road for 50 m.
The driving force of the car's engine is 3000 N.
Find the work done by the car's engine.

3 (a) A particle is pulled along a horizontal surface by a force
of 3.5 N inclined at 20° to the horizontal.
Find the work done by the force in moving the particle 10 m.

(b) The angle of the force is increased to 40°.

  (i) Explain why the force will now do less work in moving the particle.

  (ii) Find the work done in moving the particle 10 m.

4 A box is pushed for 15 m along horizontal ground by a constant force.
The work done by the force is 5250 J.
Find the magnitude of the force.

5 A box of mass 18 kg is raised 12 m vertically at constant speed.
Find the work done by the force raising the box.

6 (a) A sledge is pulled along smooth ground by a force of 90 N
inclined at 30° to the horizontal.
Find the work done by the force in moving the sledge 6 m.

(b) If the sledge had been moved 6 m with the force horizontal,
how much more work would have been done?

7 A truck is pulled along a smooth horizontal track by a force
of 150 N inclined at 60° to the horizontal.
Given that the work done by the force is 375 J, find the
distance moved by the truck.

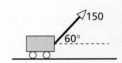

B Kinetic energy (answers p 167)

B1 A van of mass 2000 kg starts from rest and travels with constant acceleration.
After travelling a distance of 100 m its velocity is 20 m s^{-1}.
Any resistance to motion can be ignored.

  (a) Use one of the constant acceleration equations to find the acceleration of the van.

  (b) Use Newton's second law of motion to find the driving force of the van's engine.

  (c) Find the work done by the van's engine during this motion.

During the motion of the van, the van's engine has done work which has caused
an increase in the van's energy.
The energy possessed by a body due to its motion is called **kinetic energy**.

B2 A body of mass m kg is initially at rest. It is acted on by a constant force F N. After it has travelled a distance s m, its velocity is v m s^{-1}.

   (a) Use the constant acceleration equations to show that the acceleration of the body is given by $a = \dfrac{v^2}{2s}$.

   (b) Substitute this expression for a into $F = ma$, and hence show that $Fs = \frac{1}{2}mv^2$.

The expression on the left side of the equation above, Fs, is the work done by the force, measured in joules. The expression on the right side of the equation represents the kinetic energy of the body, which is also measured in joules.

> **K** The kinetic energy (k.e.) of a body of mass m kg moving with a velocity of v m s^{-1} is given by
>
> $\qquad$ k.e. $= \frac{1}{2}mv^2$
>
> The unit of energy is the joule.

B3 A car of mass 2500 kg travels with constant acceleration over a distance of 200 m. Its velocity increases from 15 m s^{-1} to 30 m s^{-1}.
Any resistance to motion can be ignored.

   (a) (i) Find the acceleration of the car.

   (ii) Use Newton's second law of motion to find the driving force of the car's engine and hence the work done by the car's engine during this motion.

   (b) (i) Find the kinetic energy of the car at the start of the motion.

   (ii) Find the kinetic energy of the car at the end of the motion.

   (iii) Find the change in the car's kinetic energy during this motion.

B4 A body of mass m kg moves with constant acceleration, increasing its velocity from u m s^{-1} to v m s^{-1} over a distance of s m.

   (a) Show that the acceleration of the body is given by $a = \dfrac{v^2 - u^2}{2s}$.

   (b) Substitute this expression for a into $F = ma$, and hence show that $Fs = \frac{1}{2}mv^2 - \frac{1}{2}mu^2$.

> **K** The work done by a force acting on a body is equal to the change in kinetic energy of the body.
>
> $\qquad Fs = \frac{1}{2}mv^2 - \frac{1}{2}mu^2$

B5 A truck of mass 10 kg is moving at a speed of 18 m s^{-1}.
It comes to rest after travelling 40 m.

Find the kinetic energy lost by the truck in coming to rest.

When the speed of an object is reduced, it loses kinetic energy and the amount of work done by the force which brings the object to rest is negative.
This force is a resisting force which acts in the opposite direction to the direction of motion.

A force acting in the direction opposite to the direction of motion does a negative amount of work.

B6 Find the magnitude of the resisting force acting on the truck in B5.

B7 A box of mass 40 kg is resting on rough horizontal ground.
It is pulled by a horizontal force of 150 N.
A constant resisting force of 80 N acts on the box.

The box moves from rest a distance of 5 m.

(a) Use Newton's second law and the constant acceleration equations to find the final velocity of the box.

(b) Hence find the gain in kinetic energy of the box.

(c) Find the work done by the 150 N force.

(d) Find the work done by the resisting force.

(e) (i) State the resultant force causing the motion of the box.

   (ii) Find the work done by the resultant force. Comment on your result.

When an object is acted upon by a number of forces, the change in kinetic energy of the object is equal to the work done by the resultant force acting on the object. If the resultant force acts in the direction of motion, the object will gain kinetic energy. If the resultant force opposes the direction of motion, the object will lose kinetic energy.

Example 2

A particle of mass 5 kg is acted upon by a horizontal force.
The initial speed of the particle is $1\,\mathrm{m\,s^{-1}}$ and the force does 200 J of work.
Find the final speed of the particle.

Solution

Work done = change in kinetic energy = $\frac{1}{2}mv^2 - \frac{1}{2}mu^2$

$\quad\quad 200 = \frac{1}{2}\times 5v^2 - \frac{1}{2}\times 5\times 1^2 = 2.5v^2 - 2.5$

$\Rightarrow \quad 2.5v^2 = 202.5$

$\Rightarrow \quad\quad v^2 = 81$

$\Rightarrow \quad\quad v = 9$

The final speed of the particle is $9\,\mathrm{m\,s^{-1}}$.

Example 3

A box of mass 25 kg is pulled 50 m along rough horizontal ground by a force of 200 N inclined at 30° to the horizontal.
The coefficient of friction between the box and the ground is 0.4.

(a) Find the work done by the 200 N force.

(b) Find the work done by the friction force.

(c) If the box started from rest, find its speed after moving 50 m.

Solution

Sketch a force diagram for the box.
Show the horizontal and vertical components of the 200 N force.

(a) *The motion is horizontal, so use* work = $Fs\cos\theta$.

Work done by 200 N force = $200 \times 50 \times \cos 30° = 8660$ J to 3 s.f.

(b) *The forces are in equilibrium vertically.*

Resolve the forces vertically. $\quad R + 200\sin 30° = 25 \times 9.8$

$\Rightarrow \qquad\qquad R = 145$ N

The box is moving, so $F = \mu R$. $\quad F = 0.4 \times 145 = 58$ N

The friction force acts in the opposite direction to the direction of motion,
so the work done by this force is negative.

Work done by the friction force = $-58 \times 50 = -2900$ J

(c) *Find the increase in kinetic energy, which is equal to the total work done on the box.*

Increase in k.e. = $8660 - 2900 = 5760$ J to 3 s.f.

Increase in k.e. = $\frac{1}{2}mv^2 - \frac{1}{2}mu^2 \qquad \frac{1}{2} \times 25 \times v^2 - 0 = 5760$

$\Rightarrow \qquad\qquad v^2 = \dfrac{2 \times 5760}{25}$

$\Rightarrow \qquad\qquad v = 21.5$ to 3 s.f.

After 50 m, the box is moving at 21.5 m s^{-1} to 3 s.f.

An alternative method would be to use Newton's second law to find the
acceleration of the box and then use $v^2 = u^2 + 2as$ *to find v.*

Exercise B (answers p 167)

1 A car of mass 2000 kg is travelling at 15 m s^{-1}.
   Find the kinetic energy of the car.

2 A cyclist on a horizontal road increases her velocity from 5 m s^{-1} to 8 m s^{-1}.
   The total mass of cyclist and bicycle is 90 kg. Resistance to motion may be ignored.

   (a) Find the change in kinetic energy.

   (b) State the work done by the cyclist.

3 A van of mass 3500 kg reduces its speed from 18 m s^{-1} to 12 m s^{-1}.
   Find the van's loss in kinetic energy.

4 A car of mass 1500 kg is travelling at 40 m s^{-1} along a horizontal road.

   (a) What is the kinetic energy of the car?

   (b) The car's brakes are applied and the car comes to rest in 100 m.
       Given that the brakes cause a constant retarding force, find the magnitude
       of this force.

5 A particle of mass 2 kg is moving at $5\,\text{m}\,\text{s}^{-1}$.
A force of 50 N acts on the particle in the direction of motion.
Find the speed of the particle after it has moved a further 4 m.

6 A van of mass 4000 kg travels along a straight horizontal road. The driving force
of the van's engine is 6500 N and the van is subject to a constant resistance.
The van's speed increases from $10\,\text{m}\,\text{s}^{-1}$ to $20\,\text{m}\,\text{s}^{-1}$ while travelling 100 m.

(a) Find the increase in the van's kinetic energy.

(b) Find the magnitude of the resistance force.

7 A sledge of mass 240 kg is pulled on level ground from rest by dogs with
a total forward force of 150 N against resistance of 45 N.
How fast will the sledge be moving after it has moved 56 m?

8 A sledge of mass 15 kg is pulled from rest along rough horizontal ground by
a horizontal force of 50 N.
The coefficient of friction between the sledge and the ground is 0.3.

(a) Draw a force diagram for the sledge.

(b) Find the magnitude of the friction force.

(c) The sledge moves 20 m. Find the work done by

    (i) the 50 N force   (ii) the friction force

(d) Find the speed of the sledge when it has moved 20 m.

9 A box of mass 18 kg is pulled from rest along rough horizontal ground
by a force of 85 N inclined at 30° to the horizontal.
The coefficient of friction between the box and the ground is 0.4.
Find the kinetic energy of the box when it has moved 6 m.

C Potential energy (answers p 168)

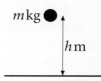

D **C1** A ball of mass 0.1 kg is dropped from a height of 2 m above ground level.

(a) What is the initial kinetic energy of the ball?

(b) Describe what happens to the kinetic energy of the ball as it falls.

(c) Use the constant acceleration equations to find the speed of the ball,
and hence its kinetic energy, as it hits the ground.

(d) (i) What force is doing work as the ball falls?

    (ii) Find the work done by this force in bringing the ball to ground level.

As the ball drops it gains kinetic energy. This is because the weight of the ball
is doing work as the ball drops.

C2 A particle of mass m kg is held at height h m above ground level
and released.
Show that the work done by the weight as the particle drops to
the ground is mgh J.

The **gravitational potential energy** of a body is defined as the work that would be done by its weight in moving the body from its current position to a fixed reference position. The reference position is an arbitrary position, often ground level, where the gravitational potential energy is taken to be zero.

A particle of mass m kg at height h m above ground level has gravitational potential energy (p.e.) mgh joules relative to the ground.

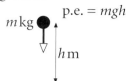

Note that 'gravitational potential energy' is often abbreviated to 'potential energy'.

C3 A particle of mass m kg is thrown vertically downwards with an initial speed u m s^{-1} from a point A that is a m above the ground. As it passes point B, which is b m above the ground, its speed is v m s^{-1}.

(a) Find an expression for the gain in kinetic energy in terms of m, u and v.

(b) Find an expression for the loss in potential energy in terms of m, a and b.

(c) Find an expression for v^2 in terms of u, g, a and b, and hence show that the gain in kinetic energy is equal to the loss in potential energy.

The result in C3 can be expressed as   k.e. at B – k.e. at A = p.e. at A – p.e. at B

This may be rearranged as   k.e. at B + p.e. at B = k.e. at A + p.e. at A

In other words, the total of the potential energy and the kinetic energy of the object is constant so long as the only force acting on the object is its weight. As the kinetic energy of the particle increases, so its potential energy decreases. Conversely, as the kinetic energy decreases, so the potential energy increases. Thus mgh represents potential energy because the particle's weight has the potential to increase the kinetic energy of the particle.

C4 A ball of mass 0.1 kg is thrown vertically upwards from ground level with initial speed 8 m s^{-1}.

(a) What is the initial kinetic energy of the ball?

(b) Describe what happens to the kinetic energy of the ball during its motion.

(c) Show that the speed of the ball when it is x m above ground level is given by $v^2 = 64 - 2gx$.

(d) Describe what happens to the potential energy of the ball during its motion.

(e) What is the potential energy of the ball when it is x m above ground level?

(f) Show that the sum of the kinetic energy and potential energy of the ball is constant.

If a particle of mass m kg is raised vertically by x m, then its potential energy is increased by mgx joules.
If it is lowered vertically by x m, then its potential energy is reduced by mgx joules.

C5 A box of mass 18 kg is lifted through a height of 2.5 m.
Find its gain in potential energy.

C6 (a) A particle of mass 5 kg falls 10 m vertically.
Find its loss in potential energy.

(b) Another particle of mass 5 kg slides down a smooth plane inclined
at 25° to the horizontal.
Its final position is 10 m vertically lower than its original position.

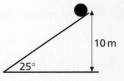

(i) Show that the distance travelled along the plane is $\dfrac{10}{\sin 25°}$ m.

(ii) Show that the work done by the weight, and hence the loss in potential
energy, in moving the particle down the plane, is 490 J.
Comment on this result.

 The change in potential energy of an object is mgh J, where h m is the
vertical distance between its initial and final positions. This value is not
affected by the path of the object between these two positions.

Example 4

A boy of mass 28 kg slides down a slide of length 4 m
inclined at 20° to the horizontal.
Calculate his loss in potential energy.

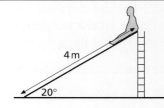

Solution

The loss in potential energy is mgh, where h is the vertical distance moved.

$\qquad h = 4\sin 20°$

Loss in p.e. $= 28 \times 9.8 \times 4\sin 20° = 375$ J to 3 s.f.

Example 5

A box of mass 15 kg is pulled for 8 m up a plane inclined at 30° to
the horizontal by a force of 50 N acting parallel to the plane.
The coefficient of friction between the box and the plane is 0.4.

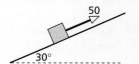

(a) Calculate the work done by the friction force.

(b) Calculate the gain in potential energy.

Solution

(a) *Sketch a force diagram.*
The friction force acts in the opposite direction to
the direction of motion, so it does negative work.

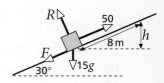

Resolve forces perpendicular to the plane. $R = 15 \times 9.8 \times \cos 30° = 147\cos 30°$

The box is moving so $F = \mu R$. $\qquad\qquad \Rightarrow F = 0.4 \times 147\cos 30° = 58.8\cos 30°$

Work done by the friction force $= -Fs = -58.8\cos 30° \times 8 = -407$ J to 3 s.f.

(b) *Calculate the vertical height, h, moved by the box.*

$$h = 8 \sin 30°$$

Gain in p.e. $= mgh = 15 \times 9.8 \times 8 \sin 30° = 588\,\text{J}$ to 3 s.f.

Exercise C (answers p 168)

1 An object of mass 8 kg is 4 m above ground level.
Find its potential energy relative to the ground.

2 A boy of mass 30 kg sits at the top of a slide of length 5 m inclined at
36° to the horizontal.
Calculate his potential energy relative to the ground.

3 A lift of mass 1500 kg travels down a vertical distance of 40 m.
Find its loss in potential energy.

4 A car of mass 1500 kg travels 50 m up a slope inclined at $\theta°$ to the horizontal,
where $\sin \theta = \frac{1}{10}$.
The driving force of the car's engine is 4000 N and the car is subject to
a constant resistance of 500 N.

  (a) Find the work done by the car's engine.

  (b) Find the work done by the resistance force.

  (c) Find the gain in potential energy of the car.

5 A sledge of mass 20 kg slides down a slope 15 m long inclined at
30° to the horizontal. It is subject to a resistance of 80 N.

  (a) Find the loss in potential energy of the sledge.

  (b) Find the work done by the resistance force.

6 A girl of mass 26 kg slides down a slide of length 4 m inclined
at 35° to the horizontal.
The coefficient of friction between the girl and the slide is 0.2.

  (a) Draw a force diagram for the girl.

  (b) Find the magnitude of the friction force.

  (c) Find the work done by the friction force.

  (d) Find the girl's loss in potential energy.

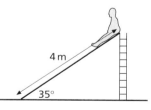

7 A box of mass 20 kg is pulled 6 m up a plane inclined at
15° to the horizontal by a force of 240 N parallel to the plane.
The coefficient of friction between the box and the plane is 0.35.

  (a) Find the work done by the 240 N force.

  (b) Find the work done by the friction force.

  (c) Find the gain in potential energy of the box.

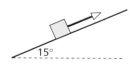

D Conservation of energy (answers p 169)

D1 A ball of mass 0.2 kg is thrown vertically upwards with initial speed $8 \, m \, s^{-1}$.

    (a) **(i)** Find the maximum height reached by the ball.

        (ii) Hence find the ball's gain in potential energy in reaching this height.

    (b) **(i)** What is the speed of the ball when it is at its maximum height?

        (ii) Find the ball's loss in kinetic energy in reaching this height. Comment on your result.

D2 A sledge of mass 15 kg slides down a smooth slope inclined at 30° to the horizontal. The slope is 10 m long and the sledge is released from rest at the top.

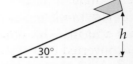

    (a) **(i)** Find the change in vertical height, h m, of the sledge during the motion.

        (ii) Hence find the loss in potential energy of the sledge during the motion.

    (b) **(i)** By resolving forces down the plane and using Newton's second law, show that the acceleration of the sledge down the plane is $4.9 \, m \, s^{-2}$.

        (ii) Find the speed of the sledge when it reaches the bottom of the slope.

        (iii) Hence find the gain in kinetic energy of the sledge during the motion. Comment on your result.

D3 A box of mass 15 kg is released from rest on a plane of length 10 m inclined at 25° to the horizontal. A constant resisting force of 50 N acts on the box.

    (a) **(i)** Find the change in vertical height, h m, of the box during the motion.

        (ii) Hence find the loss in potential energy of the box during the motion.

    (b) **(i)** By resolving forces down the plane and using Newton's second law, show that the acceleration of the box down the plane is approximately $0.808 \, m \, s^{-2}$.

        (ii) Find the speed of the box when it reaches the bottom of the slope.

        (iii) Hence find the gain in kinetic energy of the box during the motion. Comment on your result.

In the first two questions the change in kinetic energy is equal to the change in potential energy. When one is lost, the other is gained. The total mechanical energy of the system is constant. The only external force doing work is gravity.

In the third question the change in kinetic energy is not equal to the change in potential energy. This is because an external force other than gravity, that is the resisting force, is also doing work. The amount of work done by this force is negative and the total mechanical energy of the system is reduced. The normal reaction of the plane on the object is perpendicular to the direction of motion and so does no work.

> **K** The sum of the potential energy and the kinetic energy of a system will remain constant if no external force other than gravity does work.
>
> Gain in kinetic energy = loss in potential energy
>
> This is known as the **principle of conservation of mechanical energy**.

Note that if there is a loss in kinetic energy of the system, then there will be a gain in potential energy.

The principle of conservation of mechanical energy applies only if the mechanical energy of a system is not converted to another form of energy, such as light, sound or heat. For example, when a friction force acts on an object, mechanical energy is converted into heat energy.
If no external force other than gravity acts, then mechanical energy is not converted into any other form, and the principle of conservation of mechanical energy applies.

D4 (a) Find the change in energy of the box in question D3.

(b) Calculate the work done by the resisting force in question D3. Comment on your result.

> **K** If an external force other than gravity does work, then the work done by the force is equal to the change in mechanical energy of the system.
>
> Work done by force = gain in potential energy + gain in kinetic energy
>
> This is known as the **work–energy principle**.

The work–energy principle explains why work and energy have the same units.
If the work done by the force is positive, then the total mechanical energy of the system increases.
If the work done by the force is negative, then the total mechanical energy of the system decreases.

We have seen that the work–energy principle is true for situations involving constant acceleration. In fact it can be shown to be true for all situations and can thus be used to solve problems that cannot be solved using the constant acceleration equations.

D5 A stone of mass 0.2 kg is thrown vertically upwards from the top of a cliff with an initial speed of $5\,\text{m s}^{-1}$. The top of the cliff is 30 m above the water.

(a) Use the principle of conservation of mechanical energy to find the maximum height above the top of the cliff reached by the stone.

(b) Use the principle of conservation of mechanical energy to find the speed of the stone when it hits the water.

(c) Explain why you did not need to know the mass of the stone.

(d) What assumptions have been made in applying the principle of conservation of energy to this situation?

D6 A ball of mass 0.1 kg is projected up a smooth track inclined at 40° to the horizontal. The initial speed of the ball is $10\,\mathrm{m\,s^{-1}}$.

    (a) Draw a force diagram and hence explain why the principle of conservation of mechanical energy can be used in this situation.

    (b) Find the initial kinetic energy of the ball.

    (c) Assuming that the ball does not reach the end of the track, state the loss in kinetic energy of the ball in reaching its maximum height up the track.

    (d) State the increase in potential energy of the ball in reaching its maximum height up the track.

    (e) Hence find the maximum distance the ball reaches up the track.

D7 A box of mass 16 kg slides from rest down a slope of length 2.5 m inclined at 35° to the horizontal. A constant resisting force of 40 N acts on the box.

    (a) Draw a force diagram and hence explain why the principle of conservation of mechanical energy cannot be applied in this situation.

    (b) Find the work done by the resisting force during the motion.

    (c) Find the potential energy lost by the box.

    (d) Find the kinetic energy gained by the box.

    (e) Hence find the speed of the box when it reaches the bottom of the slope.

Example 6

A ball of mass 0.1 kg is projected at $1\,\mathrm{m\,s^{-1}}$ from a height of 2.5 m above ground level down a smooth curved track AB. Find the speed of the ball when it reaches B.

Solution

The normal reaction on the ball is always perpendicular to the direction of motion, so gravity is the only force doing work and the principle of conservation of mechanical energy can be used.

Gain in kinetic energy = loss in potential energy

$\frac{1}{2} \times 0.1 \times v^2 - \frac{1}{2} \times 0.1 \times 1^2 = 0.1 \times 9.8 \times 2.5$

$\Rightarrow v^2 = 50 \Rightarrow v = 7.07$ to 3 s.f.

The ball is travelling at $7.07\,\mathrm{m\,s^{-1}}$ when it reaches B.

Note that the mass of the ball was not required, as it appears in all terms in the equation.

Example 7

A load of mass 20 kg is pulled from rest up a plane inclined at 25° to the horizontal by a force of 150 N.
The coefficient of friction between the load and the plane is 0.3.

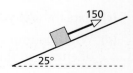

Find the kinetic energy gained by the load, and hence its speed, when it has moved 5 m up the plane.

Solution

Draw a force diagram.
The principle of conservation of mechanical energy cannot be applied
because the 150 N force and the friction force F both do work in addition
to the work done by gravity.
No work is done by R as it acts perpendicular to the direction of motion.

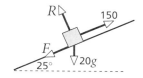

Find the magnitude of the friction force.

Resolve perpendicular to the plane. $\qquad R = 20g\cos 25°$
To retain accuracy do not substitute values for g and cos 25° until the final answer is required.

The load is moving, so $F = \mu R$. $\qquad F = 0.3 \times 20g\cos 25° = 6g\cos 25°$

Work done by 150 N force $= 150 \times 5 = 750$

Work done by friction force $= -6g\cos 25° \times 5 = -30g\cos 25°$

The height increases, so there is a gain in p.e. $\quad$ Gain in p.e. $= mgh = 20g \times 5\sin 25°$
$$= 100g\sin 25°$$

The load started from rest, so there is a gain in k.e. of $\frac{1}{2}mv^2$, where v is the speed after 5 m.

Work done = gain in p.e. + gain in k.e. $\qquad 750 - 30g\cos 25° = 100g\sin 25° + \frac{1}{2}mv^2$

$\Rightarrow \qquad\qquad\qquad \frac{1}{2}mv^2 = 750 - 30g\cos 25° - 100g\sin 25°$

$\Rightarrow \qquad\qquad\qquad \frac{1}{2}mv^2 = 69.4$ to 3 s.f.

$\qquad\qquad\qquad \frac{1}{2} \times 20 \times v^2 = 69.4$

$\Rightarrow \qquad\qquad\qquad\qquad v^2 = 6.94 \Rightarrow v = 2.63$ to 3 s.f.

When it has moved 5 m up the plane the kinetic energy gained is 69.4 J and
the load is moving at 2.63 m s⁻¹, both to 3 s.f.

Exercise D (answers p 169)

1 A stone of mass 0.2 kg is dropped from a height of 3 m above ground level.

    (a) Find the potential energy lost by the stone as it reaches the ground.

    (b) Use the principle of conservation of energy to find the kinetic energy of
the stone, and hence its velocity, as it reaches the ground.

2 A ball of mass 0.1 kg is hit vertically upwards with initial speed 15 m s⁻¹.

    (a) Find its potential energy with respect to its initial position when it has
travelled 3 m.

    (b) Find its speed at this point.

    (c) **(i)** What is the potential energy gained by the ball at its highest point?

        (ii) Find the maximum height of the ball above its initial position.

3 A particle of mass 0.1 kg on a string of length 1 m is released from rest
when the string makes an angle of 80° with the vertical as shown.
Use the principle of conservation of mechanical energy to find its speed
at the lowest point of its path.

4 A girl of mass 30 kg slides down a helter-skelter.
She starts from rest and has reached a speed of $4 \, \text{m s}^{-1}$ at the bottom.
The height of the helter-skelter is 10 m.

   (a) Find the girl's loss in potential energy.

   (b) Find her gain in kinetic energy.

   (c) Find the work done by the friction force.

5 A boy and his bicycle have a total mass of 60 kg.
At the top of a hill he is travelling at $6 \, \text{m s}^{-1}$ and he applies his brakes as
he cycles down the hill. He is travelling at $10 \, \text{m s}^{-1}$ at the bottom, having
dropped a vertical distance of 30 m.

   (a) Find the loss in potential energy.

   (b) Find the gain in kinetic energy.

   (c) Find the work done by the brakes.

   (d) Comment on the assumptions that you have made.

6 A stone of mass 0.3 kg is dropped from a height of 5 m above ground level.
The speed of the stone when it reaches the ground is $6 \, \text{m s}^{-1}$.

   (a) Find the total energy lost by the stone during the motion.

   (b) Find the magnitude of the resistance force acting on the stone.

7 A particle of mass 2 kg is projected up a slope inclined at 30° to the horizontal
with an initial speed of $8 \, \text{m s}^{-1}$. It travels 5 m up the slope before coming to rest.

   (a) Find the work done by the friction force.

   (b) Find the magnitude of the friction force.

   (c) Find the coefficient of friction between the particle and the slope.

E Power (answers p 170)

D **E1** **(a)** Tim pushes a packing case along horizontal ground with a force of 150 N.
He pushes it 5 m in 10 seconds.
How much work has he done?

   (b) Alison pushes the same packing case with a force of 150 N.
She pushes it 5 m in 15 seconds.
How much work has she done?

   (c) How could you describe the difference between the two situations?

Power is defined as the rate of doing work. This is the rate of generating or using energy.
If a person or engine can do a given amount of work in a shorter time, the energy
is generated in a shorter time and the person or engine is said to be more powerful.

$$\text{Power} = \frac{\text{work done}}{\text{time taken}}$$

The unit of power is the watt (W). This is named after James Watt (1736–1819), the Scottish inventor of the modern steam engine.
1 watt is the power which can produce 1 joule of work in 1 second.

E2 Find the power of each push in E1.

E3 A lift of mass 1000 kg travels downwards a distance of 25 m in 40 s at constant speed.
(a) Calculate the work done by the lift's motor.
(b) What is the power of the lift's motor?

Consider a vehicle whose engine is producing a driving force F N and is moving at constant speed v m s^{-1}.

The vehicle travels v m in 1 second.

Hence the work done by the driving force in 1 second is Fv J.

The power is the work done per second; hence the power of the vehicle is Fv W.

This formula applies whether or not the driving force is constant.
If the velocity of the vehicle is not constant it can be used to find the power at the instant when the velocity is v m s^{-1}.

K   Power = driving force $\times$ velocity $(P = Fv)$

E4 (a) A car's engine produces a driving force of 950 N. The car is travelling at 18 m s^{-1}. Find the power output of the car's engine.
(b) The engine of a van is operating at 5 kW. The van is travelling at 15 m s^{-1}. Find the driving force of the van's engine. (1 kW = 1000 W)

D **E5** A car's engine is running at its maximum power.
The car travels along a horizontal road at constant speed.
It reaches a hill and its speed decreases.
How does the driving force change?

The next three questions are about a car of mass 1500 kg travelling on a straight, horizontal road. It is subject to a constant resistance of 1200 N.

E6 The car is travelling at its maximum speed.
(a) What is the car's acceleration?
(b) Find the driving force of the car's engine.
(c) Given that the maximum power of the car's engine is 45 kW, find the maximum speed of the car.

E7 The speed of the car is now reduced to 25 m s^{-1}. The resistance remains constant at 1200 N.
(a) Given that the engine continues to operate at maximum power, find its driving force.
(b) Use Newton's second law to show that the acceleration of the car is 0.4 m s^{-2} when its speed is 25 m s^{-1}.

The car now travels at constant speed up a hill inclined at an angle α to the horizontal, where $\sin\alpha = \frac{1}{15}$.
It is subject to the same constant resistance.

The force diagram for the car is shown.

As the car is travelling up a hill, the engine has to do work against gravity as well as against the resistance force. Hence the driving force of the engine must be greater.

The engine is still operating at its maximum power but the speed of the car is less than when travelling on the horizontal because of the greater driving force.

E8 **(a)** By resolving the forces parallel to the plane, find the magnitude of the driving force, F N.

(b) Find the speed of the car travelling up the hill.

In the questions above, the car was subject to a constant resistance force. A resistance force need not be constant. It may vary with the speed at which the car is travelling.

E9 A van of mass 2500 kg travels along a straight horizontal road subject to a resistance of magnitude $40v$ when travelling at $v\,\mathrm{m\,s^{-1}}$.
The van has a maximum speed of $35\,\mathrm{m\,s^{-1}}$.

(a) (i) Find the magnitude of the resistance when the van is travelling at its maximum speed.

(ii) Hence show that the maximum power of the van is 49 000 W.

(b) (i) Find the magnitude of the resistance when the van is travelling at $20\,\mathrm{m\,s^{-1}}$.

(ii) If the van's engine is operating at maximum power, find the driving force of the engine when the van is travelling at $20\,\mathrm{m\,s^{-1}}$.

(iii) Use Newton's second law to find the maximum acceleration of the van when it is travelling at $20\,\mathrm{m\,s^{-1}}$.

Example 8

A car of mass 1500 kg has a power output of 40 000 W. When the car is travelling on a horizontal road at $25\,\mathrm{m\,s^{-1}}$ it is subject to a resistance of 550 N.

(a) Find the tractive force of the engine.

(b) Find the acceleration of the car.

Solution

(a) *The power and speed are known so use $P = Fv$ to calculate the tractive force. Remember that the tractive force is the driving force.*

$$40\,000 = 25F$$

$$\Rightarrow \qquad F = 1600$$

The tractive force is 1600 N.

(b) *Draw a force diagram.*
(Vertical forces balance out and are not shown.)

Apply N2L.

$$1600 - 550 = 1500a$$
$$\Rightarrow \quad 1050 = 1500a$$
$$a = 0.7$$

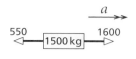

The acceleration is $0.7\,\mathrm{m\,s^{-2}}$.

Example 9

A van of mass $3000\,\mathrm{kg}$ is travelling up a slope inclined at an angle α to the horizontal, where $\sin\alpha = 0.1$. A resistance force of magnitude kv acts on the van, where k is a constant and $v\,\mathrm{m\,s^{-1}}$ is the van's speed.
When the van is travelling at a constant speed of $20\,\mathrm{m\,s^{-1}}$ up the slope its engine is operating at its maximum power output of 78 kilowatts.

(a) Find the value of k.

(b) Find the maximum speed of the van on a horizontal road.

Solution

(a) *Draw a force diagram.*

Use $P = Fv$ to calculate the driving force. Remember to use the power in watts.

$$78\,000 = 20F$$
$$\Rightarrow \quad F = 3900$$

Resolve the forces along the plane.

$$F = kv + 3000g\sin\alpha$$
$$\Rightarrow \quad 3900 = 20k + 2940$$
$$\Rightarrow \quad k = \frac{3900 - 2940}{20}$$
$$\Rightarrow \quad k = 48$$

(b) *Draw a force diagram.*
The resistance is $48v$ and the magnitude of the driving force has changed.

The van is at maximum speed, so the acceleration is zero.

Resolve the forces horizontally. $\qquad F = 48v$

At maximum speed, the power output is maximum.

$$P = Fv$$
$$78\,000 = 48v^2$$
$$\Rightarrow \quad v^2 = 1625$$
$$\Rightarrow \quad v = 40.3 \text{ to 3 s.f.}$$

The maximum speed the van is $40.3\,\mathrm{m\,s^{-1}}$ on a horizontal road.

Exercise E (answers p 170)

1 A car is travelling on a horizontal road at $27\,\mathrm{m\,s^{-1}}$.
Given that the driving force of the car's engine is $2000\,\mathrm{N}$, find its power output.

2 A weightlifter lifts a load of $55\,\mathrm{kg}$ through a height of $1.8\,\mathrm{m}$ in 2 seconds.

(a) Find the work done by the weightlifter.

(b) What is the power of this lift, assuming it is constant?

3 A crane lifts a beam of mass $240\,\mathrm{kg}$ a height of $15\,\mathrm{m}$ at a constant speed of $3\,\mathrm{m\,s^{-1}}$.
Find the power of the crane.

4 A van has a maximum power output of $45\,\mathrm{kW}$. When driving on a horizontal road it is subject to a constant resistance of magnitude $1500\,\mathrm{N}$.
Find the maximum speed of the van.

5 A pump is used to fill a tank from a reservoir $10\,\mathrm{m}$ below the pump outlet.
It pumps 50 litres of water per minute (the mass of 1 litre of water is $1\,\mathrm{kg}$).
Find the work done per second by the pump, and hence its power.

6 A car of mass $1600\,\mathrm{kg}$ has a maximum power output of $45\,000\,\mathrm{W}$.
The car travels on a horizontal road subject to a resistance of magnitude $25v\,\mathrm{N}$ when travelling at $v\,\mathrm{m\,s^{-1}}$.

(a) (i) If the car is operating at its maximum power, find the driving force of the engine when the car is travelling at $18\,\mathrm{m\,s^{-1}}$.

(ii) Find the acceleration of the car at this speed.

(b) Show that the maximum speed of the car is $42.4\,\mathrm{m\,s^{-1}}$ to 3 s.f.

7 A train of mass 450 tonnes has a maximum speed of $40\,\mathrm{m\,s^{-1}}$ on the level.
It is subject to a constant resistance of $140\,000\,\mathrm{N}$.

(a) Find the power of the engine.

(b) Assuming the same power and resistance, find the maximum speed up a slope inclined at $\theta°$ to the horizontal, where $\sin\theta = \frac{1}{120}$.

8 A car of mass $1200\,\mathrm{kg}$ has maximum power $60\,\mathrm{kW}$. A resisting force of $45v\,\mathrm{N}$ acts on the car when it is travelling at $v\,\mathrm{m\,s^{-1}}$.

(a) The car is travelling at $25\,\mathrm{m\,s^{-1}}$ on a horizontal road.

(i) Find the car's maximum driving force.

(ii) Find its maximum acceleration.

(b) The car now travels up a road inclined at $3°$ to the horizontal.
Find the car's maximum speed up this road.

9 A car of mass $1400\,\mathrm{kg}$ experiences a resistance force of magnitude $42v\,\mathrm{N}$ when travelling at $v\,\mathrm{m\,s^{-1}}$.
The car has a maximum speed of $45\,\mathrm{m\,s^{-1}}$ when travelling down a hill inclined at $\theta°$ to the horizontal, where $\sin\theta = 0.05$.
Find the maximum power of the car.

Key points

- When a constant force F N applied to an object moves it a distance s m in the direction of the force, the work done is the product of the force and the distance moved.

    Work done $= Fs$

    The unit of work is the joule. (p 92)

- The work done by a constant force moving an object in a straight line, acting at an angle θ to the direction of motion, is given by

    Work done $= Fs\cos\theta$

    A force acting perpendicular to the direction of motion does no work.
    A force acting in the direction opposite to the direction of motion does a negative amount of work. (pp 93, 96)

- The kinetic energy (k.e.) of a body of mass m kg moving with a velocity of $v\,\mathrm{m\,s^{-1}}$ is given by k.e. $= \frac{1}{2}mv^2$.
    The unit of energy is the joule. (p 95)

- The work done by a force acting on a body is equal to the change in kinetic energy of the body.

    $Fs = \frac{1}{2}mv^2 - \frac{1}{2}mu^2$ (p 95)

- The gravitational potential energy (p.e.) of a body is defined as the work that would be done by its weight in moving the body from its current position to an arbitrary fixed reference position, where the p.e. is taken to be zero.

    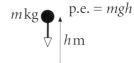

    A particle of mass m kg at height h m above ground level has gravitational potential energy mgh joules relative to the ground.

    The change in potential energy of an object is mgh joules, where h m is the vertical distance between its initial and final positions. The change in potential energy is not affected by the path of the object between these two positions. (pp 99–100)

- The principle of conservation of mechanical energy states that the sum of the potential energy and the kinetic energy of a system will remain constant if no external force other than gravity does work.

    Gain in kinetic energy = Loss in potential energy (p 103)

- The work–energy principle states that if an external force other than gravity does work, then the work done by the force is equal to the change in mechanical energy of the system.

    Work done by force = gain in potential energy + gain in kinetic energy (p 103)

- Power $= \dfrac{\text{work done}}{\text{time taken}} =$ driving force $\times$ velocity

    The unit of power is the watt. (pp 106–107)

Mixed questions (answers p 170)

1 A ball of mass 0.1 kg moves on a track as shown.
It leaves A with a speed of $2\,\text{m}\,\text{s}^{-1}$.

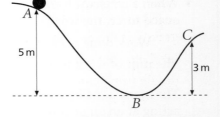

(a) Assuming that the track is smooth, use an
energy method to find

   (i) the speed of the ball at B

   (ii) the speed of the ball at C

(b) Comment on the effect that assuming the track is smooth has had on your answer.

2 A tile of mass 0.3 kg slides from rest a distance of 4 m down a roof which slopes
at 30° to the horizontal and then drops a further 6 m vertically to the ground.
The roof provides a resistance force of 1 N.

(a) Find the work done by the resistance force.

(b) Find the potential energy lost by the tile.

(c) Use an energy method to find the speed of the tile when it hits the ground.

3 A car of mass 760 kg is travelling down a straight road inclined at
an angle of $\sin^{-1}\left(\frac{1}{10}\right)$ to the horizontal. At the point A on the road,
the car is travelling with speed $10\,\text{m}\,\text{s}^{-1}$, as shown.
The point B is 200 m along the road from A.
When the car reaches B, its speed is $25\,\text{m}\,\text{s}^{-1}$ as shown.

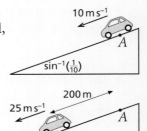

(a) Using a simple model, resistance forces are neglected and
the driving force of the car is assumed to be constant.

   (i) Find the gain in mechanical energy of the car when
it travels from A to B.

   (ii) Deduce that the driving force of the car is approximately 253 N.

(b) Using a different model, the resistance force on the car is assumed to be
1000 N and the driving force is **not** assumed to be constant.
The car reaches its maximum speed of $25\,\text{m}\,\text{s}^{-1}$ at B.

   (i) Draw a diagram to show all the forces acting on the car at B.

   (ii) Determine the driving force of the car at B using this model.   AQA 2004

4 A car of mass 1200 kg experiences a resistance force of magnitude $40v$ N when
travelling at $v\,\text{m}\,\text{s}^{-1}$.
The car travels up a slope inclined at an angle $\sin^{-1}\left(\frac{1}{10}\right)$ to the horizontal.
When its speed is $20\,\text{m}\,\text{s}^{-1}$ the car is accelerating at $1\,\text{m}\,\text{s}^{-2}$.

(a) Show that the power output of the car is 63 520 W.

(b) Assume the power calculated in part (a) is the maximum for the car.
The driver of the car finds that, when travelling up a different slope,
the maximum speed of the car is $25\,\text{m}\,\text{s}^{-1}$.
Find the angle between this slope and the horizontal.   AQA 2002

Test yourself (answers p 171)

1 A ball is projected vertically upwards, from ground level, with an initial speed of $18 \, \text{m s}^{-1}$. The ball has a mass of $0.3 \, \text{kg}$. Assume that the force of gravity is the only force acting on the ball after it is projected.

   (a) Calculate the initial kinetic energy of the ball.

   (b) By using conservation of energy, find the maximum height of the ball above ground level.

   (c) Find the kinetic energy and the speed of the ball when it is at a height of 2 metres above ground level.   AQA 2003

2 A car of mass $1200 \, \text{kg}$ is being driven up a straight road inclined at 5° to the horizontal. Resistive forces acting on the car total $1960 \, \text{N}$.

   (a) Draw a diagram showing all the forces acting on the car.

   (b) The car is moving with constant speed $15 \, \text{m s}^{-1}$.

      (i)   Show that the tractive force produced by the engine is approximately $2985 \, \text{N}$.

      (ii) Determine the rate at which the engine is doing work.

   (c) The engine has a maximum power output of $60 \, \text{kW}$. Find the maximum possible speed of the car up the same slope.   AQA 2002

3 A ball has mass $0.5 \, \text{kg}$ and is released from rest at a height of 6 metres above ground level.

   (a) Assume that no resistance force acts on the ball as it falls.

      (i)   Find the kinetic energy of the ball when it has fallen 3 metres.

      (ii) Use an energy method to find the speed of the ball when it hits the ground.

   (b) Assume that a constant resistance force acts on the ball as it falls and that the ball hits the ground travelling at $2 \, \text{m s}^{-1}$. Use an energy method to find the magnitude of the resistance force.   AQA 2003

4 A box of mass $15 \, \text{kg}$ slides from rest down a rough slope inclined at 30° to the horizontal. The slope is $5 \, \text{m}$ long and the box is moving at $6 \, \text{m s}^{-1}$ when it reaches the bottom of the slope.

   (a) Find the mechanical energy lost by the box when it travels down the slope.

   (b) Hence find the magnitude of the friction force acting on the box.

5 A car of mass $1300 \, \text{kg}$ has a maximum speed of $35 \, \text{m s}^{-1}$ when travelling on a horizontal road. The car experiences a resistance force of $kv \, \text{N}$, where $v \, \text{m s}^{-1}$ is the speed of the car and k is a constant.

   (a) Given that the maximum power of the car is $49\,000 \, \text{W}$, find the value of k.

   (b) Find the maximum possible acceleration of the car when it is travelling at $25 \, \text{m s}^{-1}$ on a horizontal road.

7 Hooke's law

In this chapter you will learn how to

- use Hooke's law
- find the work done in stretching a spring or an elastic string
- solve problems involving elastic potential energy

A Elastic springs and strings (answers p 171)

An **elastic** spring is one which will stretch when a force is applied to it.
When there is no force applied, the length of the unstretched spring is its **natural length**.
The amount that it stretches under a force is the **extension**.
When the spring is stretched there is a tension in the spring which exerts equal and opposite forces at the ends.

If the force is applied in the opposite direction, it will cause the spring to compress. The amount by which its length has been reduced is the **compression**.
When the spring is compressed there is a thrust in the spring which exerts equal and opposite forces at the ends.

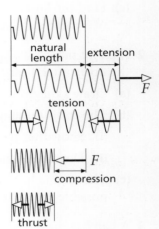

Experiments show that when a spring is stretched, the tension is directly proportional to the extension. When it is compressed the thrust is directly proportional to the compression. The tension or thrust depends on the natural length of the spring and how the spring is made.

The English scientist and architect Robert Hooke (1635–1703) discovered that the tension (or thrust) is proportional to the extension (or compression) of the spring. This fact is incorporated in a formula known as Hooke's law.

> The tension (or thrust), T N, in a spring of natural length l m is related to the extension (or compression) x m by the formula
> $$T = \frac{\lambda x}{l} \quad \text{(Hooke's law)}$$
> *T = kx   T α x   Proportional*
>
> λ is a constant for a particular spring and is known as its modulus of elasticity; it is measured in newtons.

Hooke's law also applies to elastic strings, but these can only be extended and not compressed.

A1 An elastic string of natural length 0.5 m has modulus of elasticity 15 N. Find the tension in the string when it is extended by 0.1 m.

A2 An elastic spring of natural length 0.2 m extends by 0.05 m when a force of 9 N is applied to it.

(a) What is the magnitude of the tension in the spring?

(b) Find the modulus of elasticity of the spring.

A3 Two elastic springs both have modulus of elasticity 25 N. One spring has natural length 0.4 m and the other has natural length 0.8 m. Both springs are fixed at one end and have a force of 20 N applied to the free end.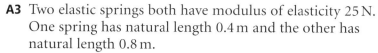

(a) Find the extension of the 0.4 m spring.

(b) Find the extension of the 0.8 m spring.

(c) Explain why the springs do not have the same extension.

A4 A spring of negligible weight is fixed at one end and has a particle of mass 0.2 kg hung on the other end. The spring hangs in equilibrium.

(a) Draw a force diagram for the particle.

(b) Find the magnitude of the tension in the spring.

(c) Given that the extension of the spring is equal to its natural length, use Hooke's law to find the modulus of elasticity of the spring. Comment on your answer.

The modulus of elasticity of a spring is equal to the force needed to double the spring's length. When the spring's extension is equal to its natural length, then the tension is equal to the modulus of elasticity. The modulus of elasticity depends on the material of the spring and on its geometric properties.

Hooke's law only applies up to a point, known as the elastic limit of the spring. If the spring is stretched further than this point, it will not return to its natural length when released, and Hooke's law no longer applies. Also a spring can only be compressed up to a certain point. None of the springs considered in this chapter will reach these limits.

A5 A spring of natural length 0.4 m is compressed by a force of 10 N. The modulus of elasticity of the spring is 40 N.

(a) Find the distance by which the spring is compressed.

(b) What is the length of the spring under the action of the force?

Example 1

An elastic spring of natural length 1.4 m is stretched to a length of 2.2 m by a force of 16 N. Find the modulus of elasticity of the spring.

Solution

Remember to use the extension, not the stretched length, in the Hooke's law equation.

Use $T = \dfrac{\lambda x}{l}$.

$$16 = \frac{(2.2 - 1.4)\lambda}{1.4} = \frac{0.8\lambda}{1.4}$$

$$\Rightarrow \lambda = \frac{16 \times 1.4}{0.8} = 28$$

The modulus of elasticity of the spring is 28 N.

Example 2

An elastic string with modulus of elasticity 7 N is fixed at one end.
A particle of mass 0.5 kg is suspended from the other end and hangs in equilibrium.
The length of the stretched string is 68 cm.
Find the natural length and extension of the string.

Solution

Draw a force diagram for the particle.
Note that in calculations all lengths should be in metres
and masses in kilograms.

The particle is in equilibrium.

$$T = 0.5g = 4.9$$

Use $T = \dfrac{\lambda x}{l}$.

$$4.9 = \frac{7x}{l}$$

$$\Rightarrow \quad x = \frac{4.9l}{7} = 0.7l$$

The stretched length is $l + x$.

$$l + x = 0.68$$

Substitute for x.

$$\Rightarrow \quad 1.7l = 0.68 \;\Rightarrow\; l = 0.4$$

$$\Rightarrow \quad x = 0.7 \times 0.4 = 0.28$$

The natural length of the string is 0.4 m and its extension is 0.28 m.

Exercise A (answers p 171)

1 An elastic string of natural length 0.8 m has modulus of elasticity 24 N.
Find the tension in the string when it is extended by

(a) 0.1 m   (b) 0.2 m   (c) 0.4 m

2 An elastic spring of natural length 0.2 m has modulus of elasticity 40 N.
Find its extension when the tension in the spring is

(a) 6 N   (b) 8 N   (c) 12 N

3 A light spring extends by 0.4 m when a particle of mass 0.5 kg
is hung on one end.
The natural length of the spring is 1.2 m.

(a) Find the tension in the spring.

(b) Find the modulus of elasticity of the spring.

4 An elastic string of natural length 0.9 m is stretched to a length of 1.5 m
by a force of 21 N.
Find the modulus of elasticity of the string.

5 A light spring of natural length 0.4 m and modulus of elasticity
20 N is compressed by a force of 8 N.
Find the compressed length of the spring.

6 A light spring has modulus of elasticity 14 N and natural length 0.05 m. A particle of mass 0.2 kg is placed on top of the spring as shown.

   (a) Find the magnitude of the thrust in the spring.

   (b) Find the amount by which the spring is compressed.

   (c) What is the compressed length of the spring?

7 An elastic string of natural length 0.3 m is fixed at one end and has a particle of mass 0.25 kg attached at the other end. The particle hangs in equilibrium 0.45 m below the fixed end. Show that the modulus of elasticity of the string is 4.9 N.

8 A spring has modulus of elasticity 16 N. It is stretched to a length of 75 cm by a force of 24 N. Find the natural length and extension of the spring.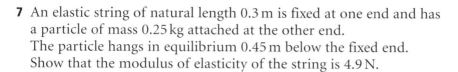

9 A light spring with modulus of elasticity 7 N is fixed at one end and has a particle of mass 0.25 kg attached at the other end. The particle hangs in equilibrium and the length of the stretched spring is 108 cm. Find the natural length and extension of the spring.

*10 A string is stretched to a length of 38 cm when a force of 15 N is applied. When the force is increased to 21 N, the string's length becomes 46 cm. Find the natural length and modulus of elasticity of the string.

B Work done by a variable force (answers p 172)

In the last chapter we learned how to find the work done by a constant force.

The graph shows the relationship between force and displacement for a constant force.

The work done by the force F is Fs, which is the area under the graph.

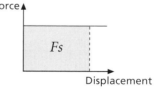

Now consider a force F_1 which acts on a body for a displacement s_1. Then it increases to F_2 and acts on the body for a displacement s_2.

The force–displacement graph is shown.

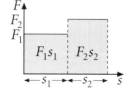

Work done by $F_1 = F_1 s_1$

Work done by $F_2 = F_2 s_2$

The total work done by the forces is therefore $F_1 s_1 + F_2 s_2$, which is the area under the step graph.

This can be generalised to give an expression for the work done by any variable force.

The work done by a variable force $F(s)$ is given by

work done $= \int F(s)\,ds$

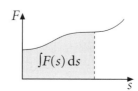

D **B1** An elastic spring is stretched by applying a force to one end.
Use Hooke's law to explain why the force is not constant as the spring stretches.

Imagine that a spring is being stretched, starting from its natural length l m.
When the extension is s m, the tension, and therefore the force F applied
to the spring, is given by $F = \dfrac{\lambda s}{l}$.

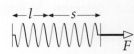

As the spring is stretched and s increases, the value of F increases,
as shown by the graph, whose equation is $F = \dfrac{\lambda s}{l}$.

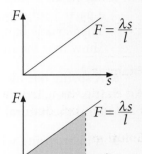

When the extension reaches x m, the work done in stretching
the spring is

$$\int_0^x F\,\mathrm{d}s = \int_0^x \frac{\lambda s}{l}\,\mathrm{d}s = \left[\frac{\lambda s^2}{2l}\right]_0^x = \frac{\lambda x^2}{2l}$$

The work done, in joules, in stretching an elastic spring with modulus of elasticity λ N
and natural length l m from its natural length to an extension x m is given by

$$\text{work done} = \frac{\lambda x^2}{2l}$$

B2 An elastic spring has natural length 0.5 m and modulus of elasticity 12 N.
Find the work done in extending the spring by 0.1 m.

B3 A spring has natural length 0.8 m and modulus of elasticity 20 N.
It is stretched from its natural length by 0.2 m.

  (a) Find the work done in stretching the spring by 0.2 m.

  (b) The spring is now stretched by a further 0.2 m.

   (i) What is the total extension of the spring?

   (ii) Find the total work done in stretching the spring to this length.

   (iii) Find the work done in stretching the spring the further 0.2 m.

  (c) Sketch a graph of force against extension for the spring and use it to
  explain why your answers to (a) and (b)(iii) were not the same.

As the spring is stretched, work is being done on it by the applied force which causes
the spring to gain energy. This energy is stored in the spring as **elastic potential energy**.
When the spring is allowed to contract, this elastic potential energy is released.

The elastic potential energy (e.p.e.), in joules, of a stretched spring with
extension x m is equal to the work done in extending the spring from
its natural length to this extension.

$$\text{e.p.e.} = \frac{\lambda x^2}{2l}$$

Note that, because of the x^2 term, the elastic potential energy of a spring is
always positive, whether the spring has been extended or compressed.

Example 3

A spring of natural length 0.9 m is compressed to a length of 0.6 m.
The modulus of elasticity of the spring is 25 N.
Find the elastic potential energy stored in the spring.

Solution

The compressed length is 0.6 m, so the spring has been compressed by 0.3 m.

$$\text{e.p.e.} = \frac{\lambda x^2}{2l} = \frac{25 \times 0.3^2}{2 \times 0.9} = 1.25\,\text{J}$$

Example 4

An elastic string has natural length 1.2 m and modulus of elasticity 40 N.
Find the work done in stretching the string from a length of 1.35 m to 1.5 m.

Solution

Find the work done to stretch the string to 1.35 m, an extension of 0.15 m.

$$\text{Work done} = \frac{\lambda x^2}{2l} = \frac{40 \times 0.15^2}{2 \times 1.2} = 0.375\,\text{J}$$

Now find the work done to stretch the string from its natural length to 1.5 m, an extension of 0.3 m.

$$\text{Work done} = \frac{\lambda x^2}{2l} = \frac{40 \times 0.3^2}{2 \times 1.2} = 1.5\,\text{J}$$

The work done in stretching from 1.35 m to 1.5 m is the difference between these two amounts.

Work done in stretching from 1.35 m to 1.5 m = 1.5 − 0.375 = 1.125 J

Exercise B (answers p 172)

1 An elastic string has modulus of elasticity 20 N and natural length 0.5 m.
   Find the work done in stretching the string from its natural length by

   (a) 0.1 m   (b) 0.2 m   (c) 0.4 m

2 An elastic string of natural length 0.75 m has modulus of elasticity 12 N.
   Find the work done in stretching the string to double its natural length.

3 Two elastic springs both have modulus of elasticity 15 N.
   One spring has natural length 0.3 m and the other has natural length 0.6 m.
   They are both stretched by a force of 10 N.

   (a) (i) Find the extension of the 0.3 m spring.

       (ii) Find the elastic potential energy stored in the spring.

   (b) (i) Find the extension of the 0.6 m spring.

       (ii) Find the elastic potential energy stored in this spring.

4 An elastic spring of natural length 0.6 m is compressed to a length of 0.4 m.
The modulus of elasticity of the spring is 6 N.
Find the elastic potential energy stored in the spring.

5 An elastic string hangs vertically in equilibrium with a particle of mass 0.1 kg attached.
The natural length of the string is 1 m and its modulus of elasticity is 14 N.

  (a) Find the extension of the string.

  (b) Find the elastic potential energy stored in the string.

6 A spring has modulus of elasticity 10 N and natural length 24 cm.

  (a) Find the work done to increase its length by 6 cm.

  (b) Find the work done to increase its length by a further 6 cm.

7 A particle of mass 0.5 kg is suspended in equilibrium from a fixed point by
an elastic string of natural length 0.8 m and modulus of elasticity 35 N.

  (a) Find the elastic potential energy stored in the string.

  (b) Find the work done in pulling the particle down a further 0.1 m.

8 An elastic string is stretched to a length of 0.75 m by a force of 5 N.
The modulus of elasticity of the string is 20 N.

  (a) Find the natural length and extension of the string.

  (b) Find the elastic potential energy stored in the string.

9 An elastic string is fixed at one end and has a particle of mass 0.25 kg
attached at the other end. The particle hangs in equilibrium 1.1 m below
the fixed point. The modulus of elasticity of the string is 24.5 N.
Find the elastic potential energy stored in the spring.

*10 A spring is stretched to a length 0.6 m.
The work done in stretching it from this length to a length of 0.8 m is 2 J.
The modulus of elasticity of the spring is 10 N.
Find its natural length.

C Mechanical energy (answers p 172)

In the previous chapter we saw that the sum of the potential energy and the kinetic
energy of a system remains constant if no external force other than gravity does work.

In the case of elastic strings and springs, elastic potential energy, another form of
mechanical energy, is introduced. Here again the principle of conservation of
mechanical energy can be applied if no external force other than gravity does work.

An elastic string is fixed at one end with a particle attached
at the free end. The particle rests on a smooth horizontal
surface and the string is slack.

A horizontal force is applied to the particle, causing the string to stretch.
The force has done work so the elastic potential energy of the string has increased.

D **C1** The force is now removed from the particle.

(a) Describe the subsequent motion and how the kinetic energy and elastic potential energy of the system change during the motion.

(b) Can the principle of conservation of mechanical energy be applied to this motion? Explain your answer.

(c) How would your answer to (b) differ if the surface had been rough rather than smooth?

(d) Describe the motion of the particle if it were resting on a smooth surface but attached to a spring rather than a string.

C2 A particle is attached to the end of a light spring and it hangs in equilibrium. The particle is pulled down a small distance and released.

(a) Describe the subsequent motion and how the kinetic energy, gravitational potential energy and elastic potential energy of the system change during the motion.

(b) Can the principle of conservation of mechanical energy be applied to this motion? Explain your answer.

K The total mechanical energy of a system remains constant if no external force other than gravity does work.
If the principle of conservation of mechanical energy applies, then the sum of the gravitational potential energy, elastic potential energy and kinetic energy of the system is constant.

Consider an elastic string of natural length 1 m and modulus of elasticity 20 N which is fixed at one end to point O and has a particle of mass 0.2 kg attached to the other end.
The particle lies on a smooth horizontal surface and is pulled to point A then released from rest.

C3 (a) When the particle is at A find

(i) the elastic potential energy (ii) the kinetic energy

(b) When the particle is 1.2 m from O find

(i) the elastic potential energy (ii) the kinetic energy

The total mechanical energy is constant throughout the motion as there is no friction force acting. The elastic potential energy has its maximum value when the particle is released. As the string contracts back to its natural length this elastic potential energy is converted to kinetic energy.
As the motion is horizontal there is no change in gravitational potential energy.

C4 (a) At what point is the kinetic energy greatest?
What is the value of the elastic potential energy at this point?

(b) Find the maximum speed of the particle.

Consider an elastic string of natural length 0.5 m and modulus of elasticity 19.6 N which is suspended from a fixed point with a particle of mass 0.4 kg attached to the free end.

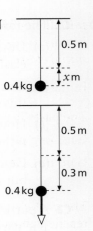

C5 Find the length of the string when the particle hangs in equilibrium.

The particle is now pulled vertically downwards, so that the length of the string is 0.8 m, then released. This is beyond the equilibrium position of the string so the particle will start to move upwards as the string contracts on release. The total mechanical energy of the system is constant because, if air resistance can be ignored, the only external force acting is the weight of the particle.

C6 (a) Find the elastic potential energy when the particle is released.

    (b) When the particle passes its equilibrium position,

        (i) find the elastic potential energy

        (ii) find the gravitational potential energy relative to the release point

        (iii) hence find the kinetic energy

    (c) When the string becomes slack,

        (i) find the elastic potential energy

        (ii) find the gravitational potential energy relative to the release point

        (iii) hence find the kinetic energy

Once the string has become slack, the elastic potential energy is zero.
The particle continues to move upwards, now acting as a projectile.

C7 (a) What is the kinetic energy of the particle when it reaches its highest point?

    (b) Find the particle's gravitational potential energy relative to the release point when the particle reaches its highest point.

    (c) What is the maximum height the particle reaches above its release point?

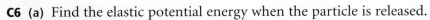

Example 5

A particle of mass 40 g is placed on top of a light spring of natural length 20 cm and modulus of elasticity 50 N resting on a horizontal surface.
The spring is compressed by 5 cm and released.
Find the maximum height above the surface reached by the particle.

Solution

All lengths must be converted to metres and masses to kilograms.
There are no external forces except gravity acting, so mechanical energy is conserved.

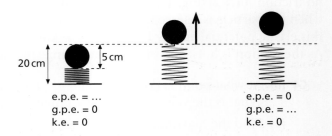

Initially the kinetic energy is zero, and it is also zero when the particle reaches its maximum height. So when the particle is at its maximum height all the initial elastic potential energy has been converted to gravitational potential energy.

$$\text{Initial e.p.e.} = \frac{\lambda x^2}{2l} = \frac{50 \times 0.05^2}{2 \times 0.2} = 0.3125$$

The particle rises h m from its initial position.

Gain in g.p.e. $= mgh = 0.04 \times 9.8h = 0.392h$

Gain in g.p.e. = loss in e.p.e. $\qquad 0.392h = 0.3125$

$$\Rightarrow \quad h = 0.797 \text{ to 3 s.f.}$$

The particle was initially 0.15 m above the surface, so the maximum height reached above the surface is 0.947 m to 3 s.f.

If the principle of conservation of mechanical energy does not apply then the problem can be solved using the work–energy principle, as demonstrated in the following example.

Example 6

One end of an elastic string is fixed to a wall and the other end is attached to a box of mass 0.5 kg. The box rests on a rough horizontal surface as shown. The string has natural length 0.4 m and modulus of elasticity 80 N. The coefficient of friction between the box and the surface is 0.25. The box is pulled so that it is 0.6 m from the wall and released from rest.

Find the speed of the box when the string becomes slack.

Solution

The motion is horizontal so the gravitational potential energy is constant.
The surface is rough so mechanical energy is not conserved.
Draw a force diagram for the box.

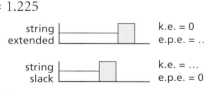

Resolve the forces vertically. $\qquad R = 0.5g = 4.9$

The box is moving, so $F = \mu R$. $\qquad F = 0.25 \times 4.9 = 1.225$

When the box is released, the extension of the string is 0.2 m.
It starts from rest so the initial kinetic energy is zero.
When the string becomes slack, the box has moved 0.2 m and the elastic potential energy is zero.
The friction force acts in the opposite direction to the direction of motion so it does negative work and the total mechanical energy has decreased.

$$\text{Initial e.p.e.} = \frac{\lambda x^2}{2l} = \frac{80 \times 0.2^2}{2 \times 0.4} = 4$$

Gain in k.e. $= \frac{1}{2}mv^2 = \frac{1}{2} \times 0.5 \times v^2 = 0.25v^2$

Work done by friction $= -1.225 \times 0.2 = -0.245$

Work done = change in energy $\qquad -0.245 = 0.25v^2 - 4$

$$\Rightarrow \quad v^2 = 15.02 \Rightarrow v = 3.88 \text{ to 3 s.f.}$$

The speed of the box when the string becomes slack is 3.88 m s^{-1} to 3 s.f.

---

1 A particle of mass 0.4 kg lies on a smooth horizontal surface attached to one end of an elastic string of natural length 0.8 m and modulus of elasticity 10 N.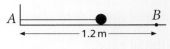
The other end of the string is fixed at point A.
The particle is pulled to point B, where $AB = 1.2$ m, and released.

   (a) Find the elastic potential energy when the particle is at B.

   (b) (i) Use the principle of conservation of energy to find the kinetic energy when the string becomes slack.

        (ii) Hence find the speed of the particle when the string becomes slack.

2 A child's toy rocket, of mass 0.04 kg, is fired by releasing a compressed spring. The natural length of the spring is 0.05 m and its modulus of elasticity is 8 N. The spring is compressed to a length of 0.02 m and released.
Find the maximum height above the surface reached by the rocket.

3 A particle of mass 0.6 kg is hung from a spring of natural length 0.2 m and modulus of elasticity 15 N.
The particle is pulled downwards until the spring's length is 0.4 m and is released from rest.

   Find the kinetic energy, and hence the speed, of the particle when the string reaches its natural length.

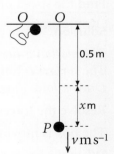

4 A particle of mass 2 kg is attached to one end of a light elastic string of natural length 0.5 m and modulus of elasticity 100 N. The other end of the string is fixed at point O. The particle is held at O and released from rest. When the particle is at point P, the extension of the string is x m and the speed of the particle is v m s^{-1}.

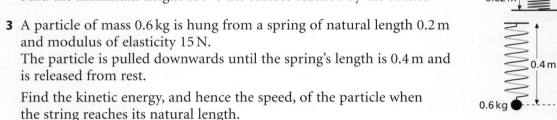

   (a) Find in terms of x and v an expression for

      (i) the gravitational potential energy lost when the particle is at P

      (ii) the kinetic energy gained when the particle is at P

      (iii) the elastic potential energy gained when the particle is at P

   (b) Use the principle of conservation of mechanical energy to show that
$$v^2 = 19.6x - 100x^2 + 9.8$$

   (c) Find the maximum value of x.

   (d) (i) What is the extension of the string when the kinetic energy is maximum?

      (ii) Hence find the maximum speed of the particle.

5 A particle of mass 0.6 kg lies on a rough horizontal surface attached to one end of an elastic string of natural length 0.25 m and modulus of elasticity 20 N. The other end of the string is fixed to a wall. The coefficient of friction between the particle and the surface is 0.4.
The particle is pulled so that it is 0.5 m from the wall and released from rest.

   Find the speed of the particle when the string becomes slack.

6 A stuntman of mass 80 kg is attached to one end of a light elastic cord of natural length 7 m and modulus of elasticity 2000 N. The other end of the cord is attached to the top of a building, 15 m above ground level. The stuntman steps off the building and falls vertically. He can be modelled as a particle throughout the motion.

   (a) Show that the speed of the stuntman at the instant the cord first becomes taut is approximately $11.7\,\mathrm{m\,s^{-1}}$.

   (b) The stuntman lands in an airbag positioned 1 m above ground level. Find his speed when he hits the airbag.

7 A particle of mass 10 kg is attached to one end of a light elastic string of natural length 2 m and modulus of elasticity 400 N. The other end of the string is fixed at point A. The particle is held at point A and released so that it drops vertically. When the string has extended x m beyond its natural length, the particle first comes instantaneously to rest.

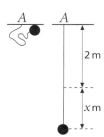

   (a) Show that $50x^2 - 49x - 98 = 0$.

   (b) Hence find the extension of the string when the particle comes to rest.

   (c) (i) Sketch a diagram showing the forces acting on the particle.

   (ii) Use Hooke's law to find the tension in the string when the particle comes to rest.

   (iii) Use Newton's second law to find the deceleration of the particle at this point.

Key points

- The tension (or thrust), T N, in a spring or elastic string of natural length l m is related to the extension (or compression) x m by the formula

    $T = \dfrac{\lambda x}{l}$ (Hooke's law)

  λ is a constant for a particular spring or elastic string and is known as its modulus of elasticity; it is measured in newtons. (p 114)

- The work done, in joules, in stretching a spring or elastic string with modulus of elasticity λ N and natural length l m by an extension x m is given by

    work done $= \dfrac{\lambda x^2}{2l}$ (p 118)

- The elastic potential energy (e.p.e.), in joules, of a stretched spring or string is equal to the work done in extending it.

    e.p.e. $= \dfrac{\lambda x^2}{2l}$ (p 118)

- The total mechanical energy of a system remains constant if no external force other than gravity does work.
  If the principle of conservation of mechanical energy applies, then the sum of the gravitational potential energy, elastic potential energy and kinetic energy of the system is constant. (p 121)

Mixed questions (answers p 173)

1 An elastic string of natural length 0.8 m is stretched to a length of 1.3 m by a force of 16 N.
Find the length of the string when a force of 24 N is applied.

2 A spring has natural length 0.3 m and modulus of elasticity 21 N.
A particle of mass 0.5 kg is attached to one end and hangs in equilibrium.
Find the work done in pulling the particle down a further 0.1 m.

3 A block, of mass 4 kg, is attached to one end of a length of elastic string. The other end of the string is fixed to a wall.
The block is placed on a horizontal surface as shown in the diagram.
The elastic string has natural length 60 cm and modulus of elasticity 60 N.
The block is pulled so that it is 1 metre from the wall and is then released from rest.

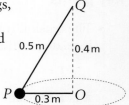

(a) Calculate the elastic potential energy when the block is 1 metre from the wall.

(b) If the surface is smooth, show that the speed of the block when it hits the wall is $2 \, \text{m s}^{-1}$.

(c) The surface is in fact rough and the coefficient of friction between the block and the surface is 0.3.

   (i) Show that the speed of the block when the string becomes slack is approximately $1.28 \, \text{m s}^{-1}$.

   (ii) Determine whether or not the block will hit the wall. AQA 2002

4 A particle of mass 0.6 kg is attached at the point P to two light strings, QP and OP. Point Q is 0.4 m vertically above O.
String QP is inextensible and of length 0.5 m. String OP is elastic and of natural length 0.25 m and modulus of elasticity λ N.
The particle moves in a horizontal circle, centre O and radius 0.3 m at a constant speed of $3 \, \text{m s}^{-1}$.

(a) Draw a diagram showing the forces acting on the particle.

(b) Show that the tension in the string QP is 7.35 N.

(c) Find the tension in the string OP in terms of λ.

(d) Find the value of λ.

5 An elastic string has natural length 2 metres and modulus of elasticity λ newtons.
One end of the string is fixed at the point O, and a particle of mass 20 kg is attached to the other end of the string.

(a) When in equilibrium the particle is 2.7 metres below O. Show that $\lambda = 560$.

(b) The particle is now held at O and released from rest. The maximum length of the string in the subsequent motion is L.

   (i) Show that L satisfies the equation $5L^2 - 27L + 20 = 0$.

   (ii) Find the maximum length of the string. AQA 2004

1 An elastic string of natural length 0.8 m is stretched to a length of 1.3 m by a force of 40 N.
Show that the modulus of elasticity of the string is 64 N.

2 An elastic string has natural length 2 m and modulus of elasticity 40 N.
One end is fixed to a smooth horizontal surface and the other end has a particle of mass 0.8 kg attached.
The string is stretched so that the particle is 2.5 m from the fixed point. The particle is released from rest and moves along the surface.
Show that the speed of the particle when the string becomes slack is 2.5 m s^{-1}.

3 A 'reverse bungee jump' consists of a 12 metre length of elastic rope, that is stretched into a V-shape ABC on a frame, as shown in the diagram. The ends of the elastic rope are fixed to the frame at the points A and C.

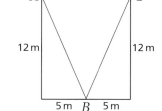

A student, of mass 85 kg, is attached to the midpoint of the elastic rope at B. The modulus of elasticity of the elastic rope is 1500 N.

(a) Show that the elastic potential energy of the elastic rope in the initial position shown in the diagram is 12 250 J.

The middle of the rope is then released from B and the student moves vertically upwards.

(b) Find the speed of the student, when at a height of 12 metres above B.

The student reaches his maximum height before the rope becomes taut again.

(c) Find the maximum height of the student above B during the motion.   AQA 2001

4 An elastic rope has natural length 4 metres and modulus of elasticity 80 N. A particle, of mass 2 kg, is attached to one end of the rope, and the other end is fixed at the point A. The particle is released from rest at A and falls vertically.

(a) When the rope first becomes taut, find
  (i) the kinetic energy of the particle
  (ii) the speed of the particle
(b) (i) The maximum extension of the rope during the motion is x metres. Show that x satisfies the equation
$$10x^2 - 19.6x - 78.4 = 0$$
  (ii) Hence find the maximum length of the rope.
(c) State clearly **one** important assumption that you have made.   AQA 2004

8 Motion in a vertical circle

In this chapter you will

- use the principle of conservation of mechanical energy to solve problems involving motion in a vertical circle
- learn about the conditions required for a body to complete a vertical circle

A Circular motion with variable speed (answers p 174)

In earlier work on circular motion we considered objects moving with constant speed. In this chapter we will extend this to objects moving with variable speed.

Consider a car accelerating around a bend in a road that is an arc of a circle. Both the magnitude and direction of the velocity of the car are changing.

There is an acceleration in the direction of the car's motion, which, at any instant, is along the tangent to the circle. This results from the change in magnitude of the velocity. This acceleration is provided by the driving force of the engine.

There is also a component of acceleration towards the centre of the circle resulting from the change in direction of the velocity. This is provided by the sideways friction of the tyres.

> **K**
>
> An object moving in a circle with variable speed $v\,\mathrm{m\,s^{-1}}$ has two components of acceleration:
>
> - a component acting towards the centre of the circle, with magnitude $\dfrac{v^2}{r}$ at any instant
>
> - a component acting along the tangent to the circle equal to the rate of change of the speed, $\dfrac{\mathrm{d}v}{\mathrm{d}t}$

D **A1** A conker, attached to the end of a piece of string, is made to rotate in a vertical circle.

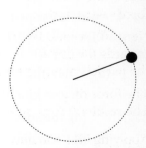

    (a) What forces act on the conker during the motion?

    (b) Describe the acceleration of the conker.

    (c) Describe how the potential energy of the conker changes as it rotates.

    (d) Describe how the kinetic energy, and hence the speed, of the conker changes as it rotates.

Assuming that air resistance is negligible, the only external force acting on the conker that does work is its weight. The tension in the string does no work because it is acting perpendicular to the direction of motion. Thus the mechanical energy of the system remains constant.

> **K**
>
> If the external forces acting on the object, apart from its weight, do no work then the principle of conservation of mechanical energy can be applied.

Consider a particle of mass 0.1 kg hanging from one end of a string of length 0.5 m, vertically below the fixed end O. The particle is given an initial speed of 8 m s^{-1} and it moves in a vertical circle as shown.

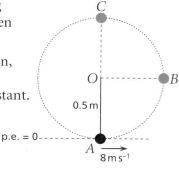

The tension in the string is at right angles to the direction of motion, so does no work. The only external force doing work is the weight of the particle, so the total mechanical energy of the particle is constant.

When the particle is at A,

$\quad$ k.e. $= \frac{1}{2}mv^2 = \frac{1}{2}\times 0.1 \times 8^2 = 3.2\,\text{J}$

$\quad$ p.e. $= mgh = 0\,\text{J}$

A2 (a) (i) Find the potential energy of the particle when it is at B.

$\quad\quad$ **(ii)** By considering the total energy of the particle, find the speed of the particle when it is at B.

$\quad$ **(b) (i)** Find the potential energy of the particle when it is at C.

$\quad\quad$ **(ii)** By considering the total energy of the particle, find the speed of the particle when it is at C.

A3 The particle is at point D, where the string makes an angle θ with the downward vertical.

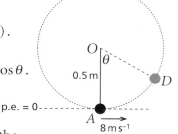

$\quad$ **(a)** Show that, when the particle is at D, p.e. $= 0.49(1 - \cos\theta)$.

$\quad$ **(b)** By considering the total energy of the particle, show that the speed of the particle at D is given by $v^2 = 54.2 + 9.8\cos\theta$.

$\quad$ **(c)** Use your answer to (b) to explain why the particle has its maximum speed at A and its minimum speed at C.

As the speed of the particle is changing throughout the motion, so the acceleration towards the centre of the circle is changing, hence the resultant force towards the centre of the circle is also changing.

Newton's second law can be applied radially (that is, along the direction towards the centre) to calculate the resultant force that must be acting on the particle at any instant during the motion.

The force diagram for the particle when it is at A is shown. The resultant force towards the centre of the circle is $T - 0.1g$.

Applying N2L radially, $\quad\quad F = \dfrac{mv^2}{r}$

$$\Rightarrow T - 0.1g = \frac{0.1 \times 8^2}{0.5}$$

$$\Rightarrow T = 12.8 + 0.98 = 13.78\,\text{N}$$

When the particle is at A, there is no component of force acting tangentially, so there is no tangential component of acceleration. The resultant acceleration acts towards the centre of the circle.

A4 The force diagram for the particle when it is at B is shown. The resultant force acting towards the centre of the circle at this point is the tension, T.

(a) Use the speed at B found in A2(a) to find the radial acceleration of the particle at this point.

(b) By applying Newton's second law radially, show that, when the particle is at B, $T = 10.8\,\text{N}$ to 3 s.f.

(c) (i) What is the resultant tangential force on the particle when it is at B?

  (ii) What is the magnitude of the tangential component of the acceleration at this point?

A5 (a) Draw a force diagram for the particle when it is at C.

(b) What is the resultant force acting towards the centre of the circle at C?

(c) Apply Newton's second law radially, and use the speed found in A2(b), to find the tension in the string at this point.

(d) (i) What is the resultant tangential force on the particle when it is at C?

  (ii) What is the direction of the resultant acceleration of the particle at this point?

A6 (a) Draw a force diagram for the particle when it is at D.

(b) Apply Newton's second law radially to show that the tension in the string when the particle is at D is given by $T = 10.84 + 2.94\cos\theta$.

(c) Hence describe how the tension in the string varies as the particle moves in a vertical circle.

Consider a bead of mass m threaded on a smooth circular wire of radius r and centre O.
The wire is fixed in a vertical plane and the bead is given an initial velocity u at K.
The bead moves round the wire in a vertical circle.

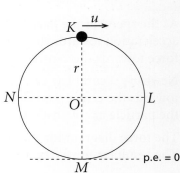

A7 What force other than its weight acts on the bead during the motion?

A8 The bead passes L with a speed v_L.

(a) Write an expression for the total energy of the bead at K.

(b) Write an expression for the total energy of the bead at L.

(c) Show that the speed of the bead at L is given by $v_L{}^2 = u^2 + 2gr$.

(d) Draw a force diagram for the bead at L.

(e) What is the resultant radial force when the bead is at L?

(f) Apply Newton's second law radially to show that the normal reaction of the wire on the bead at L is given by

$$R = \frac{m(u^2 + 2gr)}{r}$$

A9 (a) Find an expression for the speed of the bead at M in terms of u, g and r.

   (b) Draw a force diagram for the bead at M.

   (c) Find an expression for the resultant radial force when the bead is at M.

   (d) Use Newton's second law to find an expression for the normal reaction of the wire on the bead at M.

A10 Explain why the speed of the bead at N is the same as the speed at L.

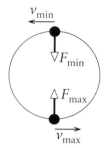

When an object moves in a vertical circle, the speed of the object changes as it moves around the circle.
The speed is maximum when the object is at its lowest point and minimum when it is at its highest point.

The resultant radial force F changes as the object moves around the circle.
The force is maximum when the object is at the lowest point and minimum when it is at its highest point.

Example 1

A smooth marble of mass 0.01 kg is released from rest at point A on the rim of a smooth hemispherical bowl of internal radius 0.4 m.

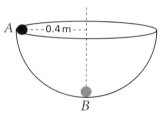

(a) Find the speed of the marble at B.

(b) Find the normal reaction of the bowl on the marble at B.

Solution

(a) *Take the potential energy at B to be zero.*
   The marble is released from rest at A, so it has zero kinetic energy at A.

   Total energy of the marble at A: k.e. + p.e. $= 0 + 0.01 \times 9.8 \times 0.4 = 0.0392$

   Total energy of the marble at B: k.e. + p.e. $= \frac{1}{2} \times 0.01 v^2 + 0 = 0.005 v^2$

   The total energy of the marble is constant. $0.005 v^2 = 0.0392$

$$\Rightarrow \quad v^2 = 7.84$$

$$\Rightarrow \quad v = 2.8$$

   The speed of the marble at B is $2.8 \, \text{m s}^{-1}$.

(b) *Draw a force diagram for the marble at B.*
   The resultant force towards the centre of the circle when the marble is at B is $R - 0.01g$.

   Apply N2L. $$F = \frac{mv^2}{r}$$

$$\Rightarrow \quad R - 0.01 \times 9.8 = \frac{0.01 \times 2.8^2}{0.4}$$

$$\Rightarrow \quad R = 0.196 + 0.098 = 0.294$$

   The normal reaction of the bowl on the marble is $0.294 \, \text{N}$.

Example 2

A bead of mass m is threaded on a smooth circular ring of radius r and centre O that is fixed in a vertical plane. The bead is moving round the wire. Its speed v, at the highest point of the path A, is one fifth of its speed at the lowest point C.

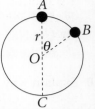

(a) Show that $v = \sqrt{\dfrac{gr}{6}}$.

(b) Find an expression for the normal reaction of the wire on the bead when the bead is at point B on the wire, where OB makes an angle θ with the vertical.

Solution

(a) *Take the potential energy at C to be zero.*

Total energy of the bead at A: k.e. + p.e. $= \frac{1}{2}mv^2 + 2mgr$

Total energy of the bead at C: k.e. + p.e. $= \frac{1}{2}m(5v)^2 + 0 = \dfrac{25mv^2}{2}$

The total energy of the bead is constant. $\frac{1}{2}mv^2 + 2mgr = \dfrac{25mv^2}{2}$

$$\Rightarrow v^2 + 4gr = 25v^2$$

$$\Rightarrow 24v^2 = 4gr \Rightarrow v^2 = \frac{gr}{6}$$

$$\Rightarrow v = \sqrt{\frac{gr}{6}}$$

(b) *Find the height of B above C.* $h = r + r\cos\theta$

Total energy of the bead at B: $\frac{1}{2}mv_B^2 + mgr(1 + \cos\theta)$

The total energy of the bead is constant. $\frac{1}{2}mv_B^2 + mgr(1 + \cos\theta) = \frac{1}{2}mv^2 + 2mgr$

$$\Rightarrow v_B^2 + 2gr(1 + \cos\theta) = v^2 + 4gr$$

$$\Rightarrow v_B^2 = v^2 + 4gr - 2gr - 2gr\cos\theta$$

$$\Rightarrow v_B^2 = v^2 + 2gr - 2gr\cos\theta$$

Draw a force diagram for the bead at B.

Apply N2L radially at B. $R + mg\cos\theta = \dfrac{mv_B^2}{r}$

$$\Rightarrow R + mg\cos\theta = \frac{m}{r}(v^2 + 2gr - 2gr\cos\theta)$$

$$\Rightarrow R = \frac{mv^2}{r} + 2mg - 2mg\cos\theta - mg\cos\theta$$

$$\Rightarrow R = \frac{mv^2}{r} + 2mg - 3mg\cos\theta$$

Exercise A (answers p 175)

1 A smooth cylinder of radius 0.5 m is placed with its axis horizontal. A particle of mass 2 kg moves in a vertical circle on the inside surface of the cylinder. If the speed of the particle is $6\,\text{m s}^{-1}$ at its lowest point, find the speed of the particle at its highest point.

2 A particle of mass 0.4 kg moves in a vertical circle on the inside surface of a smooth cylinder of radius 0.8 m. The particle is moving at $2\,\text{m s}^{-1}$ at its highest point. Find the speed of the particle at its lowest point.

3 A particle of mass 0.2 kg is fixed to one end of a string of length 0.6 m, and moves in a vertical circle about the fixed point O. The particle is moving at $5\,\text{m s}^{-1}$ at its highest point.

(a) Find the speed of the particle at its lowest point.

(b) Draw a force diagram for the particle at this point.

(c) Apply Newton's second law radially to find the tension in the string at this point.

4 A particle of mass m moves in a vertical circle on the inside surface of a smooth cylinder of radius r. The speed of the particle is u at its lowest point.

(a) Find an expression for the speed of the particle at its highest point.

(b) Draw a force diagram for the particle at this point.

(c) Find an expression for the normal reaction between the cylinder and the particle at this point.

5 A boy of mass 50 kg swings on the end of a 4 m rope. He is initially at rest with the rope at an angle of 45° with the downward vertical.

(a) (i) What angle does the rope make with the vertical when the boy is travelling at his maximum speed?

(ii) Find the maximum speed of the boy.

(iii) Find the tension in the rope at this point.

(b) (i) Find the speed of the boy when the rope makes an angle of 30° with the downward vertical.

(ii) Find the tension in the rope at this point.

(c) State the assumptions you have made in answering this question.

6 A particle of mass m kg is attached to one end of a light inextensible string of length l m. The other end of the string is fixed at point O. The particle is released from rest at point A with the string horizontal and the particle moves in a circular arc, centre O.

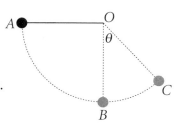

(a) Show that the tension in the string when the particle is at its lowest point, B, is $3mg\,\text{N}$.

(b) When the particle is at point C the string makes an angle θ with the vertical. Find an expression for the tension in the string at this point.

7 A bead of mass 0.25 kg is threaded on a smooth circular wire of radius 0.4 m and centre O. The wire is fixed in a vertical plane and the bead is given an initial speed of 2 m s^{-1} at A.

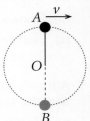

  (a) (i) Find the speed of the bead as it passes B.

     (ii) Find the normal reaction of the wire on the bead at B.

  (b) (i) Find the speed of the bead as it passes C.

     (ii) Find the normal reaction of the wire on the bead at C.

  (c) When the bead is at D, OD makes an angle $\theta°$ with the downward vertical.

    (i) Show that, when the bead is at D, the speed of the bead is given by

$$v^2 = 11.84 + 7.84\cos\theta.$$

    (ii) Find an expression for the normal reaction of the wire on the bead at D.

8 A girl swings a conker round in a vertical circle. The mass of the conker is 0.01 kg and it has velocity 3 m s^{-1} vertically downwards when the string is horizontal. The string is 0.5 m long and the conker hits another when the string makes an angle of 120° with the upward vertical.

  (a) Find the conker's velocity at this point.

  (b) Find the tension in the string at this point.

9 A particle of mass m is attached to one end of a light inextensible string of length a. The other end of the string is fixed at point O and the particle moves in a vertical circle, centre O. The speed v of the particle at the highest point of its path, A, is half of the speed at the lowest point B.

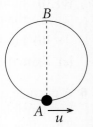

  (a) Find v in terms of a and g.

  (b) Find an expression for the tension in the string when the particle is at A.

  (c) Find an expression for the tension in the string when the particle is at B.

B Completing the circle (answers p 176)

A bead is threaded on a smooth circular wire.
The bead is given an initial speed of u m s^{-1} at A.

We saw in the previous section that the speed of the bead is maximum at the lowest point of its path, so as the bead moves round the wire to B its speed will decrease.

D **B1** Describe the subsequent motion of the bead if

  (a) its speed reaches zero before it reaches B

  (b) its speed reaches zero as it reaches B

  (c) its speed has not reached zero when it reaches B

B2 A bead of mass 0.02 kg is threaded on a smooth circular wire of radius 0.4 m and centre O. It starts at A and is given an initial velocity of $u\,\mathrm{m\,s^{-1}}$.

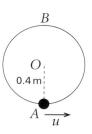

(a) (i) Use an energy equation to find the speed of the bead when it reaches B if $u = 6$.

  (ii) Describe the subsequent motion of the bead.

(b) (i) Use an energy equation to find the speed of the bead when it reaches B if $u = 3$.

  (ii) Explain your answer to (b)(i).

  (iii) Describe the motion of the bead.

(c) (i) What condition must be met for the bead to move in a complete circle?

  (ii) Find the minimum value of u for the bead to move in a complete circle.

B3 A bead of mass m is threaded on a smooth circular wire of radius r and centre O. The bead moves through A with speed u and through B with speed v.

(a) Write an expression for the total energy of the bead at A.

(b) Write an expression for the total energy of the bead at B.

(c) What condition must be met at B in order for the bead to move in a complete circle?

(d) Show that the bead will move in a complete circle if $u^2 > 4gr$.

An object which is restricted to move in a circle will move in a complete circle if the speed v at its highest point is greater than zero.

If the object comes to instantaneous rest before it reaches the highest point of the circular path, then the object will oscillate about the lowest point.

B4 A conker is attached to one end of a piece of string and the other end is held fixed. The conker is made to rotate in a vertical circle about the fixed point O.

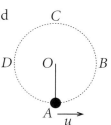

(a) Describe how the speed of the conker changes as it moves around the circle.

(b) Describe how the tension in the string changes as the conker moves around the circle.

(c) Describe what will happen to the motion of the conker if the tension in the string reduces to zero.

(d) Describe what will happen to the motion if the speed of the conker becomes zero before it reaches B.

B5 A conker of mass 0.02 kg is hanging from one end of a string of length 0.6 m, vertically below the fixed point O. The conker is given an initial speed of $u\,\text{m s}^{-1}$ at A.

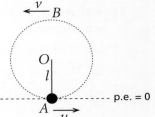

(a) (i) Use an energy equation to find the speed of the conker when it reaches B, given that $u = 7$.

   (ii) Apply Newton's second law radially to find the tension in the string at B in this case.

   (iii) Describe the motion of the conker.

(b) (i) Use an energy equation to find the speed of the conker when it reaches B, given that $u = 5$.

   (ii) Apply Newton's second law radially to find the tension in the string at B in this case. Comment on your answer.

   (iii) What does your answer to (b)(ii) tell you about the motion of the conker?

B6 A particle of mass m is attached to one end of a string of length l. The other end of the string is fixed at O. The particle moves through A with speed u and through B with speed v.

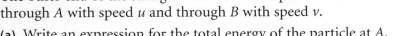

(a) Write an expression for the total energy of the particle at A.

(b) Write an expression for the total energy of the particle at B.

(c) What condition must be met at B in order for the particle to move in a complete circle?

(d) Show that, if the particle moves in a complete circle, $u^2 \geq 5gl$.

D **B7** A marble moves in a vertical circle around the inside of a smooth cylinder.

(a) What force other than weight acts on the marble during the motion?

(b) What condition must be met in order for the marble to move in a complete circle?

(c) If the marble does not move in a complete circle, describe the other possible ways in which it can move.

K A particle on a string will move in a complete circle if the string is taut throughout the motion.

$T \geq 0$

complete circles

If the tension reduces to zero before reaching the top of the circle, the particle will not continue on a circular path, but will move as a projectile.

$T = 0$
A

projectile motion

If the speed of the particle reduces to zero before it reaches A, the particle will oscillate about the lowest point of the path.

A
$v = 0$

oscillations

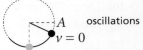

When a particle moves on the inside or the outside of a surface, the normal reaction of the surface on the particle acts as a radial force.

B8 A ball of mass 0.2 kg moves in a vertical circle around the inside surface of a smooth cylinder of radius 0.5 m and centre O. The ball passes A with speed $4\,\mathrm{m\,s^{-1}}$. When the ball is at X, the line OX makes an angle $\theta°$ with the upward vertical and the ball is moving at $v\,\mathrm{m\,s^{-1}}$.

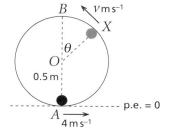

(a) Find the total energy of the ball at A.

(b) Write an expression for the total energy of the ball at X.

(c) Show that the speed of the ball at X is given by $v^2 = 6.2 - 9.8\cos\theta$.

(d) Draw a force diagram for the ball at X.

(e) Use Newton's second law radially to show that the normal reaction of the cylinder on the ball at X is given by $R = 2.48 - 5.88\cos\theta$.

(f) Explain why the ball cannot move in a complete circle.

(g) Find the value of θ when the ball loses contact with the surface.

B9 A ball of mass m moves on the inside surface of a smooth cylinder of radius r and centre O. The ball passes A with speed u and oscillates in the cylinder. When the ball is at X, the line OX makes an angle $\theta°$ with the downward vertical and the ball is moving with speed v.

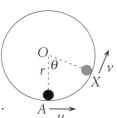

(a) Use an energy equation to show that $v^2 = u^2 - 2gr(1 - \cos\theta)$.

(b) Explain why $v = 0$ when $\theta \le 90°$ if the ball is to oscillate in the cylinder.

(c) Show that $u^2 \le 2gr$.

Example 3

A bead of mass m kg is threaded on a smooth circular ring of radius 0.5 m that is fixed in a vertical plane.
Given that the bead passes the lowest point on the ring with a speed of $u\,\mathrm{m\,s^{-1}}$, find the minimum value of u for the bead to move in a complete circle.

Solution

Take the potential energy at A to be zero.

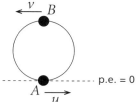

Let the speed of the bead at B be $v\,\mathrm{m\,s^{-1}}$.

Total energy of the bead at A: k.e. + p.e. $= \frac{1}{2}mu^2 + 0 = \frac{1}{2}mu^2$

Total energy of the bead at B: k.e. + p.e. $= \frac{1}{2}mv^2 + m\times9.8\times1 = \frac{1}{2}mv^2 + 9.8m$

The total energy of the bead is constant. $\frac{1}{2}mu^2 = \frac{1}{2}mv^2 + 9.8m$

$$\Rightarrow v^2 = u^2 - 9.8\times2 = u^2 - 19.6$$

For a complete circle $v^2 \ge 0$. $u^2 - 19.6 \ge 0 \Rightarrow u \ge 4.43$

The minimum value of u for the bead to move in a complete circle is $4.43\,\mathrm{m\,s^{-1}}$ to 3 s.f.

Example 4

A marble of mass m is released from rest at point A
on a smooth loop-the-loop track.
Point A is height h above the base B of the loop.
The loop is a circle with radius a.

Show that the marble performs a complete loop if $h \geq \dfrac{5a}{2}$.

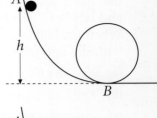

Solution

*If the marble performs a complete loop, the normal reaction, R, of the
track on the marble at C must be greater than or equal to zero.*

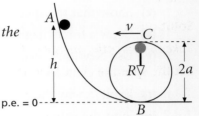

*Draw a force diagram for the marble at C, the highest point on the loop.
The resultant force towards the centre of the circle is mg + R.*

Let the speed of the marble at C be v.

Apply N2L.

$$mg + R = \frac{mv^2}{a}$$

$$\Rightarrow \quad R = \frac{mv^2}{a} - mg$$

But $R \geq 0$ for the marble to perform a complete loop.

$$\Rightarrow \quad \frac{mv^2}{a} - mg \geq 0$$

$$\Rightarrow \quad v^2 \geq ga$$

*The total energy is constant throughout the motion, so consider the energy
of the marble at A and at C. The rest of the motion need not be considered.
Take the potential energy at B to be zero.*

Total energy of the marble at A: k.e. + p.e. $= 0 + mgh$

Total energy of the marble at C: k.e. + p.e. $= \frac{1}{2}mv^2 + 2mga$

The total energy of the marble is constant. $\frac{1}{2}mv^2 + 2mga = mgh$

$$\Rightarrow \quad \frac{1}{2}v^2 = gh - 2ga$$

$$\Rightarrow \quad v^2 = 2gh - 4ga$$

But $v^2 \geq ga$. $2gh - 4ga \geq ga$

$$\Rightarrow \quad 2gh \geq 5ga$$

$$\Rightarrow \quad h \geq \frac{5a}{2}$$

Example 5

A ball of mass 0.1 kg is placed at the highest point A of a smooth hemispherical bowl of radius 0.6 m and centre O.
The ball is given an initial speed of $2\,\mathrm{m\,s^{-1}}$.
The ball loses contact with the bowl at B, where OB makes an angle $\theta°$ with the vertical as shown.

Find angle θ.

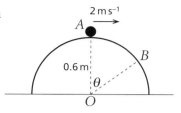

Solution

Take the potential energy at O to be zero.

Let the speed of the ball at B be $v\,\mathrm{m\,s^{-1}}$.

Total energy of the ball at A:

$$\text{k.e.} + \text{p.e.} = \tfrac{1}{2}\times0.1\times2^2 + 0.1\times9.8\times0.6 = 0.788$$

Total energy of the ball at B:

$$\text{k.e.} + \text{p.e.} = \tfrac{1}{2}\times0.1\times v^2 + 0.1\times9.8\times0.6\cos\theta$$

$$= 0.05v^2 + 0.588\cos\theta$$

The total energy of the ball is constant.

$$0.05v^2 + 0.588\cos\theta = 0.788$$

$$\Rightarrow \qquad 0.05v^2 = 0.788 - 0.588\cos\theta$$

$$\Rightarrow \qquad v^2 = 15.76 - 11.76\cos\theta$$

Draw a force diagram for the ball at B.

If the ball loses contact with the surface, then $R = 0$.
The resultant force towards the centre of the circle is $0.1g\cos\theta$.

Apply N2L.

$$F = \frac{mv^2}{r}$$

$$\Rightarrow \quad 0.1\times9.8\cos\theta = \frac{0.1(15.76 - 11.76\cos\theta)}{0.6}$$

$$\Rightarrow \qquad 5.88\cos\theta = 15.76 - 11.76\cos\theta$$

$$\Rightarrow \qquad 17.64\cos\theta = 15.76$$

$$\Rightarrow \qquad \cos\theta = 0.8934...$$

$$\Rightarrow \qquad \theta = 26.69...$$

The ball loses contact when θ is 27° to the nearest degree.

Exercise B (answers p 139)

1 A bead of mass 0.4 kg is threaded on a smooth circular wire of radius 0.6 m that is fixed in a vertical plane.
The bead passes the lowest point on the wire with a speed of $6\,\mathrm{m\,s^{-1}}$.

(a) What condition must be satisfied if the bead is to move in a complete circle?

(b) Show that the bead will move in a complete circle.

2 A smooth cylinder of radius 0.6 m is placed with its axis horizontal. A ball of mass 0.2 kg is at rest on the inside surface of the cylinder. The ball is given an initial speed of $8\,\text{m s}^{-1}$.

(a) What condition must be satisfied if the ball is to move in a complete circle?

(b) Find the speed of the ball when it passes A.

(c) Find the normal reaction of the cylinder on the ball at this instant.

3 A bead of mass 0.2 kg is threaded on a smooth circular wire of radius 0.5 m and centre O that is fixed in a vertical plane. The bead passes A with a speed of $4\,\text{m s}^{-1}$.

(a) Show that the bead does not move in a complete circle.

(b) The bead comes instantaneously to rest at B, where OB makes an angle θ with the upward vertical. By considering the energy of the bead at A and at B show that $\theta = 51°$ to the nearest degree.

4 A bridge over a river is in the form of a circular arc of radius 20 m. A motorcycle and rider have a total mass 275 kg.

(a) Assuming that the motorcycle and rider can be treated as a particle, calculate the normal reaction on the motorcycle when it is at the highest point of the bridge if its speed is

(i) $8\,\text{m s}^{-1}$ (ii) $10\,\text{m s}^{-1}$

(b) Find the greatest speed at which the motorcycle can cross the bridge without losing contact with the road at the highest point.

5 A marble of mass 0.2 kg is released from rest at point A on a smooth loop-the-loop track.
Point A is 0.5 m above the base B of the loop.
The loop is a circle with radius 0.3 m and centre O.

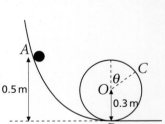

(a) Find the speed of the marble when it reaches B.

(b) The marble leaves the track when it is at point C, where OC makes an angle θ with the vertical.

(i) Find angle θ.

(ii) Find the speed of the marble at C.

6 A particle of mass 0.5 kg is attached to one end of a string of length 2 m.
The other end of the string is fixed at O.
The particle moves through A with speed $u\,\text{m s}^{-1}$.

Show that the particle oscillates about A if $u^2 \leq 39.2$.

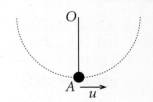

7 A marble of mass 0.01 kg is placed on the top of a smooth upturned hemispherical bowl and given an initial speed of $1\,\mathrm{m\,s^{-1}}$. The bowl has an outside radius of 0.5 m and centre O.

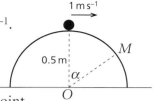

(a) Find the speed of the marble after it has descended a vertical distance of 0.1 m.

(b) Find the normal reaction of the bowl on the marble at this point.

(c) When the marble is at M the line OM makes an angle α with the vertical. The marble loses contact with the bowl at this point. Find, to the nearest degree, the angle α.

8 A particle P of mass m is attached to one end of a light inextensible string of length l.
The other end of the string is fixed at point O.
The particle is held so that the string is taut and OP is horizontal. The particle is projected vertically downwards with speed u as shown.

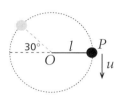

The string becomes slack when OP is inclined at an angle of $30°$ above the horizontal.

(a) Show that the speed of the particle when the string becomes slack is $\sqrt{\dfrac{gl}{2}}$.

(b) Hence find u in terms of l and g.

9 A particle of mass m is attached to one end A of a light inextensible string of length l, the other end of which is attached to a fixed point O.
The particle is projected horizontally with a velocity u when OA is vertical with A below O.

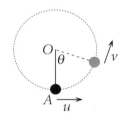

(a) Show that the velocity v of the particle when the string makes an angle θ with the downward vertical through O and the string is taut is given by
$$v^2 = u^2 - 2gl(1 - \cos\theta).$$

(b) Show that the tension in the string at this point is given by
$$T = mg(3\cos\theta - 2) + \frac{mu^2}{l}.$$

(c) Show that the particle makes complete revolutions if $u^2 \geq 5gl$.

10 A ball of mass m is placed on top of a smooth hemispherical bowl of radius r and centre O. The ball moves from rest at A. When the ball is at B, OB makes an angle θ with the vertical.

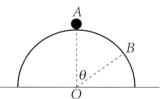

(a) Show that the normal reaction of the bowl on the ball when the ball is at B is given by $R = mg(3\cos\theta - 2)$.

(b) Show that the ball loses contact with the surface of the bowl when it has travelled a vertical distance of $\dfrac{r}{3}$.

Key points

- An object moving in a circle with variable speed $v\,\text{m}\,\text{s}^{-1}$ has two components of acceleration:

    a component acting towards the centre of the circle, with magnitude $\dfrac{v^2}{r}$ at any instant

    a component acting along the tangent to the circle equal to the rate of change of the speed, $\dfrac{\mathrm{d}v}{\mathrm{d}t}$

    If the external forces acting on the object, apart from its weight, do no work then the principle of conservation of mechanical energy can be applied. (p 128)

- When an object moves in a vertical circle, the speed of the object changes as it moves around the circle.
  The speed is maximum when the object is at its lowest point and minimum when it is at its highest point.

  The resultant radial force F changes as the object moves around the circle.
  The force is maximum when the object is at the lowest point and minimum when it is at its highest point.

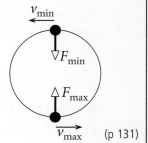

(p 131)

- An object which is restricted to move in a circle will move in a complete circle if the speed v at its highest point is greater than zero.

  If the object comes to instantaneous rest before it reaches the highest point of the circular path, then the object will oscillate about the lowest point.

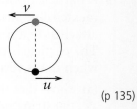

(p 135)

- A particle on a string will move in a complete circle if the string is taut throughout the motion.

  $T \geq 0$

  complete circles

  If the tension reduces to zero before reaching the top of the circle, the particle will not continue on a circular path, but will move as a projectile.

  $T = 0$

  A

  projectile motion

  If the speed of the particle reduces to zero before it reaches A, the particle will oscillate about the lowest point of the path.

  A

  $v = 0$

  oscillations

  When a particle moves on the inside or the outside of a surface, the normal reaction of the surface on the particle acts as a radial force.

(p 136)

Mixed questions (answers p 178)

1 The diagram shows a vertical cross-section of a new adventure slide at a theme park.
It consists of three section, AB, BC and CD.
Section AB is smooth and vertical and has length r.
Section BC is smooth and forms a quarter of a circle.
The circle has centre O and radius r.
The radius OB is horizontal and OC is vertical.
Section CD is rough, straight and horizontal.
It is of length $4r$.

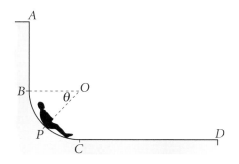

Steve, who has mass m, starts from rest at A and reaches speed u at the point B.
He remains in contact with the surface until he reaches D.

It can be assumed that Steve can be modelled as a particle throughout the motion.

(a) Find u^2 in terms of g and r.

(b) Steve reaches the point P between B and C where angle $POB = \theta$, as shown in the diagram. His speed at P is v.

   (i) Show that $v^2 = 2gr(1 + \sin\theta)$.

   (ii) Draw a diagram showing the forces acting on Steve when he is at the point P.

   (iii) Find an expression for the normal reaction, R, on Steve when he is at the point P. Give your answer in terms of m, g and θ.

(c) Show that, as Steve crosses C, there is a reduction in the normal reaction of magnitude $4mg$.

(d) Between C and D, Steve decelerates uniformly and comes to rest at the point D. Find his retardation.
AQA 2003

2 A stuntman S stands initially on a platform P. He holds a rope which is attached to a fixed support O. The points O and P are at the same horizontal level. The man then steps off the platform with the rope taut and horizontal. He swings through a circular arc, as shown in the diagram.

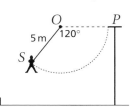

The mass of the man is $70\,\text{kg}$ and the length of the rope is $5\,\text{m}$.
The man may be modelled as a particle throughout the motion.

(a) The man releases his grip on the rope when it has swung through an angle of $120°$.

   (i) Show that the speed of the man when he is about to let go of the rope is approximately $9.21\,\text{m s}^{-1}$.

   (ii) Find the tension in the rope when the man is about to let go of the rope.

(b) After letting go of the rope, the stuntman moves freely under gravity.
He rises a distance d before beginning to fall into the safety net. Show that d is approximately 1 metre.

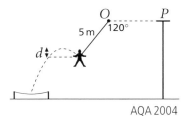

(c) Comment on the assumption that the man can be modelled as a particle.
AQA 2004

3 Maria is modelling the motion of a toy car along a 'loop-the-loop' track.

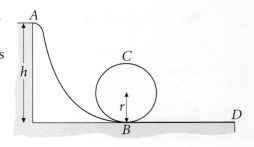

The track, $ABCD$, can be modelled as a continuous smooth surface contained in a vertical plane. The highest point on the track is A, which is a distance h above the floor. The loop is a circle of radius r with BC as a diameter, and with C vertically above B. The track ends at the point D, as shown in the diagram.

Maria is trying to determine a connection between h and r in the case where the car stays only just in contact with the track at C.

Maria models the car as a particle of mass m, which starts from rest at A. In the case where the car stays only just in contact with the track at C, it has speed u at B and speed v at C.

(a) By considering the forces on the car at C, show that $v^2 = rg$.

(b) Find an expression for u^2 in terms of g and r.

(c) Show that $h = kr$, where k is a constant to be determined.

(d) Suggest one improvement that could be made to the model in order to refine the solution.

AQA 2003

4 Adam has set up an experiment for his Mechanics coursework. He has attached a small ball B, of mass m, to one end of a light inextensible string of length $5a$. The other end of the string is attached to a fixed point O. The ball is released from rest with the string taut and horizontal, as shown in the diagram. The ball subsequently passes through point C, which is a vertical distance $5a$ below O.

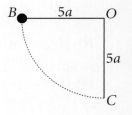

(a) Find an expression, in terms of a and g, for the speed of B when it reaches C.

(b) A small smooth peg P is fixed at a distance d vertically above C. When the string reaches the vertical position, B begins to move in a vertical circle with centre P and radius d, as shown in the diagram.

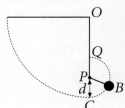

The ball reaches Q, the point at a distance d vertically above P, with speed v. At Q, the string is taut.

(i) Show that $v^2 = 2g(5a - 2d)$.

(ii) Find, in terms of a, d, g and m, the tension in the string when the ball is at Q.

(iii) Hence show that $d < 2a$.

(c) State **one** modelling assumption used in this question.

AQA 2004

1 A bead, of mass m, is threaded on a smooth circular ring, of radius r, which is fixed in a vertical plane. The bead is moving on the wire so that its speed at the lowest point of its path is four times its speed, v, at the highest point.

(a) Find v in terms of r and g.

(b) Find the reaction of the wire on the bead when the bead is at its lowest point.

AQA 2002

2 In crazy golf, a golf ball is fired along a smooth track and loops the loop inside a section of track.
Model this loop as a vertical circle of radius a and centre Q, as shown in the diagram.
The golf ball is travelling at speed u as it enters the circle at the lowest point.
Model the ball as a particle P, of mass m.

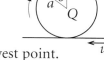

(a) Show that the reaction of the track on the particle when QP makes an angle of θ with the upward vertical is $\dfrac{mu^2}{a} - 3mg\cos\theta - 2mg$.

(b) Given that the ball completes a vertical circle inside the track, show that $u \geq \sqrt{5ag}$.

AQA 2004

3 A girl of mass $35\,\text{kg}$ swings on one end of a rope of length $4\,\text{m}$. The motion is in a vertical plane. Initially the rope makes an angle of $45°$ with the downward vertical and the girl has a speed of $2\,\text{m s}^{-1}$ at right angles to the rope.

(a) Show that the maximum speed of the girl during the motion is approximately $5.2\,\text{m s}^{-1}$.

(b) Find, to the nearest degree, the maximum angle that the rope makes with the downward vertical.

(c) State one modelling assumption you have used in answering this question.

4 A solid smooth hemisphere, of radius r, has its plane face fixed to a horizontal table. The centre of the plane face is O. A particle P, of mass m, is placed at the highest point of the hemisphere. The particle is then given a horizontal velocity of $\frac{1}{2}\sqrt{rg}$. At the instant when OP makes an angle θ with the vertical through O, and P is still in contact with the hemisphere, the speed of P is v.

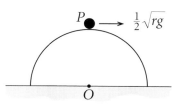

(a) Show that $v^2 = \frac{1}{4}rg(9 - 8\cos\theta)$.

(b) (i) Find, in terms of m, g and θ, the normal reaction between the particle and the hemisphere.

(ii) Determine whether or not P is still in contact with the hemisphere when $\cos\theta = \frac{4}{5}$.

(iii) Find the value of $\cos\theta$ when P loses contact with the hemisphere.

(iv) Show that the speed at which P leaves the hemisphere is $\frac{1}{2}\sqrt{3rg}$.

AQA 2002

Answers

1 Moments

Answers are given to three significant figures where appropriate.

A Moment of a force (p 6)

A1 In the first case the ruler remains stationary on the table.
In the second case the ruler rotates on the table.

A2 (a) The force will cause the spanner to turn anticlockwise and loosen the nut.

(b) The force will again cause the spanner to turn anticlockwise, but the turning effect will not be as great as in (a). The nut will again loosen.

(c) The force will cause the spanner to turn clockwise and tighten the nut.

A3 (a) 12 N m anticlockwise   (b) 20 N m clockwise

(c) 12 N m anticlockwise

A4 (a) Less because the distance of the line of action from A is less.

(b) $0.2 \sin 30° = 0.1$ m

(c) 0.8 N m anticlockwise

A5 (a) $5 \times 3 \sin 45° = 10.6$ N m clockwise

(b) $10 \times 4 \sin 60° = 34.6$ N m clockwise

(c) $7 \times 1.5 \sin 50° = 8.04$ N m anticlockwise

A6 (a) 20 N m clockwise   (b) 0 N m   (c) 0 N m

A7 (a) 0 N m   (b) 0 N m

(c) 20 N m anticlockwise

(d) 20 N m anticlockwise

Exercise A (p 9)

1 (a) 8 N m anticlockwise

(b) 4.5 N m clockwise

(c) 17.5 N m anticlockwise

(d) 2.54 N m clockwise

(e) 5.79 N m clockwise

(f) 17.3 N m anticlockwise

2 (a) 16 N m clockwise   (b) 16 N m clockwise

(c) 0 N m   (d) 0 N m

3 (a) 25 N m clockwise   (b) 10 N m clockwise

(c) 5 N m clockwise

4 (a) 8 N m anticlockwise   (b) 4 N m clockwise

5 (a) 0 N m

(b) 5.20 N m anticlockwise

(c) 8.66 N m anticlockwise

6 6

B Equilibrium of a rigid body (p 10)

B1 (a) The seesaw will not balance. It will rotate so that Sasha's feet rest on the ground and Kieran is in the air.

(b) Sasha should move towards the pivot, or Kieran should move away from it, to make the seesaw balance.

B2 Resolve vertically: $R = 25g + 30g + 20g$
$$R = 75g = 735$$

B3 (a) Total moment about S
$= 75g \times 1.6 - 25g \times 0 - 30g \times 1.6 - 20g \times 3.6$
$= 120g - 48g - 72g = 0$ N m

(b) Total moment about K
$= 25g \times 3.6 + 30g \times 2 + 20g \times 0 - 75g \times 2$
$= 90g + 60g - 150g = 0$ N m

(c) Total moment about O
$= 75g \times 2 - 25g \times 0.4 - 30g \times 2 - 20g \times 4$
$= 150g - 10g - 60g - 80g = 0$ N m

(d) The total moment of the forces is zero about each of the points. The seesaw is in equilibrium, so the total moment of the forces about any point will be zero.

B4 (a) Total moment about A
$= R_B \times 4 - 50 \times 2.5 = 4R_B - 125 = 0$
$\Rightarrow R_B = 31.25$

(b) Total moment about B
$= 50 \times 1.5 - R_A \times 4 = 75 - 4R_A = 0$
$\Rightarrow R_A = 18.75$

(c) Resolve vertically: $R_A + R_B = 50$
Substitute calculated values:
$18.75 + 31.25 = 50$, which is correct, so the forces are in equilibrium.

B5 (a)

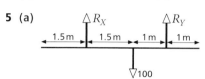

(b) M(B): $50 \times 0.5 = R_A \times 2 \implies R_A = 12.5$
Reaction at $A = 12.5\,N$

(c) M(A): $R_B \times 2 = 50 \times 1.5 \implies R_B = 37.5$
Reaction at $B = 37.5\,N$

(d) Moving the supports has changed the magnitudes of the reactions, but the sum of the reactions must remain as $50\,N$ for the rod to remain in equilibrium.

B6 (a)

(b) M(B): $50 \times 0.5 = 10 \times 1 + R_A \times 2$
$\implies \qquad R_A = 7.5$
Reaction at $A = 7.5\,N$

(c) M(A): $R_B \times 2 = 50 \times 1.5 + 10 \times 3$
$\implies \qquad R_B = 52.5$
Reaction at $B = 52.5\,N$

B7 (a)

(b) M(Q): $75 \times 4 = R_P \times 6$
$\implies \qquad R_P = 50$
Reaction at $P = 50\,N$

(c) M(P): $R_Q \times 6 = 75 \times 2$
$\implies \qquad R_Q = 25$
Reaction at $Q = 25\,N$

B8 (a) M(Q): $75 \times 4 + 30 \times 3 = R_P \times 6$
$\implies \qquad R_P = 65$
Reaction at $P = 65\,N$

(b) M(P): $R_Q \times 6 = 75 \times 2 + 30 \times 3$
$\implies \qquad R_Q = 40$
Reaction at $Q = 40\,N$

Exercise B (p 13)

1 (a) $A = 24,\ B = 16$ **(b)** $C = 12,\ D = 19$
(c) $E = 19.2,\ F = 7.2$ **(d)** $G = 0.5,\ H = 2.5$

2 $40\,kg$

3 (a)

(b) $4\,N$ **(c)** $8\,N$

4 (a) $8\,N$ **(b)** $6\,N$

5 (a)

(b) $40\,N$ **(c)** $60\,N$

6 (a) $20\,N$ **(b)** $5\,N$

7 The centre of mass of the rod is $1.6\,m$ from P.

8 $0.5\,m$

C Tilting (p 15)

C1 (a) The beam could remain in equilibrium or tilt with B as the pivot.

(b) The beam will remain in equilibrium.

(c) The beam could remain in equilibrium or tilt with C as the pivot.

C2 (a) $2W + 6R_C = 600$

(b) As W increases, R_C decreases.

(c) The maximum value of W for the beam to remain in equilibrium is 300.

(d) M(C): $8W + 600 = 6R_B$
As W increases, R_B increases.

(e) $R_C = 0,\ R_B = 500$

C3 (a) C

(b) M(C): $200 \times 3.4 = 1.6W \implies W = 425$
Neeta's weight is $425\,N$.

(c) $R_B = 0,\ R_C = 625$

Exercise C (p 17)

1 (a) $0\,N$ **(b)** $20\,N$ **(c)** $80\,N$

2 (a) B **(b)** $500\,N$ **(c)** $900\,N$

3 $37.5\,N$

4 $0.875\,m$

5 225 N

6 (a) 0.36 m   **(b)** 28 N

D Non-parallel forces (p 18)

D1 (a) The distance d is $4\sin 45°$, so the moment of T about P is $4T\sin 45°$.

(b) $500g \times 3 = 4T\sin 45° \Rightarrow 1500g = 4T\sin 45°$

(c) $T = 5200$

D2 (a) $Y + T\sin 45° = 500g \Rightarrow Y = 1225$

(b) $X = T\cos 45° \Rightarrow X = 3675$

(c) $R = \sqrt{1223^2 + 3677^2}$
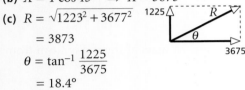
$= 3873$

$\theta = \tan^{-1}\dfrac{1225}{3675}$

$= 18.4°$

D3 (a)
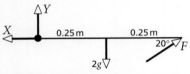

(b) $2g \times 0.25 = F \times 0.5\sin 20° \Rightarrow F = 28.7$

(c) $X = F\cos 20° = 26.9$

$Y + F\sin 20° = 2g \Rightarrow Y = 9.8$

Magnitude of reaction $= \sqrt{26.9^2 + 9.8^2} = 28.6\,\text{N}$

Direction $= \tan^{-1}\dfrac{9.8}{26.9} = 20.0°$ to the horizontal

D4 (a)

(b) There is no horizontal force to balance the reaction at the wall, R_W, so the ladder will slip.

D5 (a)
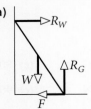

(b) The ladder will remain in equilibrium if $F = R_W$. If R_W is greater than the limiting value of the friction force, then the ladder will slip.

D6 The lines of action of F and R_B pass through B, so their moments about B are zero, and R_A is the only unknown in the equation.

D7 As the man climbs up the ladder, the reaction at the wall increases which causes the friction force to increase. The reaction at the ground is constant. If the friction force reaches its limiting value, then the ladder will slip.

D8 (a) $R_B = 850$

(b) $R_A = F$

(c) $R_A \times 4\sin 60° = 100 \times 2\cos 60° + 750 \times x\cos 60°$

(d) $F_{\text{max}} = 0.4 \times 850 = 340 \Rightarrow R_A = 340$

(e) $x = 2.87$

The man can climb 2.87 m up the ladder before it slips.

Exercise D (p 21)

1 (a)
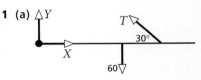

(b) The distance of A from the line of action of T is $3\sin 30°$, so the moment of T about A is $3T\sin 30°$.

(c) 80

2 $\dfrac{W}{3}$

3 (a)
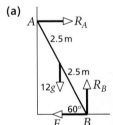

(b) 33.9 N   **(c)** 33.9 N   **(d)** 0.289

4 (a)

(b) 19.6 N

(c) 27.7 N at 45° to the horizontal

5 (a)

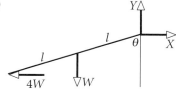

(b) $X = 4W$, $Y = W$

(c) $\sqrt{17}\,W$ at $14.0°$ to the horizontal

(d) $82.9°$

6 $5.31\,\text{m}$

7 (a)

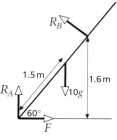

(b) $34.5\,\text{N}$ (c) 0.441

Mixed questions (p 23)

1 (a) $259\,\text{N}$ (b) $182\,\text{N}$ (c) $61.7\,\text{kg}$

2 (a) (i) $2T = 10g \times 0.5 \;\Rightarrow\; T = 24.5$

    (ii) $612.5\,\text{N}$

  (b) There would be no change, as the ratio of the distances from the pivot would be the same.

3 (a) $30\,\text{N}$ (b) $10\,\text{N}$ (c) $1.2\,\text{m}$

4 $\dfrac{\sqrt{3}\,mg}{6}$

5 (a) M(B): $W(x - 2) + 100 = 6R$ (1)

    M(C): $W(8 - x) + 200 = 18R$ (2)

    Subtract (2) from (1)×3:

    $3W(x - 2) + 300 - W(8 - x) - 200 = 0$

    $14W - 4Wx = 100$

    $\Rightarrow\; W = \dfrac{50}{7 - 2x}$

  (b) $0 \leq x < 3.5$

6 (a) Resolve vertically: $R_B = 5W$

    Limiting equilibrium, so $F = \mu R_B$

    $\Rightarrow\; F = \tfrac{1}{4} \times 5W = \dfrac{5W}{4}$

  (b) $P = \dfrac{5W}{18}$

Test yourself (p 24)

1 Reaction at $A = 98\,\text{N}$, reaction at $B = 196\,\text{N}$

2 (a)

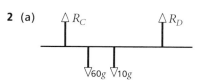

  (b) Reaction at $C = 490\,\text{N}$, reaction at $D = 196\,\text{N}$

3 (a) Reaction at $A = 408\,\text{N}$, reaction at $B = 2042\,\text{N}$

  (b) $1.56\,\text{m}$

4 (a)   **(b)** $102\,\text{N}$

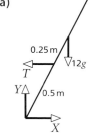

5 (a)

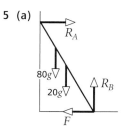

  (b) (i) Resolve vertically: $R_B = 100g$

         Resolve horizontally: $R_A = F$

         Limiting equilibrium, so $F = \mu R_B$

         $\Rightarrow\; F = 0.4 \times 100g = 392 \;\Rightarrow\; R_A = 392$

    (ii) $3.71\,\text{m}$

2 Centre of mass

A Centre of mass of a system of particles
(p 26)

A1 (a)

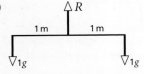

(b) Total moment about support
$= g \times 1 - g \times 1 = 0$
The total moment about the support is zero, so the system is in equilibrium.

A2 M(support): $2g \times x = g(2 - x) \Rightarrow 2gx = 2g - gx$
$\Rightarrow 3x = 2 \Rightarrow x = \frac{2}{3}$
The centre of mass is $\frac{2}{3}$ m from A.

A3 (a) 19.6 N m clockwise
(b) $3g \times \frac{2}{3} = 19.6$ N m clockwise

A4 (a) 39.2 N m anticlockwise
(b) $3g \times \left(2 - \frac{2}{3}\right) = 39.2$ N m anticlockwise

A5 (a) $2g \times 1 - g \times 1 = 9.8$ N m anticlockwise
(b) $3g \times \frac{1}{3} = 9.8$ N m anticlockwise

Exercise A (p 28)

1 (a) 1.125 m **(b)** 1.15 m **(c)** 0.84 m **(d)** 0.5 m

2 3.75 m

3 (a) 3.4 m **(b)** 3.75 m from A

4 30

5 6

6 2.25 m

7 4.25 m

B A system of particles in a plane

Exercise B (p 30)

1 (a) (3.25, 1.75) **(b)** (4, 3.7)
(c) (3.2, 2.6) **(d)** (3.4, 1.8)

2 (1.4, 2)

3 (a) 0.53 m (to 2 d.p.) **(b)** 2 m

4 (a) (1.5, 1.5) **(b)** (1.5, 1)

5 (a) 8 **(b)** 0.625

6 (a) 1.2 m **(b)** 2 m
(c) 1 m from PQ, 1.5 m from PS

7 $p = 8, q = 4$

C Centre of mass by symmetry (p 32)

C1 (a) (2, 1)
(b) The lines $x = 2$ and $y = 1$ are lines of symmetry of the system. The centre of mass lies at the point of intersection of these lines as the masses are symmetrically distributed about this point.

C2 (a) The centre of the circle
(b) The centre of the square

(c) The centre of the rectangle

Exercise C (p 32)

1 (a) (2.5, 2.5) **(b)** (1.5, 1.6)

2 (a) (2.5, 3) **(b)** (3.5, 2.5)
(c) (−0.5, 0.5) **(d)** (2.5, 1.5)

D Centre of mass of a composite body (p 33)

D1 (a) (1, 2) **(b)** (5, 1)

D2 (a) $8a$ kg **(b)** $12a$ kg

D3 Using $M\bar{x} = \sum mx$, $20a\bar{x} = 8a \times 1 + 12a \times 5$
$\Rightarrow 20\bar{x} = 68 \Rightarrow \bar{x} = 3.4$
Using $M\bar{y} = \sum my$, $20a\bar{y} = 8a \times 2 + 12a \times 1$
$\Rightarrow 20\bar{y} = 28 \Rightarrow \bar{y} = 1.4$
The centre of mass is at (3.4, 1.4).

D4 (a) (3, 1.5)
(b) (3, 4.5)
(c) By symmetry, $\bar{x} = 3$
Using $M\bar{y} = \sum my$,
$(18 + 6)\bar{y} = 18 \times 1.5 + 6 \times 4.5$
$\Rightarrow 24\bar{y} = 54 \Rightarrow \bar{y} = 2.25$
The centre of mass of the lamina is at (3, 2.25).

D5 (a)

	Area	Distance from AD	Distance from AB
$ABCD$	$24\,\text{m}^2$	**3 m**	**2 m**
$EFGH$	$4\,\text{m}^2$	**3 m**	**1.5 m**
Lamina	$20\,\text{m}^2$	x_{L} m	y_{L} m

(b) (i) Using $M\bar{x} = \sum mx$, $24\times3 = 4\times3 + 20x_{\text{L}}$
$\Rightarrow 72 = 12 + 20x_{\text{L}}$

(ii) Using $M\bar{y} = \sum my$, $24\times2 = 4\times1.5 + 20y_{\text{L}}$
$\Rightarrow 48 = 6 + 20y_{\text{L}}$

(iii) $20x_{\text{L}} = 60 \Rightarrow x_{\text{L}} = 3$
$20y_{\text{L}} = 42 \Rightarrow y_{\text{L}} = 2.1$
The centre of mass is at $(3, 2.1)$.

Exercise D (p 36)

1 (a) $(2.5, 1)$ **(b)** $(4, 2.5)$ **(c)** $(2.75, 1.25)$

2 (a) $(0.83, 0.83)$ (to 2 d.p.)

(b) $(1.7, 0.7)$

(c) $(2, 1.3)$

(d) $(2.78, 1.61)$ (to 2 d.p.)

3 (a) AD is a line of symmetry of the lamina.

(b) $(2.71, 2.71)$ (to 2 d.p.)

4 (a)

	Length	Distance from AC	Distance from AB
Side AB	0.3 m	0.15 m	0 m
Side BC	0.5 m	**0.15 m**	**0.2 m**
Side AC	0.4 m	**0 m**	**0.2 m**
Triangle	**1.2 m**	$\bar{x}$ m	$\bar{y}$ m

(b) 0.1 m   **(c)** 0.15 m

5 (a) 0.14 m (to 2 d.p.)   **(b)** 0.4 m

6 (a) $(2, 1.5)$ **(b)** $(1, 2)$ **(c)** $(2.07, 1.46)$

7 (a) $(1.98, 2.02)$ (to 2 d.p.)

(b) $(3.88, 2)$ (to 2 d.p.)

8 0.75 m

9 (a) Using $M\bar{y} = \sum my$,
$(1.5 + 4 + 2)\bar{y} = 1.5\times1 + 4\times2 + 2\times2$
$\Rightarrow 7.5\bar{y} = 13.5 \Rightarrow \bar{y} = 1.8$
So the centre of mass is 1.8 m from AB.

(b) 1.1 m

10 (a) 0.225 m   **(b)** 0.45 m

11 1.5625 cm

E Suspended objects (p 38)

E1 (a) It would not stay in this position because the weight of the lamina, acting at its centre of mass, has a resultant moment about A, causing the lamina to rotate.

(b) Again, the lamina will not stay in this position, because there is still a resultant moment of the weight of the lamina about A.

(c) When the centre of mass of the lamina is vertically below A, the moment of the weight about A is zero, and so the lamina is in equilibrium.

(d) $\theta = \tan^{-1}\frac{1}{2} = 26.6°$ (to 3 s.f.)

E2 (a) (i) 2 m   **(ii)** 2.5 m

(b) (i)

(ii) $\theta = \tan^{-1}\frac{2}{2.5} = 38.7°$ (to 3 s.f.)

(c) (i)

(ii) $51.3°$ (to 3 s.f.)

E3

$\theta = \tan^{-1}\frac{3.5}{1.5} = 66.8°$ (to 3 s.f.)

E4 (a)

	Area	Distance from AG	Distance from AB
$ABFG$	$9\,\text{m}^2$	$1.5\,\text{m}$	$1.5\,\text{m}$
$CDEF$	$3\,\text{m}^2$	$4.5\,\text{m}$	$2.5\,\text{m}$
Lamina	$12\,\text{m}^2$	$\bar{x}\,\text{m}$	$\bar{y}\,\text{m}$

$12\bar{x} = 9 \times 1.5 + 3 \times 4.5 \implies 12\bar{x} = 27$
$\implies \bar{x} = 2.25$

(b) $12\bar{y} = 9 \times 1.5 + 3 \times 2.5 \implies 12\bar{y} = 21$
$\implies \bar{y} = 1.75$

(c) (i)

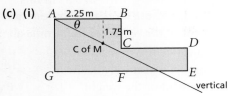

(ii) $\theta = \tan^{-1}\frac{1.75}{2.25} = 38°$ to the nearest degree

Exercise E (p 40)

1 (a) G is the point of intersection of the lines of symmetry of the framework.

(b)

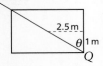

$\theta = \tan^{-1}\frac{2.5}{1} = 68.198... = 68°$ to the nearest degree

2 (a) (i) $1.5\,\text{m}$ **(ii)** $1\,\text{m}$

(b) $56.3°$ (to 3 s.f.)

(c) $71.6°$ (to 3 s.f.)

3 (a)

	Area	Distance from AB	Distance from AF
$ABCG$	$6\,\text{m}^2$	$0.5\,\text{m}$	$3\,\text{m}$
$DEFG$	$2\,\text{m}^2$	$1.5\,\text{m}$	$1\,\text{m}$
Lamina	$8\,\text{m}^2$	$\bar{y}\,\text{m}$	$\bar{x}\,\text{m}$

$8\bar{y} = 6 \times 0.5 + 2 \times 1.5 \implies 8\bar{y} = 6$
$\implies \bar{y} = 0.75$

(b) $2.5\,\text{m}$ **(c)** $77.9°$ (to 3 s.f.)

4 (a) (i) $1.5\,\text{m}$ **(ii)** $3.125\,\text{m}$

(b) $64.4°$ (to 3 s.f.)

5 (a) (i) $0.1875\,\text{m}$ **(ii)** $0.1\,\text{m}$

(b) $58.0°$ (to 3 s.f.)

6 (a) $3.5\,\text{m}$ **(b)** $1.78\,\text{m}$ (to 3 s.f.)

7 3

Mixed questions (p 42)

1 (a) $2.2\,\text{m}$

(b) $176\,\text{N}$ at A, $216\,\text{N}$ at B (both to 3 s.f.)

2 (a) $5\,\text{cm}$

(b) Using $M\bar{x} = \sum mx$,
$(2m + 1)\bar{x} = m \times 6 + m \times 6 + 1 \times 3$
$\implies (2m + 1)\bar{x} = 12m + 3 \implies \bar{x} = \frac{12m + 3}{2m + 1}$

(c) 1

Test yourself (p 43)

1 (a) Using $M\bar{y} = \sum my$,
$(1 + 3 + m) \times 3 = 1 \times 3 + 3 \times 1 + m \times 6$
$\implies 12 + 3m = 6 + 6m \implies m = 2$

(b) 5

2 (a) AP is a line of symmetry.

(b) $7.75\,\text{cm}$ **(c)** $32°$

3 (a) (i) $28.4\,\text{cm}$ (to 3 s.f.)

     (ii) $41.3\,\text{cm}$ (to 3 s.f.)

(b) $28.4\,\text{cm}$

(c) $24.8\,\text{cm}$

3 Variable acceleration

A Motion in one dimension

Exercise A (p 46)

1 $v = 12t^3 - 2t, \quad a = 36t^2 - 2$

2 (a) $v = 3e^{3t} + 2e^{2t}$
$a = 9e^{3t} + 4e^{2t}$

(b) $v = 3\cos 3t - 2\sin 2t$
$a = -9\sin 3t - 4\cos 2t$

3 (a) $0.25t^2 + 0.5t^3 + c$

(b) (i) $c = 1$
$x = 0.25t^2 + 0.5t^3 + 1$

(ii) 6

4 (a) $2\cos 2t + \frac{3}{2}e^{\frac{1}{2}t}$

(b) (i) $-\frac{1}{2}\cos 2t + 6e^{\frac{1}{2}t} + c$

(ii) $c = -5\frac{1}{2}$
$x = -\frac{1}{2}\cos 2t + 6e^{\frac{1}{2}t} - 5\frac{1}{2}$

5 (a) (i) $6t^2 - 6$ **(ii)** $\frac{1}{2}t^4 - 3t^2$
(iii) $13\frac{1}{2}$

(b) (i) $4t^3 - 6t$ **(ii)** $\frac{1}{5}t^5 - t^3$
(iii) $21\frac{3}{5}$

(c) (i) $-12e^{-3t}$ **(ii)** $\frac{4}{3}(1 - e^{-3t})$
(iii) 1.33 (to 3 s.f.)

(d) (i) $-6\sin 2t$ **(ii)** $\frac{3}{2}\sin 2t$
(iii) -0.419 (to 3 s.f.)

(e) (i) $\frac{\pi}{2}\cos\frac{\pi t}{2}$ **(ii)** $\frac{2}{\pi}\left(1 - \cos\frac{\pi t}{2}\right)$
(iii) $\frac{2}{\pi}$

(f) (i) $-\pi\sin\frac{\pi t}{4}$ **(ii)** $\frac{16}{\pi}\sin\frac{\pi t}{4}$
(iii) $\frac{8\sqrt{2}}{\pi} = 3.60$ (to 3 s.f.)

6 (a) (i) $2t + 6\cos 3t$ **(ii)** $2 - 18\sin 3t$

(b) $\sin 3t = \frac{1}{9}$
$\Rightarrow t = \frac{1}{3}\sin^{-1}\frac{1}{9}$
$\Rightarrow t = 0.0371$

(c) $2 - 18\sin 3t = 11$
$\Rightarrow \sin 3t = -\frac{1}{2}$
$\Rightarrow 3t = \frac{7\pi}{6}$
$\Rightarrow t = \frac{7\pi}{18}$

7 (a) (i) $3t + \frac{4}{3}\sqrt{t^3} + 4$
(ii) $\frac{3}{2}t^2 + \frac{8}{15}\sqrt{t^5} + 4t$

(b) Speed $= 13.8 \, \text{m s}^{-1}$ (to 3 s.f.)
Position $= 17.0 \, \text{m}$ (to 3 s.f.)

8 (a)

(b) 6

(c) $v = \frac{5\pi}{6}\cos\frac{\pi t}{6}$

(d) (i) $\frac{5\pi}{6}$ **(ii)** 0 **(iii)** $-\frac{5\pi}{6}$

(e) The point P oscillates between positions -5 and 5. The period of the oscillation is 12. When $t = 0$, the point is at $x = 0$ where it has maximum speed.

9 (a) $p = -\frac{5}{2}, \quad q = 7$

(b) $x = -\frac{5}{6}t^3 + \frac{7}{2}t^2 - \frac{7}{3} \Rightarrow x = \frac{1}{3}$ when $t = 4$

10 (a) $p = 5, \quad q = -\frac{3}{\pi}$

(b) $x = \frac{5}{\pi}(1 - \cos\pi t) + \frac{3}{2\pi^2}(\cos 2\pi t - 1)$
$\Rightarrow x = \frac{10}{\pi} = 3.18$ (to 3 s.f.) when $t = 1$

B Motion in two dimensions 1 (p 48)

B1 When $t = 1$, $\frac{1}{2}t^2 = 0.5$ and $10\sin\frac{1}{2}t = 4.79$ (to 3 s.f.)
So $\mathbf{r} = 0.5\mathbf{i} + 4.79\mathbf{j}$
$t = 2$, $\mathbf{r} = 2\mathbf{i} + 8.41\mathbf{j}$
$t = 3$, $\mathbf{r} = 4.5\mathbf{i} + 9.97\mathbf{j}$
$t = 4$, $\mathbf{r} = 8\mathbf{i} + 9.09\mathbf{j}$
$t = 5$, $\mathbf{r} = 12.5\mathbf{i} + 5.98\mathbf{j}$

B2

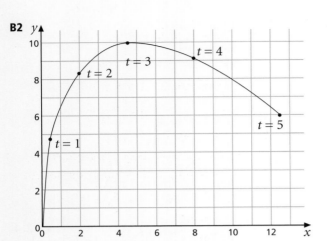

B3 When $t = 0$, $5\cos\frac{1}{2}t = 5\cos 0 = 5$
So $\mathbf{v} = 0\mathbf{i} + 5\mathbf{j} = 5\mathbf{j}$
$t = 1$, $\mathbf{v} = 1\mathbf{i} + 4.39\mathbf{j}$
$t = 2$, $\mathbf{v} = 2\mathbf{i} + 2.70\mathbf{j}$
$t = 3$, $\mathbf{v} = 3\mathbf{i} + 0.35\mathbf{j}$
$t = 4$, $\mathbf{v} = 4\mathbf{i} - 2.08\mathbf{j}$
$t = 5$, $\mathbf{v} = 5\mathbf{i} - 4.01\mathbf{j}$

B4 $t = 0$, $\mathbf{a} = \mathbf{i}$
$t = 1$, $\mathbf{a} = \mathbf{i} - 1.20\mathbf{j}$
$t = 2$, $\mathbf{a} = \mathbf{i} - 2.10\mathbf{j}$
$t = 3$, $\mathbf{a} = \mathbf{i} - 2.49\mathbf{j}$
$t = 4$, $\mathbf{a} = \mathbf{i} - 2.27\mathbf{j}$
$t = 5$, $\mathbf{a} = \mathbf{i} - 1.50\mathbf{j}$

B5 3.14

B6 (a)

t	t^2	$\cos\frac{1}{3}\pi t$	$4(1 + \cos\frac{1}{3}\pi t)$	$\mathbf{r}$
0	0	1	8	$8\mathbf{j}$
1	1	0.5	6	$1\mathbf{i} + 6\mathbf{j}$
2	4	−0.5	2	$4\mathbf{i} + 2\mathbf{j}$
3	9	−1	0	$9\mathbf{i} + 0\mathbf{j}$
4	16	−0.5	2	$16\mathbf{i} + 2\mathbf{j}$

(b) $\mathbf{v} = 2t\mathbf{i} - \frac{4}{3}\pi\sin\frac{1}{3}\pi t\mathbf{j}$

(c) $t = 0$, $\mathbf{v} = 0\mathbf{i} + 0\mathbf{j}$
$t = 1$, $\mathbf{v} = 2\mathbf{i} - 3.63\mathbf{j}$
$t = 2$, $\mathbf{v} = 4\mathbf{i} - 3.63\mathbf{j}$
$t = 3$, $\mathbf{v} = 6\mathbf{i} + 0\mathbf{j}$
$t = 4$, $\mathbf{v} = 8\mathbf{i} + 3.63\mathbf{j}$
The results at $t = 1, 2, 3, 4, 5$ are reasonable because they are tangent vectors.

(d) The component in the $\mathbf{j}$-direction is 0 so the object is moving in the $\mathbf{i}$-direction.

(e) $\mathbf{a} = 2\mathbf{i} - \frac{4}{9}\pi^2\cos\frac{1}{3}\pi t\mathbf{j}$

(f) $t = 0$, $\mathbf{a} = 2\mathbf{i} - 4.39\mathbf{j}$
$t = 1$, $\mathbf{a} = 2\mathbf{i} - 2.19\mathbf{j}$
$t = 2$, $\mathbf{a} = 2\mathbf{i} + 2.19\mathbf{j}$
$t = 3$, $\mathbf{a} = 2\mathbf{i} + 4.39\mathbf{j}$
$t = 4$, $\mathbf{a} = 2\mathbf{i} + 2.19\mathbf{j}$
The acceleration moves the object away from rest and gives it a curved path.

B7 (a) $\mathbf{v} = 10t\mathbf{i} + 4\mathbf{j}$
$\mathbf{a} = 10\mathbf{i}$

(b) $\mathbf{v} = (4t - 3)\mathbf{i} + 12t^2\mathbf{j}$
$\mathbf{a} = 4\mathbf{i} + 24t\mathbf{j}$

(c) $\mathbf{v} = 5e^t\mathbf{i} + 2t\mathbf{j}$
$\mathbf{a} = 5e^t\mathbf{i} + 2\mathbf{j}$

(d) $\mathbf{v} = 2e^{2t}\mathbf{i} + 3e^{3t}\mathbf{j}$
$\mathbf{a} = 4e^{2t}\mathbf{i} + 9e^{3t}\mathbf{j}$

(e) $\mathbf{v} = \cos t\mathbf{i} + 2\cos 2t\mathbf{j}$
$\mathbf{a} = -\sin t\mathbf{i} - 4\sin 2t\mathbf{j}$

(f) $\mathbf{v} = -\frac{1}{2}\pi\sin\frac{1}{2}\pi t\mathbf{i} + \frac{1}{3}\pi\cos\frac{1}{3}\pi t\mathbf{j}$
$\mathbf{a} = -\frac{1}{4}\pi^2\cos\frac{1}{2}\pi t\mathbf{i} - \frac{1}{9}\pi^2\sin\frac{1}{3}\pi t\mathbf{j}$

B8 (a) $8\mathbf{i} + 3\mathbf{j}$

(b) $v = |\mathbf{v}| = \sqrt{8^2 + 3^2} = 8.5440...$
Speed $= 8.54\,\text{m s}^{-1}$ (to 3 s.f.)

(c) Angle $= \tan^{-1}\frac{3}{8} = 0.359$ (to 3 s.f.)

(d) $3\mathbf{i} + 2t\mathbf{j}$

(e) When $t = 2$, $\mathbf{a} = 3\mathbf{i} + 4\mathbf{j}$
$a = |\mathbf{a}| = \sqrt{3^2 + 4^2} = 5$
Acceleration $= 5\,\text{m s}^{-2}$

(f) Angle $= \tan^{-1}\frac{4}{3} = 0.927$ (to 3 s.f.)

Exercise B (p 52)

1 (a) $(5 - 2t)\mathbf{i} + 3t^2\mathbf{j}$

(b) $\sqrt{1^2 + 12^2} = 12.04...$
Speed $= 12.0\,\text{m s}^{-1}$ (to 3 s.f.)

(c) $-2\mathbf{i} + 6t\mathbf{j}$

(d) $\sqrt{(-2)^2 + 12^2} = 12.16...$
Acceleration $= 12.2\,\text{m s}^{-2}$ (to 3 s.f.)

2 (a) $(1 + 3t^2)\mathbf{i} - 8t\mathbf{j}$

(b) $36.9\,\text{m s}^{-2}$ (to 3 s.f.)

3 (a) $32t\mathbf{i} + (3t^2 - 48)\mathbf{j}$

(b) $3t^2 - 48 = 0 \Rightarrow t = 4\,\text{s}$

(c) $32t = -(3t^2 - 48) \Rightarrow 3t^2 + 32t - 48 = 0$
$\Rightarrow (3t - 4)(t + 12) = 0 \Rightarrow t = \frac{4}{3}\,\text{s}$

4 (a) $(3t^2 - 14t)\mathbf{i} + (2t - 6)\mathbf{j}$

(b) $2t - 6 = 0 \Rightarrow t = 3$

(c) $15\,\text{m s}^{-1}$

(d) The **i**-component of $\mathbf{v} = 0$
So $3t^2 - 14t = 0 \Rightarrow t(3t - 14) = 0$
$\Rightarrow t = 0$ or $4\frac{2}{3}$

(e) At $t = 0$, speed $= 6\,\text{m s}^{-1}$
At $t = 4\frac{2}{3}$, speed $= 3\frac{1}{3}\,\text{m s}^{-1}$

5 (a) $\left(\frac{1}{4}e^t - 1\right)\mathbf{i} + \left(\frac{1}{2}e^{\frac{1}{2}t} - 3\right)\mathbf{j}$

(b) When $t = \ln 4$, horizontal component of $\mathbf{v}$
$= \frac{1}{4}e^{\ln 4} - 1 = \frac{1}{4}(4) - 1 = 0$
As the horizontal component of $\mathbf{v}$ is 0, the velocity is vertical.

(c) $\frac{1}{2}e^{\frac{1}{2}t} - 3 = 0 \Rightarrow e^{\frac{1}{2}t} = 6 \Rightarrow \frac{1}{2}t = \ln 6$
$\Rightarrow t = 2\ln 6$

6 (a) $5\cos 5t\,\mathbf{i} + 4\mathbf{j}$

(b) If $\cos 5t = 0.8$ then $v = 5\times0.8\mathbf{i} + 4\mathbf{j} = 4\mathbf{i} + 4\mathbf{j}$
$= 4(\mathbf{i} + \mathbf{j})$, which is in the direction $\mathbf{i} + \mathbf{j}$

(c) (i) 0.129 (to 3 s.f.)

(ii) Acceleration $= -25\sin 5t\,\mathbf{i}$
Magnitude of acceleration $= 15\,\text{m s}^{-2}$

7 (a) $\frac{1}{3}\cos\frac{t}{30}\mathbf{i} + \frac{1}{3}\cos\frac{t}{45}\mathbf{j}$

(b) $0.430\,\text{m s}^{-1}$

(c) (i) $47\,\text{s}$

(ii) $0.167\,\text{m s}^{-1}$

(iii) $16.4\,\text{m}$

(iv) Acceleration $= -\frac{1}{90}\sin\frac{t}{30}\mathbf{i} - \frac{1}{135}\sin\frac{t}{45}\mathbf{j}$
Magnitude of acceleration $= 0.0128\,\text{m s}^{-2}$

8 (a) $\frac{5\sqrt{2}}{2} = 3.54\,\text{m}$ (to 3 s.f.)

(b) $\mathbf{v} = -3\pi\sin\pi t\,\mathbf{i} + 4\pi\cos\pi t\,\mathbf{j}$

(c) $\frac{5\sqrt{2}}{2}\pi = 11.1\,\text{m s}^{-1}$ (to 3 s.f.)

(d) (i) $\frac{5\sqrt{2}}{2}\pi^2 = 34.9\,\text{m s}^{-2}$ (to 3 s.f.)

(ii) $4\pi^2 = 39.5\,\text{m s}^{-2}$ (to 3 s.f.)

(iii) $3\pi^2 = 29.6\,\text{m s}^{-2}$ (to 3 s.f.)

9 (a) $5\,\text{m s}^{-1}$ **(b)** $7.21\,\text{m s}^{-2}$

10 (a) $2e^{0.5t}\mathbf{i} + 4.8e^{0.2t}\mathbf{j}$

(b) If the particle is moving in the direction $\mathbf{i} + \mathbf{j}$ then the **i**-component = the **j**-component
$\Rightarrow 2e^{0.5T} = 4.8e^{0.2T} \Rightarrow \frac{e^{0.5T}}{e^{0.2T}} = 2.4$
$\Rightarrow e^{0.3T} = 2.4$
$\Rightarrow T = \frac{\ln 2.4}{0.3} = 2.92$ (to 3 s.f.)

11 (a) $\mathbf{v} = 2Ae^{2t}\mathbf{i} + 3Be^{3t}\mathbf{j}$ gives $20^2 = 4A^2 + 9B^2$
$\mathbf{a} = 4Ae^{2t}\mathbf{i} + 9Be^{3t}\mathbf{j}$ gives $50^2 = 16A^2 + 81B^2$
Solving gives $A^2 = 55$ and $B^2 = 20$
$\Rightarrow A = 7.42$ (to 3 s.f.) and $B = 4.47$ (to 3 s.f.)

(b) $5\sqrt{3} = 8.66$ (to 3 s.f.)

12 (a) Velocity $= \dfrac{d\mathbf{r}}{dt}$
$= (2\pi - 2\pi\cos 2\pi t)\mathbf{i} + (0 + 2\pi\sin 2\pi t)\mathbf{j}$
$= 2\pi(1 - \cos 2\pi t)\mathbf{i} + 2\pi\sin 2\pi t\,\mathbf{j}$
Speed $= \sqrt{(2\pi(1 - \cos 2\pi t))^2 + (2\pi\sin 2\pi t)^2}$
$= \sqrt{4\pi^2(1 - 2\cos 2\pi t + \cos^2 2\pi t + \sin^2 2\pi t)}$
$= 2\pi\sqrt{2 - 2\cos 2\pi t}$
$= 2\pi\sqrt{4\sin^2 \pi t} = 4\pi\sin\pi t$

(b) Highest position is when the **j**-component $= 2$
So $1 - \cos 2\pi t = 2 \Rightarrow \cos 2\pi t = -1 \Rightarrow t = \frac{1}{2}$
(the first time). When $t = \frac{1}{2}$, speed $= 4\pi\,\text{m s}^{-1}$

C Motion in two dimensions 2 (p 55)

C1 $\mathbf{r} = \int \mathbf{v}\,dt = \int (6t^2\mathbf{i} + (4t - 3)\mathbf{j})\,dt$
$= 2t^3\mathbf{i} + (2t^2 - 3t)\mathbf{j} + \mathbf{c}$
When $t = 0$, $\mathbf{r} = 2\times0^3\mathbf{i} + (2\times0^2 - 3\times0)\mathbf{j} + \mathbf{c} = \mathbf{c}$
so $\mathbf{c} = \mathbf{i} + \mathbf{j}$
so $\mathbf{r} = (2t^3 + 1)\mathbf{i} + (2t^2 - 3t + 1)\mathbf{j}$

C2 $\mathbf{r} = \int \mathbf{v}\,dt = \int (e^{3t}\mathbf{i} + \sin 2t\,\mathbf{j})\,dt$
$= \frac{1}{3}e^{3t}\mathbf{i} - \frac{1}{2}\cos 2t\,\mathbf{j} + \mathbf{c}$
When $t = 0$, $\mathbf{r} = \mathbf{0}$ so $\frac{1}{3}e^0\mathbf{i} - \frac{1}{2}\cos 0\,\mathbf{j} + \mathbf{c} = 0$
$\Rightarrow \mathbf{c} = -\frac{1}{3}\mathbf{i} + \frac{1}{2}\mathbf{j}$ so $\mathbf{r} = \frac{1}{3}e^{3t}\mathbf{i} - \frac{1}{2}\cos 2t\,\mathbf{j} - \frac{1}{3}\mathbf{i} + \frac{1}{2}\mathbf{j}$
$= \frac{1}{3}(e^{3t} - 1)\mathbf{i} - \frac{1}{2}(\cos 2t - 1)\mathbf{j}$

C3 $\mathbf{v} = \int \mathbf{a}\,dt = \int (3(t^2-4)\mathbf{i} + (t+2)\mathbf{j})\,dt$
$= 3\left(\tfrac{1}{3}t^3 - 4t\right)\mathbf{i} + \left(\tfrac{1}{2}t^2 + 2t\right)\mathbf{j} + \mathbf{c}$
When $t = 0$, $\mathbf{v} = 0\mathbf{i} + 0\mathbf{j} + \mathbf{c} = 2\mathbf{i} - \mathbf{j} \Rightarrow \mathbf{c} = 2\mathbf{i} - \mathbf{j}$
so $\mathbf{v} = 3\left(\tfrac{1}{3}t^3 - 4t\right)\mathbf{i} + \left(\tfrac{1}{2}t^2 + 2t\right)\mathbf{j} + 2\mathbf{i} - \mathbf{j}$
$\Rightarrow \mathbf{v} = (t^3 - 12t + 2)\mathbf{i} + \left(\tfrac{1}{2}t^2 + 2t - 1\right)\mathbf{j}$

Exercise C (p 56)

1 $(4t^2 - 2t^3)\mathbf{i} + (2t^2 + t^3)\mathbf{j}$

2 $\left(2 + 2t + \tfrac{5}{2}t^2\right)\mathbf{i} + \left(2t^2 + \tfrac{1}{3}t^3\right)\mathbf{j}$

3 (a) $\left(\tfrac{1}{2}t^2 - t\right)\mathbf{i} + \left(\tfrac{1}{4}t^4 - \tfrac{1}{2}t^2 + 5\right)\mathbf{j}$
   (b) $\left(\tfrac{1}{6}t^3 - \tfrac{1}{2}t^2\right)\mathbf{i} + \left(\tfrac{1}{20}t^5 - \tfrac{1}{6}t^3 + 5t\right)\mathbf{j}$

4 $6\sin\tfrac{1}{2}t\,\mathbf{i} + 4\left(1 - \cos\tfrac{1}{2}t\right)\mathbf{j}$

5 (a) $\mathbf{v} = (3t^3 + 2t + 1)\mathbf{i} + (4t^3 - t + 1)\mathbf{j}$
   $\mathbf{r} = \left(\tfrac{3}{4}t^4 + t^2 + t\right)\mathbf{i} + \left(t^4 - \tfrac{1}{2}t^2 + t\right)\mathbf{j}$
   (b) $\mathbf{v} = \tfrac{3}{4}\sin 4t\,\mathbf{i} + (7 - \cos 2t)\mathbf{j}$
   $\mathbf{r} = \tfrac{3}{16}(1 - \cos 4t)\mathbf{i} + \left(7t - \tfrac{1}{2}\sin 2t\right)\mathbf{j}$
   (c) $\mathbf{v} = (1 - e^{-t})\mathbf{i} + \tfrac{1}{2}(2t - 1 + e^{-2t})\mathbf{j}$
   $\mathbf{r} = (t - 1 + e^{-t})\mathbf{i} + \tfrac{1}{4}(2t^2 - 2t + 1 - e^{-2t})\mathbf{j}$
   (d) $\mathbf{v} = 12\sin\tfrac{1}{6}t\,\mathbf{i} + 12\left(1 - \cos\tfrac{1}{6}t\right)\mathbf{j}$
   $\mathbf{r} = 72\left(1 - \cos\tfrac{1}{6}t\right)\mathbf{i} + 12\left(t - 6\sin\tfrac{1}{6}t\right)\mathbf{j}$

6 (a) $0, 3$ (b) $(3 - 2t)\mathbf{i} + 24t^2\mathbf{j}$
   (c) $\left(\tfrac{3}{2}t^2 - \tfrac{1}{3}t^3\right)\mathbf{i} + 2t^4\mathbf{j}$

D Motion in three dimensions (p 57)

D1 (a) $\mathbf{a} = \dfrac{d\mathbf{v}}{dt} = 4\mathbf{i} + (6t + 8)\mathbf{j} - 2\mathbf{k}$
   (b) $\mathbf{r} = \int \mathbf{v}\,dt = (2t^2 - 5t)\mathbf{i} + (t^3 + 4t^2)\mathbf{j} + (7t - t^2)\mathbf{k} + \mathbf{c}$
   When $t = 0$, $\mathbf{r} = 0\mathbf{i} + 0\mathbf{j} + 0\mathbf{k} + \mathbf{c} = 5\mathbf{i}$
   $\Rightarrow \mathbf{r} = (2t^2 - 5t + 5)\mathbf{i} + (t^3 + 4t^2)\mathbf{j} + (7t - t^2)\mathbf{k}$

Exercise D (p 58)

1 (a) $2t\mathbf{i} + 8t\mathbf{j} + (3t^2 - 2t)\mathbf{k}$
   (b) $3t^2 - 2t = 0 \Rightarrow$ time is $0\,\text{s}$ or $\tfrac{2}{3}\,\text{s}$
   (c) When $t = 2$, $\mathbf{v} = 4\mathbf{i} + 16\mathbf{j} + 8\mathbf{k}$
   $|\mathbf{v}| = \sqrt{4^2 + 16^2 + 8^2} = 18.330\ldots$
   Speed $= 18.3\,\text{m s}^{-1}$ (to 3 s.f.)
   (d) $2\mathbf{i} + 8\mathbf{j} + (6t - 2)\mathbf{k}$
   (e) $t = \tfrac{1}{3}$
   (f) When $t = 0$, $\mathbf{a} = 2\mathbf{i} + 8\mathbf{j} - 2\mathbf{k}$
   $|\mathbf{a}| = \sqrt{2^2 + 8^2 + (-2)^2} = 8.485\ldots$
   $a = 8.49\,\text{m s}^{-2}$ (to 3 s.f.)

2 (a) $\cos\tfrac{1}{4}\pi t = 0 \Rightarrow t = 2\,\text{s}$
   (b) $\mathbf{v} = 8\mathbf{i} + 6\mathbf{j} \Rightarrow$ speed $= 10\,\text{m s}^{-1}$
   (c) $t = 6 \Rightarrow \mathbf{v} = 24\mathbf{i} + 18\mathbf{j} \Rightarrow$ speed $= 30\,\text{m s}^{-1}$
   (d) $\mathbf{a} = 4\mathbf{i} + 3\mathbf{j} - \tfrac{1}{4}\pi\sin\tfrac{1}{4}\pi t\,\mathbf{k}$
   (e) $\mathbf{r} = 2t^2\mathbf{i} + \tfrac{3}{2}t^2\mathbf{j} + \dfrac{4}{\pi}\sin\tfrac{1}{4}\pi t\,\mathbf{k}$

3 (a) It increases rapidly initially and then levels out as the height approaches $20\,\text{m}$. It never quite reaches $20\,\text{m}$.
   (b) The horizontal distance is given by the $\mathbf{i}$-component and the $\mathbf{j}$-component of $\mathbf{r}$. Horizontal distance
   $= \sqrt{(50\cos 0.1t)^2 + (50\sin 0.1t)^2}$
   $= \sqrt{2500(\cos^2 0.1t + \sin^2 0.1t)}$
   $= \sqrt{2500}$
   $= 50$
   So the horizontal distance is constant. The aircraft spirals around the surface of an imaginary vertical cylinder as it rises.
   (c) $-5\sin 0.1t\,\mathbf{i} + 5\cos 0.1t\,\mathbf{j} + 5e^{-0.5t}\mathbf{k}$
   (d) $v = |\mathbf{v}|$
   $= \sqrt{(-5\sin 0.1t)^2 + (5\cos 0.1t)^2 + (5e^{-0.5t})^2}$
   $= \sqrt{25(\sin^2 0.1t + \cos^2 0.1t) + 25e^{-t}}$
   $= \sqrt{25(1 + e^{-t})}$
   So speed $= 5\sqrt{1 + e^{-t}}\,\text{m s}^{-1}$
   (e) The speed decreases and gets closer to $5\,\text{m s}^{-1}$.
   (f) $\mathbf{a} = -0.5\cos 0.1t\,\mathbf{i} - 0.5\sin 0.1t\,\mathbf{j} - 2.5e^{-0.5t}\mathbf{k}$
   (g) $a = |\mathbf{a}| = 0.5\sqrt{1 + 25e^{-t}}$
   When $t = 0$, acceleration $= 2.55\,\text{m s}^{-2}$
   (h) As t increases, $25e^{-t}$ approaches 0
   $\Rightarrow 1 + 25e^{-t}$ becomes closer and closer to 1
   $\Rightarrow 0.5\sqrt{1 + 25e^{-t}}$ becomes closer and closer to $0.5\,\text{m s}^{-2}$

E Using Newton's laws in one dimension (p 59)

E1 (a) $6t - 6t^2$
   (b) $6 - 12t$
   (c) $F = m(6 - 12t) = 2.5(6 - 12t) = 15 - 30t$
   (d) $F = -45 \Rightarrow |F| = 45\,\text{N}$
   (e) $2.5(6 - 12t) = 0 \Rightarrow t = 0.5\,\text{s}$

E2 (a) N2L: $F = ma \Rightarrow 6\sqrt{t} - 2 = 0.4a$

$\Rightarrow a = 15\sqrt{t} - 5$

(b) $15\sqrt{t} - 5 = 0 \Rightarrow \sqrt{t} = \frac{1}{3} \Rightarrow t = \frac{1}{9}$

(c) $v = \int a \, dt = \int (15\sqrt{t} - 5) \, dt = 10t^{\frac{3}{2}} - 5t + c$

$v = 0$ when $t = 0 \Rightarrow c = 0$

so $v = 10t^{\frac{3}{2}} - 5t$

(d) Displacement $= \int v \, dt = \int (10t^{\frac{3}{2}} - 5t) \, dt$

$= 4t^{\frac{5}{2}} - \frac{5}{2}t^2 + c$

Displacement $= 0$ when $t = 0 \Rightarrow c = 0$

So displacement $= 4t^{\frac{5}{2}} - \frac{5}{2}t^2$

(e) Particle at rest when $10t^{\frac{3}{2}} - 5t = 0$

$\Rightarrow 5t(2t^{\frac{1}{2}} - 1) = 0$

$\Rightarrow t^{\frac{1}{2}} = \frac{1}{2}$ (or $t = 0$)

$\Rightarrow t = \frac{1}{4}$

(f) When $t = 0$, $F = -2\,\text{N}$

When $t = 4$, $F = 1\,\text{N}$

Exercise E (p 60)

1 (a) $2t^2 - 6t$ **(b)** $\frac{2}{3}t^3 - 3t^2$ **(c)** $4.5\,\text{s}$

(d) $\frac{1}{6}t^4 - t^3$ **(e)** $6\,\text{s}$ **(f)** $36\,\text{m s}^{-1}$

2 (a) $\sin 0.2t$

(b) $0.2 \cos 0.2t$

(c) $0.06 \cos 0.2t$

(d) $0.2t = \frac{\pi}{2} \Rightarrow$ time $= 7.85\,\text{s}$

3 (a) $30 - 5kt$

(b) $30t - \frac{5}{2}kt^2$

(c) $15t^2 - \frac{5}{6}kt^3$

(d) (i) When $t = 4$, $x = 0 \Rightarrow 240 - \dfrac{160k}{3} = 0$

$\Rightarrow k = 4.5$

(ii) $v = 30t - \frac{45}{4}t^2$

When $t = 4$, velocity $= -60\,\text{m s}^{-1}$

4 (a) $6t + 3 - 12e^{-2t}$

(b) $6 + 24e^{-2t}$

(c) $F = 1.2(6 + 24e^{-2t})$

When $t = 0$, $F = 36\,\text{N}$

(d) The magnitude of the force decreases and gets closer and closer to $7.2\,\text{N}$.

5 (a) $30\sqrt{t}$ **(b)** $20t^{\frac{3}{2}} + 2$

(c) $2.25\,\text{s}$ **(d)** $8t^{\frac{5}{2}} + 2t$

(e) $65.25\,\text{m}$

6 (a) $0.1 - 0.05e^{0.1t}$ **(b)** $4 - 2e^{0.1t}$

(c) $10 \ln 2$

7 Acceleration $= \dfrac{d^2x}{dt^2} = -6 - 3t$

Force $= 0.05(-6 - 3t) = -0.3 - 0.15t$

Magnitude $= |-0.3 - 0.15t|$

F Using Newton's laws in two or three dimensions (p 62)

F1 (a) $(10t - 2)\mathbf{i} + 6t^2\mathbf{j} + 10\mathbf{k}$

(b) N2L: $\mathbf{F} = m\mathbf{a} \Rightarrow \mathbf{F} = 3((10t - 2)\mathbf{i} + 6t^2\mathbf{j} + 10\mathbf{k})$

$= (30t - 6)\mathbf{i} + 18t^2\mathbf{j} + 30\mathbf{k}$

$= 6(5t - 1)\mathbf{i} + 18t^2\mathbf{j} + 30\mathbf{k}$

(c) When $t = 1$, $\mathbf{F} = 6(5(1) - 1)\mathbf{i} + 18(1)^2\mathbf{j} + 30\mathbf{k}$

$= 24\mathbf{i} + 18\mathbf{j} + 30\mathbf{k}$

$|\mathbf{F}| = \sqrt{24^2 + 18^2 + 30^2} = \sqrt{1800}$

$= \sqrt{900 \times 2} = 30\sqrt{2}$

F2 (a) N2L: $\mathbf{F} = m\mathbf{a} \Rightarrow 15t^2\mathbf{i} = 2.5\mathbf{a}$

$\Rightarrow \mathbf{a} = 6t^2\mathbf{i}$

(b) $\mathbf{v} = \int 6t^2\mathbf{i} \, dt = 2t^3\mathbf{i} + \mathbf{c}$

(c) When $t = 0$, $\mathbf{v} = 2(0)^3\mathbf{i} + \mathbf{c} = \mathbf{c}$

Also, when $t = 0$, $\mathbf{v} = 3\mathbf{i} - 2\mathbf{j} \Rightarrow \mathbf{c} = 3\mathbf{i} - 2\mathbf{j}$

So $\mathbf{v} = 2t^3\mathbf{i} + 3\mathbf{i} - 2\mathbf{j} = (2t^3 + 3)\mathbf{i} - 2\mathbf{j}$

(d) $\mathbf{r} = \int \mathbf{v} \, dt = (\frac{1}{2}t^4 + 3t)\mathbf{i} - 2t\mathbf{j} + \mathbf{c}$

When $t = 0$, $\mathbf{r} = \mathbf{0} \Rightarrow \mathbf{c} = \mathbf{0}$

$\Rightarrow \mathbf{r} = (\frac{1}{2}t^4 + 3t)\mathbf{i} - 2t\mathbf{j}$

(e) When $t = 2$, $\mathbf{r} = 14\mathbf{i} - 4\mathbf{j}$

Distance from origin $= \sqrt{14^2 + (-4)^2} = 14.6\,\text{m}$

Exercise F (p 63)

1 $(1.6 - 2t)\mathbf{i} + 0.4(t - t^2)\mathbf{j}$

2 (a) $(10 - 2t)\mathbf{i} + 7\mathbf{j}$ **(b)** $(2 - 0.4t)\mathbf{i} + 1.4\mathbf{j}$

3 (a) $(2t^2 - 4)\mathbf{i} + (4t + 6)\mathbf{j}$

(b) $(\frac{2}{3}t^3 - 4t + 4)\mathbf{i} + (2t^2 + 6t)\mathbf{j}$

4 (a) $3t^2\mathbf{i} + (2t - 2)\mathbf{j} + 2t\mathbf{k}$

(b) $6t\mathbf{i} + 2\mathbf{j} + 2\mathbf{k}$

(c) $12t\mathbf{i} + 4\mathbf{j} + 4\mathbf{k}$

(d) $24.7\,\text{N}$ (to 3 s.f.)

5 (a) $5\mathbf{i} - 2\mathbf{j} + \frac{5}{2}\pi\cos\frac{1}{8}\pi t\,\mathbf{k}$

   (b) $0.5\mathbf{i} - 0.2\mathbf{j} + 0.25\pi\cos\frac{1}{8}\pi t\,\mathbf{k}$

   (c) $0.539\,\text{N}$ (to 3 s.f.)

6 (a) $\mathbf{F} = 1.2\cos 2t\,\mathbf{j} - 1.2\sin 2t\,\mathbf{k}$

   (b) $|\mathbf{F}| = \sqrt{(1.2\cos 2t)^2 + (-1.2\sin 2t)^2}$
   $= \sqrt{1.2^2(\cos^2 2t + \sin^2 2t)}$
   $= \sqrt{1.2^2}$
   $= 1.2$
   The magnitude is constant and has value $1.2\,\text{N}$.

7 (a) $4t\mathbf{i} + 6t^2\mathbf{j} + (8 - 4e^{0.2t})\mathbf{k}$

   (b) $5\ln 2$

   (c) $73.4\,\text{m s}^{-1}$

Mixed questions (p 64)

1 (a) $4 - 2e^{-t}$

   (b) $2e^{-t}$

   (c) The acceleration decreases and gets closer and closer to zero.

2 (a) $(3t^2 - 6t)\mathbf{i} + (4 + 4t)\mathbf{j}$

   (b) $\sqrt{(6t-6)^2 + 4^2}$

   (c) Minimum when $t = 1$, $4\,\text{m s}^{-2}$

3 (a) $-4\sin t\mathbf{i} + \left(\frac{7}{2} - 3\cos t\right)\mathbf{j} + \frac{1}{2}t\mathbf{k}$

   (b) $4\cos t\mathbf{i} + \left(\frac{7}{2}t - 3\sin t\right)\mathbf{j} + \frac{1}{4}t^2\mathbf{k}$

   (c) The position vector is $\left(\frac{7}{4}\pi - 3\right)\mathbf{j} + \frac{1}{16}\pi^2\mathbf{k}$ so the distance is $2.57\,\text{m}$.

4 (a) (i) 2 (ii) $8 - 2t$

   (b) $8t - t^2 - 14$

5 (a) $0.8t\mathbf{i} + 0.8t^2\mathbf{j} + (t + 100e^{-0.01t} - 100)\mathbf{k}$

   (b) $0.4t^2\mathbf{i} + \frac{4}{15}t^3\mathbf{j} + \left(\frac{1}{2}t^2 - 10\,000e^{-0.01t} - 100t + 10\,000\right)\mathbf{k}$

6 (a) $-2\sin\dfrac{t}{20}\,\mathbf{i} + 4\cos\dfrac{t}{20}\,\mathbf{j}$

   (b) When $t = 0$, velocity $= 0\mathbf{i} + 4\mathbf{j}$
   The boat is travelling north as the component of the velocity in the east direction is zero.

   (c) Just after $t = 62.8\,\text{s}$

7 (a) $5(1 - \cos 4t)$ (b) $5t - \frac{5}{4}\sin 4t + \frac{4}{5}$

8 (a) (i) 75 (ii) $10\,\text{m s}^{-1}$ (iii) $0\,\text{m s}^{-2}$

   (b) When $t = 10$, velocity $= 10\,\text{m s}^{-1}$
   $v = \dfrac{ds}{dt} = h$ so $h = 10$
   When $t = 10$, displacement $s = ht - k = 75$
   Hence $100 - k = 75$ so $k = 25$

9 (a) $30e^{-2t}\mathbf{i} + (50e^{-2t} - 5)\mathbf{j}$

   (b) $54.1\,\text{m s}^{-1}$ (to 3 s.f.)

   (c) Horizontally

   (d) $\frac{1}{2}\ln 10 = 1.15\,\text{s}$ (to 3 s.f.)

   (e) $3\,\text{m s}^{-1}$

   (f) $16.7\,\text{m}$ (to 3 s.f.)

   (g) $-6\mathbf{i} - 10\mathbf{j}$

   (h) The ball returns to the ground when the vertical component of the position vector is zero.
   $25(1 - e^{-2T}) - 5T = 0$
   $\Rightarrow 1 - e^{-2T} = \dfrac{5T}{25} = \dfrac{1}{5}T$
   Horizontal distance travelled $= 15(1 - e^{-2T})$
   $\qquad\qquad\qquad\qquad\qquad = 15\left(\frac{1}{5}T\right)$
   $\qquad\qquad\qquad\qquad\qquad = 3T$
   So the distance travelled is $3T\,\text{m}$.

10 (a) $\left(12 - 6\cos\frac{1}{2}t\right)\mathbf{i} + 6\sin\frac{1}{2}t\mathbf{j} + t^2\mathbf{k}$

   (b) $\frac{3}{10}\cos\frac{1}{2}t\mathbf{i} - \frac{3}{10}\sin\frac{1}{2}t\mathbf{j} + \frac{4}{10}\mathbf{k}$

   (c) $|\mathbf{F}| = \sqrt{\left(\frac{3}{10}\cos\frac{1}{2}t\right)^2 + \left(-\frac{3}{10}\cos\frac{1}{2}t\right)^2 + \left(\frac{4}{10}\right)^2}$
   $= \sqrt{\frac{9}{100}\left(\cos^2\frac{1}{2}t + \sin^2\frac{1}{2}t\right) + \frac{16}{100}}$
   $= \sqrt{\frac{9}{100} + \frac{16}{100}} = \sqrt{\frac{25}{100}} = 0.5$
   The magnitude is constant and has value $0.5\,\text{N}$

Test yourself (p 67)

1 (a) $v = \int a\,dt = \int(2 - 2e^{-t})\,dt = 2t + 2e^{-t} + c$
   When $t = 0$, $v = 4$ so $2\times 0 + 2e^0 + c = 4$
   $\Rightarrow 2 + c = 4$
   $\Rightarrow c = 2$
   $\Rightarrow v = 2t + 2e^{-t} + 2$

   (b) $t^2 - 2e^{-t} + 2t + 2$

2 (a) The horizontal component starts at $70\,\text{m}\,\text{s}^{-1}$ and decreases, getting closer and closer to $0\,\text{m}\,\text{s}^{-1}$. The vertical component starts at $0\,\text{m}\,\text{s}^{-1}$ and decreases, getting closer and closer to $-40\,\text{m}\,\text{s}^{-1}$.

(b) $700(1 - e^{-0.1t})\mathbf{i} + 400(1 - e^{-0.1t} - 0.1t)\mathbf{j}$

3 (a) $\frac{1}{2}t\mathbf{i} - \frac{5}{2}\mathbf{j}$

(b) $\mathbf{v} = \int \mathbf{a}\,dt = \int\left(\frac{1}{2}t\mathbf{i} - \frac{5}{2}\mathbf{j}\right)dt = \int \frac{1}{2}t\mathbf{i}\,dt - \int \frac{5}{2}\mathbf{j}\,dt$

$= \dfrac{t^2}{4}\mathbf{i} - \dfrac{5t}{2}\mathbf{j} + \mathbf{c}$

When $t = 0$, $\mathbf{v} = 6\mathbf{j} \Rightarrow \dfrac{0^2}{4}\mathbf{i} - \dfrac{5\times 0}{2}\mathbf{j} + \mathbf{c} = 6\mathbf{j}$

$\Rightarrow \mathbf{c} = 6\mathbf{j}$

So $\mathbf{v} = \dfrac{t^2}{4}\mathbf{i} - \dfrac{5t}{2}\mathbf{j} + 6\mathbf{j} = \dfrac{t^2}{4}\mathbf{i} + \left(6 - \dfrac{5t}{2}\right)\mathbf{j}$

(c) $\dfrac{t^3}{12}\mathbf{i} + \left(6t - \dfrac{5t^2}{4}\right)\mathbf{j}$

4 Differential equations

A Forming and solving a differential equation
(p 68)

A1 (a) Using N2L,

$$-0.1v^3 = 0.4\frac{dv}{dt}$$

Separating the variables,

$$\frac{dv}{dt} = -\tfrac{1}{4}v^3$$

$$\Rightarrow \quad \frac{1}{v^3}\,dv = -\tfrac{1}{4}\,dt$$

Integrating both sides,

$$\int \frac{1}{v^3}\,dv = -\int \tfrac{1}{4}\,dt$$

$$\int v^{-3}\,dv = -\int \tfrac{1}{4}\,dt$$

$$-\tfrac{1}{2}v^{-2} = -\tfrac{1}{4}t + c$$

$$\Rightarrow \quad \frac{1}{2v^2} = \tfrac{1}{4}t - c$$

$v = 5$ when $t = 0$, so

$$\frac{1}{2(5)^2} = \tfrac{1}{4}(0) - c$$

$$\Rightarrow \quad c = -\tfrac{1}{50}$$

The equation becomes

$$\frac{1}{2v^2} = \tfrac{1}{4}t + \tfrac{1}{50}$$

$$\Rightarrow \quad \frac{50}{v^2} = 25t + 2$$

$$\Rightarrow \quad v^2 = \frac{50}{25t + 2}$$

(b) 0.498 (to 3 s.f.)   **(c)** 0.42

A2 (a)

$$-0.1v^4 = 0.4\frac{dv}{dt}$$

$$\frac{dv}{dt} = -\tfrac{1}{4}v^4$$

$$\Rightarrow \quad \frac{1}{v^4}\,dv = -\tfrac{1}{4}\,dt$$

Hence

$$\int \frac{1}{v^4}\,dv = -\int \tfrac{1}{4}\,dt$$

$$\int v^{-4}\,dv = -\int \tfrac{1}{4}\,dt$$

$$-\tfrac{1}{3}v^{-3} = -\tfrac{1}{4}t + c$$

$$\Rightarrow \quad \frac{1}{3v^3} = \tfrac{1}{4}t - c$$

$v = 5$ when $t = 0$, so

$$\frac{1}{3(5)^3} = \tfrac{1}{4}(0) - c$$

$$\Rightarrow \quad c = -\tfrac{1}{375}$$

The equation becomes

$$\frac{1}{3v^3} = \tfrac{1}{4}t + \tfrac{1}{375}$$

$$\Rightarrow \quad \frac{500}{v^3} = 375t + 4$$

$$\Rightarrow \quad v^3 = \frac{500}{375t + 4}$$

(b) 1.18 (to 3 s.f.)

(c) 0.156

A3

$$-0.1v^{\frac{1}{2}} = 0.4\frac{dv}{dt}$$

$$\frac{dv}{dt} = -\tfrac{1}{4}v^{\frac{1}{2}}$$

$$\Rightarrow \quad \frac{1}{v^{\frac{1}{2}}}\,dv = -\tfrac{1}{4}\,dt$$

Hence

$$\int \frac{1}{v^{\frac{1}{2}}}\,dv = -\int \tfrac{1}{4}\,dt$$

$$\int v^{-\frac{1}{2}}\,dv = -\int \tfrac{1}{4}\,dt$$

$$2v^{\frac{1}{2}} = -\tfrac{1}{4}t + c$$

$v = 5$ when $t = 0$, so

$$2(5)^{\frac{1}{2}} = -\tfrac{1}{4}(0) + c$$

$$\Rightarrow \quad c = 2(5)^{\frac{1}{2}}$$

The equation becomes

$$2v^{\frac{1}{2}} = -\tfrac{1}{4}t + 2(5)^{\frac{1}{2}}$$

$$\Rightarrow \quad v^{\frac{1}{2}} = -\tfrac{1}{8}t + 5^{\frac{1}{2}}$$

A4 As t increases, v decreases and gets closer and closer to 0.

A5 (a)

$$-kv^4 = m\frac{dv}{dt}$$

$$\Rightarrow \quad -m\frac{dv}{dt} = kv^4$$

$$\Rightarrow \quad -\frac{m}{v^4}\,dv = k\,dt$$

(b) $\int -\dfrac{m}{v^4}\,dv = \int k\,dt$

$$\Rightarrow \quad \frac{m}{3v^3} = kt + c$$

(c) $v = U$ when $t = 0$, so $c = \dfrac{m}{3U^3}$

(d) The equation becomes

$$\frac{m}{3v^3} = kt + \frac{m}{3U^3}$$

$$\Rightarrow \quad \frac{3mU^3}{3v^3} = 3ktU^3 + m$$

$$\Rightarrow \quad v^3 = \frac{mU^3}{3ktU^3 + m}$$

A6 As t increases, the displacement increases and gets closer and closer to 20 m.

Exercise A (p 72)

1

$$-60v^2 = 750\frac{dv}{dt}$$

$$\Rightarrow \quad \frac{1}{v^2}\,dv = -\tfrac{2}{25}\,dt$$

Hence

$$\int \frac{1}{v^2}\,dv = -\int \tfrac{2}{25}\,dt$$

$$\Rightarrow \quad -\frac{1}{v} = -\tfrac{2}{25}t + c$$

$$\Rightarrow \quad \frac{1}{v} = \tfrac{2}{25}t - c$$

$v = 8$ when $t = 0$, so

$$c = -\tfrac{1}{8}$$

The equation becomes

$$\frac{1}{v} = \tfrac{2}{25}t + \tfrac{1}{8}$$

$$\Rightarrow \quad \frac{200}{v} = 16t + 25$$

$$\Rightarrow \quad v = \frac{200}{16t + 25}$$

(b) 1.5625 s

2 (a)

$$-40v = 500\frac{dv}{dt}$$

$$\Rightarrow \quad \frac{1}{v}\,dv = -0.08\,dt$$

Hence

$$\int \frac{1}{v}\,dv = -\int 0.08\,dt$$

$$\ln v = -0.08t + c$$

$$\Rightarrow \quad v = e^{-0.08t + c} = Ae^{-0.08t}$$

where $A = e^c$

$v = 20$ when $t = 0$, so $\quad 20 = Ae^0$

$$\Rightarrow \quad A = 20$$

The equation becomes $\quad v = 20e^{-0.08t}$

(b) $x = \int v\,dt = \int 20e^{-0.08t}\,dt = -\dfrac{20}{0.08}e^{-0.08t} + c$

When $t = 0$, $x = 0$, so $\quad 0 = -\dfrac{20}{0.08}e^0 + c$

$$\Rightarrow \quad c = \tfrac{20}{0.08}$$

The equation becomes $\quad x = -\dfrac{20}{0.08}e^{-0.08t} + \dfrac{20}{0.08}$

$$= 250(1 - e^{-0.08t})$$

(c) As t increases, the speed decreases and gets closer and closer to $0\,\text{m s}^{-1}$. The distance increases and gets closer and closer to 250 m.

3 (a)

$$-kmv^3 = m\frac{dv}{dt}$$

$$\frac{1}{v^3}\,dv = -k\,dt$$

Hence
$$\int \frac{1}{v^3}\,dv = -\int k\,dt$$

$$\Rightarrow \int v^{-3}\,dv = -\int k\,dt$$

$$\Rightarrow -\frac{1}{2v^2} = -kt + c$$

$$\Rightarrow \frac{1}{2v^2} = kt - c$$

$v = U$ when $t = 0$, so
$$\frac{1}{2U^2} = k(0) - c$$

$$\Rightarrow c = -\frac{1}{2U^2}$$

The equation becomes
$$\frac{1}{2v^2} = kt + \frac{1}{2U^2}$$

$$\Rightarrow kt = \frac{1}{2v^2} - \frac{1}{2U^2}$$

$$\Rightarrow t = \frac{1}{2k}\left(\frac{1}{v^2} - \frac{1}{U^2}\right)$$

(b) Let T be the time when the speed is $20\,\mathrm{m\,s^{-1}}$.

Form two equations.
$$T = \frac{1}{2k}\left(\frac{1}{20^2} - \frac{1}{U^2}\right)$$

$$T + 10 = \frac{1}{2k}\left(\frac{1}{10^2} - \frac{1}{U^2}\right)$$

Solving gives
$$k = \frac{3}{8000}$$

4 (a)

$$-0.05v = 0.4\frac{dv}{dt}$$

$$\Rightarrow \frac{1}{v}\,dv = -0.125\,dt$$

Hence
$$\int \frac{1}{v}\,dv = -\int 0.125\,dt$$

$$\Rightarrow \ln v = -0.125t + c$$

$$\Rightarrow v = e^{-0.125t + c} = Ae^{-0.125t}$$
where $A = e^c$

$v = 80$ when $t = 0$, so $80 = Ae^0$

$$\Rightarrow A = 80$$

The equation becomes $v = 80e^{-0.125t}$

(b) $x = \int v\,dt = \int 80e^{-0.125t}\,dt = -\frac{80}{0.125}e^{-0.125t} + c$

$x = 0$ when $t = 0$, so $\quad 0 = -\frac{80}{0.125}e^0 + c$

$$\Rightarrow c = \frac{80}{0.125} = 640$$

The equation becomes $x = -\frac{80}{0.125}e^{-0.125t} + 640$

$$= 640(1 - e^{-0.125t})$$

5 (a)

$$-km\sqrt{v} = m\frac{dv}{dt}$$

$$\Rightarrow \frac{1}{\sqrt{v}}\,dv = -k\,dt$$

Hence
$$\int \frac{1}{\sqrt{v}}\,dv = -\int k\,dt$$

$$\Rightarrow 2\sqrt{v} = -kt + c$$

$v = U$ when $t = 0$, so
$$2\sqrt{U} = -k(0) + c$$

$$\Rightarrow c = 2\sqrt{U}$$

The equation becomes
$$2\sqrt{v} = -kt + 2\sqrt{U}$$

$$\Rightarrow \sqrt{v} = \sqrt{U} - \tfrac{1}{2}kt$$

$$\Rightarrow v = \left(\sqrt{U} - \tfrac{1}{2}kt\right)^2$$

(b) The particle comes to rest. It will stay at rest because it is not acted on by any external forces.

(c)
$$x = \int v\,dt = \int \left(\sqrt{U} - \tfrac{1}{2}kt\right)^2\,dt$$

$$= \frac{1}{3(-\frac{1}{2}k)}\left(\sqrt{U} - \tfrac{1}{2}kt\right)^3 + c$$

$x = 0$ when $t = 0$, so $\quad 0 = -\frac{2}{3k}\left(\sqrt{U} - \tfrac{1}{2}k(0)\right)^3 + c$

$$\Rightarrow c = \frac{2}{3k}\left(\sqrt{U}\right)^3$$

The equation becomes
$$x = -\frac{2}{3k}\left(\sqrt{U} - \tfrac{1}{2}kt\right)^3 + \frac{2}{3k}\left(\sqrt{U}\right)^3$$

$$= -\frac{2}{3k}\left(\left(\sqrt{U}\right)^3 - \tfrac{3}{2}k\left(\sqrt{U}\right)^2 t + \tfrac{3}{4}k^2\sqrt{U}t^2 - \tfrac{1}{8}k^3t^3\right)$$
$$\quad + \frac{2}{3k}\left(\sqrt{U}\right)^3$$

$$= -\frac{2}{3k}\left(\sqrt{U}\right)^3 + Ut - \tfrac{1}{2}k\sqrt{U}t^2 + \tfrac{1}{12}k^2t^3 + \frac{2}{3k}\left(\sqrt{U}\right)^3$$

$$= Ut - \tfrac{1}{2}k\sqrt{U}t^2 + \tfrac{1}{12}k^2t^3$$

6 (a)

$$\frac{100}{v} = 8\frac{dv}{dt}$$

$$\Rightarrow \quad v\,dv = \tfrac{25}{2}\,dt$$

Hence

$$\int v\,dv = \tfrac{25}{2}\,dt$$

$$\Rightarrow \quad \tfrac{1}{2}v^2 = \tfrac{25}{2}t + c$$

$v = 5$ when $t = 0$, so

$$\tfrac{1}{2} \times 25 = \tfrac{25}{2}(0) + c$$

$$\Rightarrow \quad c = \tfrac{25}{2}$$

The equation becomes

$$\tfrac{1}{2}v^2 = \tfrac{25}{2}t + \tfrac{25}{2}$$

$$\Rightarrow \quad v^2 = 25(t+1)$$

$$\Rightarrow \quad v = 5(t+1)^{\frac{1}{2}}$$

(b) 63 s

(c) $x = \int v\,dt = \int 5(t+1)^{\frac{1}{2}}\,dt = \frac{10}{3}(t+1)^{\frac{3}{2}} + c$

When $t = 0$, $x = 0$, so

$$0 = \tfrac{10}{3}(0+1)^{\frac{3}{2}} + c$$

$$\Rightarrow \quad c = -\tfrac{10}{3}$$

The equation becomes

$$x = \tfrac{10}{3}\left((t+1)^{\frac{3}{2}} - 1\right)$$

7 (a) $-kv^2 = \dfrac{dv}{dt}$

(b) $\dfrac{1}{v} = kt + c \ \Rightarrow \ k = 0.025$

Test yourself (p 73)

1

$$-kv^2 = m\frac{dv}{dt}$$

$$\Rightarrow \quad \frac{1}{v^2}\,dv = -\frac{k}{m}\,dt$$

Hence

$$\int \frac{1}{v^2}\,dv = -\int \frac{k}{m}\,dt$$

$$\Rightarrow \quad -\frac{1}{v} = -\frac{kt}{m} + c$$

$$\Rightarrow \quad \frac{1}{v} = \frac{kt}{m} - c$$

$v = U$ when $t = 0$, so

$$\frac{1}{U} = \frac{k}{m} \times 0 - c$$

$$\Rightarrow \quad c = -\frac{1}{U}$$

The equation becomes

$$\frac{1}{v} = \frac{k}{m}t + \frac{1}{U}$$

$$\Rightarrow \quad \frac{1}{v} = \frac{Ukt + m}{mU}$$

$$\Rightarrow \quad v = \frac{mU}{Ukt + m}$$

2 (a)

$$-mkv^3 = m\frac{dv}{dt}$$

$$\Rightarrow \quad \frac{1}{v^3}\,dv = -k\,dt$$

Hence

$$\int \frac{1}{v^3}\,dv = -\int k\,dt$$

$$\Rightarrow \quad -\frac{1}{2v^2} = -kt + c$$

$$\Rightarrow \quad \frac{1}{2v^2} = kt - c$$

$v = U$ when $t = 0$, so

$$\frac{1}{2U^2} = k(0) - c$$

$$\Rightarrow \quad c = -\frac{1}{2U^2}$$

The equation becomes

$$\frac{1}{2v^2} = kt + \frac{1}{2U^2}$$

$$\Rightarrow \quad \frac{1}{2v^2} = \frac{2kU^2t + 1}{2U^2}$$

$$\Rightarrow \quad v^2 = \frac{U^2}{2kU^2t + 1}$$

(b) As t increases, v gets closer and closer to 0.

3

$$\frac{P}{v} = m\frac{dv}{dt}$$

$$\Rightarrow \quad v\,dv = \frac{P}{m}\,dt$$

Hence

$$\tfrac{1}{2}v^2 = \frac{P}{m}t + c$$

$v = U$ when $t = 0$, so

$$\tfrac{1}{2}U^2 = \frac{P}{m}(0) + c$$

$$\Rightarrow \quad c = \tfrac{1}{2}U^2$$

The equation becomes

$$\tfrac{1}{2}v^2 = \frac{P}{m}t + \tfrac{1}{2}U^2$$

$$\Rightarrow \quad v^2 = U^2 + \frac{2Pt}{m}$$

5 Uniform circular motion

Answers are given to three significant figures where appropriate.

A Angular speed (p 74)

A1 (a) Although the magnitude of the velocity is constant, its direction is continuously changing.

(b) It is directed along a tangent to the circle.

A2 (a) 0.2π m (b) 0.1π m s^{-1}

A3 (a) 15 r.p.m. (b) 0.2 r.p.m.

A4 (a) 0.4π rad s^{-1} (b) 0.011π rad s^{-1}

A5 (a) 8.38 rad s^{-1} (b) 0.75 s

A6 (a) 47.7 r.p.m. (b) 1.26 s

A7 (a) 0.0167 r.p.m. (b) 1.75×10^{-3} rad s^{-1}

A8 (a) (i) The penny moves in the arc of a circle which subtends an angle of 1 radian at the centre of the circle.
Length of arc $= r\theta = 0.1 \times 1 = 0.1$ m
(ii) 0.4 m s^{-1}

(b) (i) This penny moves a distance of 0.2 m when the turntable rotates through 1 radian, so its speed is greater.
(ii) 0.8 m s^{-1}

(c) The distance travelled, and hence the speed, of the penny is proportional to the distance from the centre of the turntable. If it is 0.05 m from the centre, the speed will be half that of the first penny.

Exercise A (p 76)

1 (a) 10.5 rad s^{-1} (b) 0.6 s

2 (a) 76.4 r.p.m. (b) 0.785 s

3 1.26 rad s^{-1}

4 (a) 60 s (b) 0.105 rad s^{-1}
(c) 9.42×10^{-3} m s^{-1}

5 (a) 5.24 rad s^{-1} (b) 20.9 m s^{-1}

6 (a) 0.157 rad s^{-1} (b) 0.0314 m s^{-1}

7 (a) 11.9 (b) 10 m s^{-1} (c) 7.5 m s^{-1}

8 18.8 m s^{-1}

9 0.213 m s^{-1}

10 (a) 464 m s^{-1} (b) 0 m s^{-1}

11 (a) 1.02×10^{-5} rad s^{-1} (b) 10 900 m s^{-1}

B Velocity and acceleration (p 78)

B1 (a) $\mathbf{v} = \dfrac{d\mathbf{r}}{dt} = -\omega r \sin \omega t \, \mathbf{i} + \omega r \cos \omega t \, \mathbf{j}$
$\mathbf{v} = \omega r(-\sin \omega t \, \mathbf{i} + \cos \omega t \, \mathbf{j})$

(b) $|\mathbf{v}| = \omega r \sqrt{\sin^2 \omega t + \cos^2 \omega t} = \omega r$

(c) $\mathbf{a} = \dfrac{d\mathbf{v}}{dt} = \omega r(-\omega \cos \omega t \, \mathbf{i} - \omega \sin \omega t \, \mathbf{j})$
$\mathbf{a} = -\omega^2 r(\cos \omega t \, \mathbf{i} + \sin \omega t \, \mathbf{j})$

(d) $|\mathbf{a}| = \omega^2 r \sqrt{\cos^2 \omega t + \sin^2 \omega t} = \omega^2 r$

(e) $\mathbf{a} = -\omega^2 r \cos \omega t \, \mathbf{i} - \omega^2 r \sin \omega t \, \mathbf{j}$
$\mathbf{a} = -\omega^2(r \cos \omega t \, \mathbf{i} + r \sin \omega t \, \mathbf{j}) = -\omega^2 \mathbf{r}$
The position vector $\mathbf{r}$ is directed out from the centre of the circle, so the acceleration vector is directed towards the centre of the circle.

B2 $v = r\omega \implies \omega = \dfrac{v}{r}$
$a = \omega^2 r = \left(\dfrac{v}{r}\right)^2 \times r \implies a = \dfrac{v^2}{r}$

B3 $a = r\omega^2 = 0.2 \times 5^2 = 5$ m s^{-2}

B4 $a = \dfrac{v^2}{r} = \dfrac{9^2}{20} = 4.05$ m s^{-2}

Exercise B (p 79)

1 (a) 6.4 m s^{-2} (b) 12.8 m s^{-2}

2 (a) (i) 4 m s^{-1}
(ii) Along the tangent to the wheel
(b) (i) 40 m s^{-2}
(ii) Towards the centre of the wheel

3 0.0375 m s^{-2}

4 (a) 33.3 m s^{-1} (b) 37.0 m

5 4.14 rad s^{-1}

6 (a) (i) 0.628 m s^{-1} (ii) 0.395 m s^{-2}
(b) (i) 0.942 m s^{-1} (ii) 0.592 m s^{-2}

7 1.52×10^{-7} m s^{-2}

8 (a) $2.66 \times 10^{-6}\,\mathrm{rad\,s^{-1}}$ (b) $2.72 \times 10^{-3}\,\mathrm{m\,s^{-2}}$

9 $37.7\,\mathrm{m\,s^{-2}}$

C Forces in circular motion (p 80)

C1 (a) The tension in the string

(b) The gravitational force between the earth and the satellite

(c) The friction force between the wheels and the road

C2 (a) $F = ma$ and $a = r\omega^2 \Rightarrow F = mr\omega^2$

(b) $F = ma$ and $a = \dfrac{v^2}{r} \Rightarrow F = \dfrac{mv^2}{r}$

C3 (a)

(b) $mr\omega^2$

(c) If ω is doubled, T is multiplied by 4.

(d) If the string breaks, there will be no force acting towards the centre of the circle, so the particle will no longer move in a circle.
The particle will move in a straight line in the direction of the tangent to the circle at the instant the string broke.

C4 (a) $a = \dfrac{v^2}{r} = \dfrac{1.2^2}{0.4} = 3.6\,\mathrm{m\,s^{-2}}$

(b) $T = ma = 2 \times 3.6 = 7.2\,\mathrm{N}$

(c) $T_{\mathrm{max}} = \dfrac{mv^2}{r} \Rightarrow 20 = \dfrac{2v^2}{0.4} \Rightarrow v = 2\,\mathrm{m\,s^{-1}}$

(d) $v_{\mathrm{max}} = r\omega_{\mathrm{max}} \Rightarrow 2 = 0.4\omega_{\mathrm{max}}$
$\Rightarrow \omega_{\mathrm{max}} = 5\,\mathrm{rad\,s^{-1}}$

C5 (a)

(b) $F = 0.2 \times 0.05 \times 6^2$
$= 0.36\,\mathrm{N}$

(c) $F = 0.2 \times 0.1 \times 6^2$
$= 0.72\,\mathrm{N}$

C6 (a) $\omega = \dfrac{2\pi \times 30}{60} = 3.14\,\mathrm{rad\,s^{-1}}$

(b) $a = r\omega^2 = 0.2 \times 3.14^2 = 1.97\,\mathrm{m\,s^{-2}}$

(c) $F = ma = 0.4 \times 1.97 = 0.790\,\mathrm{N}$

(d) $R = 0.4g = 3.92\,\mathrm{N}$

(e) $F = \mu R \Rightarrow \mu = \dfrac{F}{R} = 0.201$

Exercise C (p 83)

1 $200\,\mathrm{N}$ towards the centre of the circle

2 $0.48\,\mathrm{N}$

3 $2250\,\mathrm{N}$

4 $112\,\mathrm{N}$

5 (a) (i) $2\,\mathrm{m\,s^{-1}}$

(ii) Along the tangent to the circle

(b) (i) $8\,\mathrm{m\,s^{-2}}$

(ii) Towards the centre of the circle

(c) $24\,\mathrm{N}$

(d) The particle moves in a straight line along the surface in the direction of the tangent to the circle at the instant the string broke.

6 (a)

(b) $0.32\,\mathrm{N}$ (c) 0.408

7 (a) $F = \dfrac{mv^2}{r} = \dfrac{1400 \times 24^2}{120} = 6720\,\mathrm{N}$

(b) 0.490

8 $18.6\,\mathrm{rad\,s^{-1}}$

9 (a)

(b) The person will not slip if $F = mg$. The maximum value of F is μR. As the speed increases, the normal reaction R increases and hence F can increase.

(c) $2.21\,\mathrm{rad\,s^{-1}}$

10 Resolve vertically: $R = mg$

The particle does not slip if $F \leq \mu R$

$\Rightarrow F \leq \mu mg$

But $F = mr\omega^2$

So $mr\omega^2 \leq \mu mg \Rightarrow \omega^2 \leq \dfrac{\mu g}{r}$

$\Rightarrow \omega \leq \sqrt{\dfrac{\mu g}{r}}$

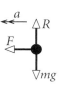

D Problems needing resolving of forces (p 84)

D1 (a) As the angular speed increases, the radius increases.

(b) As the length of the string increases, the radius increases.

D2 (a) $\sin\theta = \dfrac{r}{l}$

$\Rightarrow r = l\sin\theta$

(b) $T\cos\theta = mg \Rightarrow T = \dfrac{mg}{\cos\theta}$

(c) $T\sin\theta = mr\omega^2$

$\Rightarrow \dfrac{mg}{\cos\theta} \times \sin\theta = ml\sin\theta \times \omega^2$

$\Rightarrow \omega^2 = \dfrac{g}{l\cos\theta}$

D3 (a) As ω increases, $\cos\theta$ decreases, so θ increases.

(b) $T\cos\theta = mg \Rightarrow \cos\theta = \dfrac{mg}{T}$

If the string is horizontal, $\cos\theta = 0$, but $\dfrac{mg}{T}$ must be greater than zero, so the string cannot be horizontal.

(c) If l is increased for a given ω, then $\cos\theta$ must decrease and hence θ must increase.

D4 (a)

(b) $T\cos 30° = 0.01g \Rightarrow T = 0.113\,\text{N}$

(c) $T\sin 30° = 0.01a \Rightarrow a = 5.66\,\text{m s}^{-2}$

(d) $a = \dfrac{v^2}{r} \Rightarrow 5.66 = \dfrac{v^2}{0.4\sin 30°}$

$\Rightarrow v = 1.06\,\text{m s}^{-1}$

D5 (a)

(b) The horizontal component of the normal reaction force of the bowl on the ball

(c) Letting θ be the angle between R and the vertical, $R\cos\theta = 0.3g \Rightarrow R = \dfrac{0.3g}{0.6} = 4.9\,\text{N}$

(d) $R\sin\theta = mr\omega^2 \Rightarrow 4.9 \times 0.8 = 0.3 \times 0.4\omega^2$

$\Rightarrow \omega = 5.72\,\text{rad s}^{-1}$

Exercise D (p 87)

1 (a)

(b) 22°   (c) 5.29 N

(d) 3.96 m s^{-2} (e) 1.09 m s^{-1}

2 (a)

(b) 3.92 N   (c) 6.51 rad s^{-1}

(d) 0.965 s

3 0.046 m (to 2 s.f.)

4 (a)

(b) Resolve vertically: $R\cos 30° = 100g$

$\Rightarrow R = 1130\,\text{N}$

(c) 7.52 m s^{-1}

(d) The cyclist and bicycle can be modelled as a particle and air resistance can be ignored.

5 (a) Resolve vertically: $R\sin\theta = mg$

N2L horizontally: $R\cos\theta = mr\omega^2$

$\Rightarrow \dfrac{R\sin\theta}{R\cos\theta} = \dfrac{mg}{mr\omega^2} \Rightarrow \tan\theta = \dfrac{g}{r\omega^2}$

$\Rightarrow r = \dfrac{g}{\omega^2\tan\theta}$

(b) $\dfrac{g}{4\omega^2\tan\theta}$

6 (a) 3.36 rad s^{-1} (b) 3.36 rad s^{-1}

7 (a) (i) Letting θ be the angle between the string and the vertical,

$T\sin\theta = mr\omega^2$ and $r = l\sin\theta$

$\Rightarrow T\sin\theta = ml\sin\theta \times \omega^2 \Rightarrow T = ml\omega^2$

(ii) As ω increases, T increases.

(b) (i) $T\cos\theta = mg$ and $\cos\theta = \dfrac{h}{l} \Rightarrow \dfrac{Th}{l} = mg$

But $T = ml\omega^2$, so $ml\omega^2\dfrac{h}{l} = mg$

$\Rightarrow h = \dfrac{g}{\omega^2}$

(ii) As ω increases, h decreases.

8 (a) (i) $r = 0.75\sin\theta = 0.75 \times 0.6 = 0.45\,\text{m}$

(ii) $4.9\,\text{N}$

(iii) $4.04\,\text{rad s}^{-1}$

(b) $0.15\,\text{m}$

9 (a) As the angular speed increases, the tension increases.

(b) $3.87\,\text{rad s}^{-1}$

(c) $49.2°$

10 (a) $32.7\,\text{N}$ (b) $6.76\,\text{m s}^{-1}$

11 $T_A = 24.2\,\text{N}$, $T_B = 4.6\,\text{N}$

Mixed questions (p 90)

1 (a) $98\,\text{N}$

(b) $3.70\,\text{m s}^{-1}$

(c) The particle moves in a straight line with constant speed along a tangent to the circle.

2 Resolve vertically: $R = mg$
The car doesn't slip, so $F \leq \mu R \Rightarrow F \leq \mu mg$
N2L horizontally:
$F = \dfrac{mv^2}{r} \Rightarrow \dfrac{mv^2}{r} \leq \mu mg \Rightarrow \mu \geq \dfrac{v^2}{rg}$

3 (a)

(b) $r = 0.5\sin 30° = 0.25$
N2L horizontally: $T\sin 30° = \dfrac{mv^2}{r}$

$\Rightarrow T\sin 30° = \dfrac{2 \times 0.3^2}{0.25} \Rightarrow T = 1.44\,\text{N}$

(c) $18.4\,\text{N}$

4 (a) Let θ be the angle between the string and the vertical.
Resolve vertically: $T\cos\theta = mg$

$\Rightarrow \dfrac{T\sqrt{l^2 - r^2}}{l} = mg$

$\Rightarrow T = \dfrac{mgl}{\sqrt{l^2 - r^2}}$

(b) $\dfrac{gr^2}{\sqrt{l^2 - r^2}}$

(c) $\dfrac{ml}{2}\left(\dfrac{V^2}{r^2} + \dfrac{g}{\sqrt{l^2 - r^2}}\right)$

Test yourself (p 91)

1 (a) $0.0392\,\text{N}$

(b) $26.7\,\text{r.p.m.}$

(c) It is reduced by a factor of 4.

2 (a) $\omega = \dfrac{1}{19.5 \times 24 \times 60} \times \dfrac{2\pi}{60} = 3.729 \times 10^{-6}\,\text{rad s}^{-1}$
$v = r\omega = 1.22 \times 10^9 \times 3.729 \times 10^{-6}$
$= 4550\,\text{m s}^{-1}$

(b) $2.27 \times 10^{21}\,\text{N}$

3 (a) (i) Resolve vertically: $R\sin 30° = 3g$
$\Rightarrow R = 58.8\,\text{N}$

(ii) $2.91\,\text{m s}^{-1}$

(b) (i) There is no change.

(ii) The speed is increased, because v^2 is proportional to the radius.

4 (a) $ml\omega^2$

(b) Resolve vertically: $T\cos\theta = mg$
$\Rightarrow ml\omega^2\cos\theta = mg \Rightarrow \cos\theta = \dfrac{g}{l\omega^2}$

(c) (i) $T \leq 16 \Rightarrow 0.1 \times 0.4\omega^2 \leq 16$
$\Rightarrow \omega^2 \leq 400 \Rightarrow \omega \leq 20$

(ii) $86°$

6 Work, energy and power

A Work (p 92)

A1 You will do twice as much work.

A2 Work done $= 40 \times 10 = 400\,\text{J}$

A3 (a) $Fd\,\text{J}$

(b) (i)

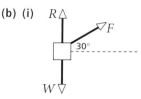

(ii) The horizontal component, $F\cos 30°$, of the force F

(iii) $Fd\cos 30°\,\text{J}$

A4 (a) $0\,\text{J}$

(b) $25 \times 10 \times \cos 40° = 192\,\text{J}$ (to 3 s.f.)

A5 $2500 \times 50 = 125\,000\,\text{J}$

Exercise A (p 94)

1 $120\,\text{J}$

2 $150\,000\,\text{J}$

3 (a) $32.9\,\text{J}$ (to 3 s.f.)

(b) (i) The magnitude of the horizontal component of the force is now less.

(ii) $26.8\,\text{J}$ (to 3 s.f.)

4 $350\,\text{N}$

5 $2120\,\text{J}$ (to 3 s.f.)

6 (a) $468\,\text{J}$ (to 3 s.f.)   (b) $72.3\,\text{J}$ (to 3 s.f.)

7 $5\,\text{m}$

B Kinetic energy (p 94)

B1 (a) $u = 0$, $v = 20$, $s = 100$
Using $v^2 = u^2 + 2as$, $20^2 = 0^2 + 200a$
$\Rightarrow a = 2\,\text{m s}^{-2}$

(b) $F = ma = 2000 \times 2 = 4000\,\text{N}$

(c) Work done $= Fs = 4000 \times 100 = 400\,000\,\text{J}$

B2 (a) Using $v^2 = u^2 + 2as$ with $u = 0$,
$v^2 = 2as \Rightarrow a = \dfrac{v^2}{2s}$

(b) $F = ma = \dfrac{mv^2}{2s} \Rightarrow Fs = \tfrac{1}{2}mv^2$

B3 (a) (i) $u = 15$, $v = 30$, $s = 200$
Using $v^2 = u^2 + 2as$, $30^2 = 15^2 + 400a$
$\Rightarrow a = 1.6875\,\text{m s}^{-2}$

(ii) $F = ma = 2500 \times 1.6875 = 4218.75\,\text{N}$
Work done $= Fs = 4218.75 \times 200$
$= 843\,750\,\text{J}$

(b) (i) $\tfrac{1}{2}mu^2 = \tfrac{1}{2} \times 2500 \times 15^2 = 281\,250\,\text{J}$

(ii) $\tfrac{1}{2}mv^2 = \tfrac{1}{2} \times 2500 \times 30^2 = 1\,125\,000\,\text{J}$

(iii) Change in k.e. $= 1\,125\,000 - 281\,250$
$= 843\,750\,\text{J}$

B4 (a) $v^2 = u^2 + 2as \Rightarrow v^2 - u^2 = 2as$
$\Rightarrow a = \dfrac{v^2 - u^2}{2s}$

(b) $F = ma = \dfrac{m(v^2 - u^2)}{2s} \Rightarrow Fs = \tfrac{1}{2}mv^2 - \tfrac{1}{2}mu^2$

B5 $\tfrac{1}{2} \times 10 \times 18^2 - 0 = 1620\,\text{J}$

B6 $40F = -1620 \Rightarrow F = -40.5$
The magnitude of the force is $40.5\,\text{N}$.

B7 (a) $150 - 80 = 40a \Rightarrow a = 1.75\,\text{m s}^{-2}$
$v^2 = u^2 + 2as$ gives $v^2 = 0 + 2 \times 1.75 \times 5 = 17.5$
so $v = 4.18\,\text{m s}^{-1}$ (to 3 s.f.)

(b) Gain in k.e. $= \tfrac{1}{2}mv^2 - \tfrac{1}{2}mu^2 = \tfrac{1}{2} \times 40 \times 17.5 - 0$
$= 350\,\text{J}$

(c) Work done $= 150 \times 5 = 750\,\text{J}$

(d) Work done by resistance $= -80 \times 5 = -400\,\text{J}$

(e) (i) Resultant force $= 150 - 80 = 70\,\text{N}$

(ii) Work done by resultant $= 70 \times 5 = 350\,\text{J}$
The sum of the work done by the $150\,\text{N}$ force and the work done by the $80\,\text{N}$ force is equal to the work done by the resultant force. The work done by the resultant is equal to the gain in kinetic energy of the box.

Exercise B (p 97)

1 $225\,000\,\text{J}$

2 (a) $1755\,\text{J}$ (b) $1755\,\text{J}$

3 $315\,000\,\text{J}$

4 (a) 1 200 000 J   **(b)** 12 000 N

5 15 m s^{-1}

6 (a) 600 000 J   **(b)** 500 N

7 7 m s^{-1}

8 (a)

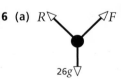

(b) 44.1 N

(c) (i) 1000 J   **(ii)** −882 J

(d) 3.97 m s^{-1} (to 3 s.f.)

9 120 J (to 3 s.f.)

C Potential energy (p 98)

C1 (a) 0 J

(b) As the ball drops, its speed, and hence its kinetic energy, increases.

(c) $u = 0$, $a = 9.8$, $s = 2$
$v^2 = u^2 + 2as$ gives $v^2 = 0 + 2 \times 9.8 \times 2 = 39.2$
so $v = 6.26$ m s^{-1} (to 3 s.f.)
k.e. $= \frac{1}{2}mv^2 = \frac{1}{2} \times 0.1 \times 39.2 = 1.96$ J

(d) (i) The weight of the ball

     (ii) Work done $= Fs = 0.1 \times 9.8 \times 2 = 1.96$ J

C2 The weight of the particle is mg N and the distance moved is h m.
Work done $= Fs = mgh$ J

C3 (a) $\frac{1}{2}mv^2 - \frac{1}{2}mu^2$

(b) $mga - mgb$

(c) $v^2 = u^2 + 2as \Rightarrow v^2 = u^2 + 2g(a - b)$
$\Rightarrow$ gain in k.e. $= \frac{1}{2}m(u^2 + 2g(a - b)) - \frac{1}{2}mu^2$
$= \frac{1}{2}mu^2 + mg(a - b) - \frac{1}{2}mu^2$
$= mga - mgb =$ loss in p.e.

C4 (a) $\frac{1}{2} \times 0.1 \times 8^2 = 3.2$ J

(b) As the ball moves upwards, its speed, and hence its kinetic energy, decreases until it reaches its maximum height, at which point its speed and kinetic energy are zero. The ball then moves downwards with increasing speed and hence increasing kinetic energy.

(c) Using $v^2 = u^2 + 2as$, $v^2 = 8^2 + 2 \times (-g) \times x$
$\Rightarrow v^2 = 64 - 2gx$

(d) As the ball's height increases, its potential energy increases. It has maximum potential energy when it is at its maximum height. As the ball drops, its potential energy decreases.

(e) p.e. $= 0.1gx$ J

(f) k.e. + p.e. $= \frac{1}{2} \times 0.1 \times (64 - 2gx) + 0.1gx$
$= 3.2 - 0.1gx + 0.1gx = 3.2$ J
The sum of the k.e. and p.e. is independent of x and hence constant.

C5 Gain in p.e. $= 18 \times 9.8 \times 2.5 = 441$ J

C6 (a) Loss in p.e. $= 5 \times 9.8 \times 10 = 490$ J

(b) (i) $\sin 25° = \dfrac{10}{d}$

$\Rightarrow d = \dfrac{10}{\sin 25°}$

     (ii) Only the component of the weight acting down the plane does work.
Work done $= 5g \sin 25° \times \dfrac{10}{\sin 25°} = 490$ J
The loss of potential energy when the particle slides down the plane is the same as when it falls the same distance vertically.

Exercise C (p 101)

1 313.6 J

2 864 J (to 3 s.f.)

3 588 000 J

4 (a) 200 000 J   **(b)** −25 000 J   **(c)** 73 500 J

5 (a) 1470 J   **(b)** −1200 J

6 (a)

(b) 41.7 N (to 3 s.f.)

(c) −167 J (to 3 s.f.)

(d) 585 J (to 3 s.f.)

7 (a) 1440 J   **(b)** −398 J (to 3 s.f.)

(c) 304 J (to 3 s.f.)

D Conservation of energy (p 102)

D1 (a) (i) $u = 8$, $v = 0$, $a = -9.8$
$v^2 = u^2 + 2as$ gives $0 = 8^2 - 2 \times 9.8 \times s$
so $s = 3.27$ m (to 3 s.f.)

   (ii) Gain in p.e. $= 0.2 \times 9.8 \times 3.27 = 6.4$ J

   (b) (i) $0 \, \text{m s}^{-1}$

   (ii) Loss in k.e. $= \frac{1}{2} \times 0.2 \times 8^2 - 0 = 6.4$ J
The loss in k.e. is equal to the gain in p.e.

D2 (a) (i) $h = 10 \sin 30° = 5$

   (ii) Loss in p.e. $= 15 \times 9.8 \times 5 = 735$ J

   (b) (i) Using $F = ma$, $15g \sin 30° = 15a$
$\Rightarrow a = 9.8 \sin 30° = 4.9 \, \text{m s}^{-2}$

   (ii) $u = 0$, $s = 10$, $a = 4.9$
$v^2 = u^2 + 2as$ gives $v^2 = 2 \times 4.9 \times 10 = 98$
So $v = 9.90 \, \text{m s}^{-1}$ (to 3 s.f.)

   (iii) Gain in k.e. $= \frac{1}{2} \times 15 \times 98 = 735$ J
The gain in k.e. is equal to the loss in p.e.

D3 (a) (i) $h = 10 \sin 25° = 4.23$ m (to 3 s.f.)

   (ii) Loss in p.e. $= 15 \times 9.8 \times 4.23 = 621$ J (to 3 s.f.)

   (b) (i) Using $F = ma$, $15g \sin 25° - 50 = 15a$
So $a = 0.808 \, \text{m s}^{-2}$ (to 3 s.f.)

   (ii) $u = 0$, $s = 10$, $a = 0.808$
$v^2 = u^2 + 2as$ gives $v^2 = 2 \times 0.808 \times 10 = 16.2$
So $v = 4.02 \, \text{m s}^{-1}$ (to 3 s.f.)

   (iii) Gain in k.e. $= \frac{1}{2} \times 15 \times 16.2 = 121$ J (to 3 s.f.)
The gain in k.e. is less than the loss in p.e. in this case.

D4 (a) Total gain in energy = gain in k.e. − loss in p.e.
$= 121 - 621 = -500$ J
There is an overall energy loss of 500 J.

   (b) Work done by resisting force $= -50 \times 10$
$= -500$ J
The work done by the resisting force is equal to the change in energy of the box.

D5 (a) At its maximum height the speed, and hence the kinetic energy of the stone, is zero.
Gain in p.e. = loss in k.e.
$0.2 \times 9.8 \times h = \frac{1}{2} \times 0.2 \times 5^2$
So $h = 1.28$ m (to 3 s.f.)

   (b) When it hits the water, the stone is a vertical distance of 30 m below its starting point.
Gain in k.e. = loss in p.e.
$\frac{1}{2} \times 0.2 \times v^2 - \frac{1}{2} \times 0.2 \times 5^2 = 0.2 \times 9.8 \times 30$
$\Rightarrow v^2 = 613 \Rightarrow v = 24.8 \, \text{m s}^{-1}$ (to 3 s.f.)

   (c) Each term in the energy equation contains the mass, so it cancels out and was not required.

   (d) The stone can be treated as a particle and there is no air resistance.

D6 (a) The only external force doing work is gravity, so mechanical energy is conserved. The normal reaction does no work as it is perpendicular to the direction of motion.

   (b) $\frac{1}{2} \times 0.1 \times 10^2 = 5$ J

   (c) 5 J

   (d) 5 J

   (e) When the ball is at its maximum distance d up the slope, the increase in height is $d \sin 40°$.
Increase in p.e. $= 0.1 \times 9.8 \times d \sin 40° = 5$
So $d = 7.94$ m (to 3 s.f.)

D7 (a) Gravity is not the only external force doing work; the resistance also does work, so the principle of conservation of mechanical energy does not apply.

   (b) $-40 \times 2.5 = -100$ J

   (c) $16 \times 9.8 \times 2.5 \sin 35° = 225$ J (to 3 s.f.)

   (d) Work done = gain in p.e. + gain in k.e.
$-100 = -225 +$ gain in k.e.
$\Rightarrow$ gain in k.e. $= 125$ J

   (e) $\frac{1}{2} \times 16 \times v^2 = 125 \Rightarrow v = 3.95 \, \text{m s}^{-1}$ (to 3 s.f.)

Exercise D (p 105)

1 (a) 5.88 J

   (b) k.e. = 5.88 J, $v = 7.67 \, \text{m s}^{-1}$ (to 3 s.f.)

2 (a) 2.94 J

   (b) $12.9 \, \text{m s}^{-1}$ (to 3 s.f.)

   (c) (i) 11.25 J   (ii) 11.5 m (to 3 s.f.)

3 $4.02 \, \text{m s}^{-1}$ (to 3 s.f.)

4 (a) 2940 J   (b) 240 J   (c) −2700 J

5 (a) $17\,640\,\text{J}$

(b) $1920\,\text{J}$

(c) $-15\,720\,\text{J}$

(d) It has been assumed that there is no air resistance acting. Air resistance would also help to slow the boy down.

6 (a) $9.3\,\text{J}$ **(b)** $1.86\,\text{N}$

7 (a) $-15\,\text{J}$ **(b)** $3\,\text{N}$

(c) 0.177 (to 3 s.f.)

E Power (p 106)

E1 (a) $750\,\text{J}$

(b) $750\,\text{J}$

(c) They have both done the same amount of work, but Tim's push had more power, as he did the work in a shorter time.

E2 Tim's push: power $= \frac{750}{10} = 75\,\text{W}$

Alison's push: power $= \frac{750}{15} = 50\,\text{W}$

E3 (a) $1000 \times 9.8 \times 25 = 245\,000\,\text{J}$

(b) $\frac{245\,000}{40} = 6125\,\text{W}$

E4 (a) $950 \times 18 = 17\,100\,\text{W}$

(b) $\frac{5000}{15} = 333\,\text{N}$ (to 3 s.f.)

E5 The power is constant, so when the speed decreases the driving force increases.

E6 (a) $0\,\text{m s}^{-2}$ **(b)** $1200\,\text{N}$

(c) $\frac{45\,000}{1200} = 37.5\,\text{m s}^{-1}$

E7 (a) $\frac{45\,000}{25} = 1800\,\text{N}$

(b) $F = ma \Rightarrow 1800 - 1200 = 1500a$
$\Rightarrow a = 0.4\,\text{m s}^{-2}$

E8 (a) $F = 1200 + 1500g\sin\alpha = 2180\,\text{N}$

(b) $\frac{45\,000}{2180} = 20.6\,\text{m s}^{-1}$ (to 3 s.f.)

E9 (a) (i) $40 \times 35 = 1400\,\text{N}$

(ii) Max. power $=$ resistance $\times$ max. speed
$= 1400 \times 35 = 49\,000\,\text{W}$

(b) (i) $40 \times 20 = 800\,\text{N}$

(ii) $\frac{49\,000}{20} = 2450\,\text{N}$

(iii) $F = ma \Rightarrow 2450 - 800 = 2500a$
$\Rightarrow a = 0.66\,\text{m s}^{-2}$

Exercise E (p 110)

1 $54\,000\,\text{W}$

2 (a) $970.2\,\text{J}$ **(b)** $485.1\,\text{W}$

3 $7056\,\text{W}$

4 $30\,\text{m s}^{-1}$

5 Work done per second $= 81.7\,\text{J}$ (to 3 s.f.)
Power $= 81.7\,\text{W}$

6 (a) (i) $2500\,\text{N}$ **(ii)** $1.28\,\text{m s}^{-2}$ (to 3 s.f.)

(b) At maximum speed, driving force $=$ resistance
Power $=$ driving force $\times$ velocity $= 25v \times v$
So $45\,000 = 25v^2 \Rightarrow v^2 = 1800$
So $v = 42.4\,\text{m s}^{-1}$ (to 3 s.f.)

7 (a) $5\,600\,000\,\text{W}$ **(b)** $31.7\,\text{m s}^{-1}$ (to 3 s.f.)

8 (a) (i) $2400\,\text{N}$ **(ii)** $1.0625\,\text{m s}^{-2}$

(b) $30.3\,\text{m s}^{-1}$ (to 3 s.f.)

9 $54\,180\,\text{W}$

Mixed questions (p 112)

1 (a) (i) $10.1\,\text{m s}^{-1}$ (to 3 s.f.)

(ii) $6.57\,\text{m s}^{-1}$ (to 3 s.f.)

(b) If the track is smooth the only external force doing work is the weight of the ball, so the principle of conservation of mechanical energy can be applied. If the track were rough, the friction force would be doing work, causing the ball to lose energy, and its speed at C would be lower.

2 (a) $-4\,\text{J}$ **(b)** $23.52\,\text{J}$

(c) $11.4\,\text{m s}^{-1}$ (to 3 s.f.)

3 (a) (i) $50\,540\,\text{J}$

(ii) Work done $=$ change in energy
$200F = 50\,540$
So $F = 252.7 = 253\,\text{N}$ (to 3 s.f.)

(b) (i)   **(ii)** $255.2\,\text{N}$

4 (a) Using N2L,
$$F - 40 \times 20 - 1200 \times 9.8 \times \tfrac{1}{10} = 1200 \times 1$$
$$\Rightarrow F = 3176\,\text{N}$$
Using $P = Fv$, $P = 3176 \times 20 = 63\,520\,\text{W}$

(b) $7.53°$ (to 3 s.f.)

Test yourself (p 113)

1 (a) 48.6 J

(b) 16.5 m

(c) k.e. = 42.72 J, speed = 16.9 m s^{-1} (to 3 s.f.)

2 (a)

(b) (i) $F = 1960 + 1200g \sin 5°$
So $F = 2985\,\text{N}$ (to 4 s.f.)

(ii) 44 774 W

(c) 20.1 m s^{-1} (to 3 s.f.)

3 (a) (i) 14.7 J   **(ii)** 10.8 m s^{-1} (to 3 s.f.)

(b) 4.73 N (to 3 s.f.)

4 (a) 97.5 J   **(b)** 19.5 N

5 (a) 40   **(b)** 0.738 m s^{-2} (to 3 s.f.)

7 Hooke's law

A Elastic strings and springs (p 114)

A1 $T = \dfrac{\lambda x}{l} = \dfrac{15 \times 0.1}{0.5} = 3\,\text{N}$

A2 (a) 9 N

(b) $9 = \dfrac{0.05\lambda}{0.2} \Rightarrow \lambda = 36\,\text{N}$

A3 (a) $20 = \dfrac{25x}{0.4} \Rightarrow x = 0.32\,\text{m}$

(b) $20 = \dfrac{25x}{0.8} \Rightarrow x = 0.64\,\text{m}$

(c) Hooke's law can be rearranged to give $x = \dfrac{Tl}{\lambda}$, so for a given T and λ, the extension is proportional to the natural length of the spring. As the natural length of one spring is double that of the other, the extension is also double.

A4 (a)

$\uparrow T$

●

$\downarrow 0.2g$

(b) $T = 0.2g = 1.96\,\text{N}$

(c) $x = l$, so $1.96 = \dfrac{\lambda l}{l} \Rightarrow \lambda = 1.96\,\text{N}$
The modulus of elasticity is equal to the tension in the string when the extension is equal to the natural length.

A5 (a) $10 = \dfrac{40x}{0.4} \Rightarrow x = 0.1\,\text{m}$ **(b)** 0.3 m

Exercise A (p 116)

1 (a) 3 N   **(b)** 6 N   **(c)** 12 N

2 (a) 0.03 m   **(b)** 0.04 m   **(c)** 0.06 m

3 (a) 4.9 N   **(b)** 14.7 N

4 31.5 N

5 0.24 m

6 (a) 1.96 N   **(b)** 0.007 m   **(c)** 0.043 m

7 $T = 0.25g = 2.45$
$x = 0.45 - 0.3 = 0.15$
$T = \dfrac{\lambda x}{l} \Rightarrow 2.45 = \dfrac{0.15\lambda}{0.3} \Rightarrow \lambda = 4.9\,\text{N}$

8 Natural length = 0.3 m, extension = 0.45 m

9 Natural length $= 0.8\,\text{m}$, extension $= 0.28\,\text{m}$

10 Natural length $= 18\,\text{cm}$,
modulus of elasticity $= 13.5\,\text{N}$

B Work done by a variable force (p 117)

B1 The force applied to the spring is equal to the tension in the spring, which is given by $T = \dfrac{\lambda x}{l}$. As the extension increases, the tension and hence also the applied force increases.

B2 Work done $= \dfrac{12 \times 0.1^2}{2 \times 0.5} = 0.12\,\text{J}$

B3 (a) Work done $= \dfrac{20 \times 0.2^2}{2 \times 0.8} = 0.5\,\text{J}$

 (b) (i) $0.4\,\text{m}$

 (ii) Work done $= \dfrac{20 \times 0.4^2}{2 \times 0.8} = 2\,\text{J}$

 (iii) $1.5\,\text{J}$

 (c) The work done in stretching the spring by $0.2\,\text{m}$ is the area under the graph from $s = 0$ to $s = 0.2$. The work 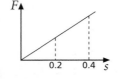 done in stretching the spring the further $0.2\,\text{m}$ is the area under the graph from $s = 0.2$ to $s = 0.4$. These areas are not equal, so the work done in each case is not the same.

Exercise B (p 119)

1 (a) $0.2\,\text{J}$ (b) $0.8\,\text{J}$ (c) $3.2\,\text{J}$

2 $4.5\,\text{J}$

3 (a) (i) $0.2\,\text{m}$ (ii) $1\,\text{J}$
 (b) (i) $0.4\,\text{m}$ (ii) $2\,\text{J}$

4 $0.2\,\text{J}$

5 (a) $0.07\,\text{m}$ (b) $0.0343\,\text{J}$

6 (a) $0.075\,\text{J}$ (b) $0.225\,\text{J}$

7 (a) $0.274\,\text{J}$ (to 3 s.f.)
 (b) $0.709\,\text{J}$ (to 3 s.f.)

8 (a) Natural length $= 0.6\,\text{m}$, extension $= 0.15\,\text{m}$
 (b) $0.375\,\text{J}$

9 $0.1225\,\text{J}$

10 $0.35\,\text{m}$

C Mechanical energy (p 120)

C1 (a) The particle moves back towards the fixed point, its k.e. increases and its e.p.e. decreases, reaching zero when the string reaches its natural length. From this point the particle continues to move with constant velocity as there is no force acting in the direction of motion.

 (b) Yes, because no external force is doing work

 (c) If the surface had been rough, the friction force would be doing work, so the principle of conservation of mechanical energy would not apply.

 (d) If the particle were attached to a spring, once the spring reached its natural length the particle would continue moving and the spring would go into compression, causing an increase in e.p.e. and a corresponding decrease in k.e. until the k.e. became zero, at which point the spring would begin to return to its natural length, with a decrease in e.p.e. and increase in k.e. The spring would continue to oscillate, centred on its natural length.

C2 (a) On release, the particle moves upwards, its e.p.e. decreases and its k.e. and g.p.e. increase. When it reaches its natural length the e.p.e is zero and the k.e. is maximum. The particle continues to move upwards; the g.p.e. and e.p.e. increase and the k.e. decreases until it reaches zero when the particle is at its maximum height. The particle then moves downwards; the g.p.e. and e.p.e. decrease and the k.e. increases. The particle oscillates about its equilibrium position.

 (b) Yes, because the only external force doing work is gravity

C3 (a) (i) e.p.e. $= \dfrac{20 \times 0.5^2}{2 \times 1} = 2.5\,\text{J}$
 (ii) k.e. $= 0\,\text{J}$
 (b) (i) e.p.e. $= \dfrac{20 \times 0.2^2}{2 \times 1} = 0.4\,\text{J}$
 (ii) Gain in k.e. $=$ loss in e.p.e
 $\Rightarrow$ k.e. $= 2.5 - 0.4 = 2.1\,\text{J}$

C4 (a) The k.e. is greatest when the string reaches its natural length. The e.p.e. is zero at this point.

  (b) Max k.e. = 2.5 J $\Rightarrow \frac{1}{2} \times 0.2 \times v^2 = 2.5$
$\Rightarrow v = 5\,\text{m s}^{-1}$

C5 $0.4g = \frac{19.6x}{0.5} \Rightarrow x = 0.1$
Hence the length of the string is 0.6 m.

C6 (a) e.p.e. $= \frac{19.6 \times 0.3^2}{2 \times 0.5} = 1.764\,\text{J}$

  (b) (i) e.p.e. $= \frac{19.6 \times 0.1^2}{2 \times 0.5} = 0.196\,\text{J}$

    (ii) g.p.e. $= 0.4 \times 9.8 \times 0.2 = 0.784\,\text{J}$

    (iii) Energy is conserved so
$1.764 = 0.196 + 0.784 + \text{k.e.}$
$\Rightarrow$ k.e. $= 0.784\,\text{J}$

  (c) (i) e.p.e. = 0 J

    (ii) g.p.e. $= 0.4 \times 9.8 \times 0.3 = 1.176\,\text{J}$

    (iii) Energy is conserved so
$1.764 = 1.176 + \text{k.e.} \Rightarrow$ k.e. $= 0.588\,\text{J}$

C7 (a) k.e. = 0 J

  (b) Energy is conserved, so g.p.e. = 1.764 J

  (c) $0.4 \times 9.8 \times h = 1.764 \Rightarrow h = 0.45\,\text{m}$

Exercise C (p 124)

1 (a) 1 J

  (b) (i) 1 J   **(ii)** 2.24 m s^{-1} (to 3 s.f.)

2 0.204 m (to 3 s.f.)

3 k.e. = 0.324 J, speed = 1.04 m s^{-1}

4 (a) (i) $9.8 + 19.6x$ **(ii)** v^2 **(iii)** $100x^2$

  (b) Energy is conserved,
so g.p.e lost = k.e. gained + e.p.e. gained
$\Rightarrow 9.8 + 19.6x = v^2 + 100x^2$
$\Rightarrow v^2 = 19.6x - 100x^2 + 9.8$

  (c) 0.426 m (to 3 s.f.)

  (d) (i) 0.098 m   **(ii)** 3.28 m s^{-1} (to 3 s.f.)

5 2.52 m s^{-1} (to 3 s.f.)

6 (a) When the string becomes taut,
k.e. gained $= \frac{1}{2} \times 80 \times v^2 = 40v^2$
g.p.e. lost $= 80 \times 9.8 \times 7 = 5488$
Energy is conserved, so k.e. gained = g.p.e. lost
$\Rightarrow 40v^2 = 5488 \Rightarrow v = 11.7\,\text{m s}^{-1}$ (to 3 s.f.)

  (b) 9.97 m s^{-1} (to 3 s.f.)

7 (a) e.p.e. gained $= \frac{400x^2}{2 \times 2} = 100x^2$
g.p.e lost $= 10 \times 9.8 \times (2 + x) = 196 + 98x$
k.e. gained = 0
Energy is conserved,
so e.p.e gained = g.p.e. lost, giving
$100x^2 = 196 + 98x \Rightarrow 50x^2 - 49x - 98 = 0$

  (b) 1.97 m (to 3 s.f.)

  (c) (i)

    (ii) 395 N

    (iii) 29.7 m s^{-2} (to 3 s.f.)

Mixed questions (p 126)

1 1.55 m

2 0.84 J

3 (a) 8 J

  (b) Initial k.e. = 0, e.p.e. = 8
At the wall, e.p.e. = 0, k.e. $= \frac{1}{2} \times 4v^2 = 2v^2$
Energy is conserved
so $2v^2 = 8 \Rightarrow v = 2\,\text{m s}^{-1}$

  (c) (i) When the string is slack, the work done by
friction $= -0.3 \times 4 \times 9.8 \times 0.4 = -4.704$
k.e. $= \frac{1}{2} \times 4v^2 = 2v^2$
Work done = gain in k.e. – loss in e.p.e.
so $-4.704 = 2v^2 - 8$
$\Rightarrow v = 1.28\,\text{m s}^{-1}$ (to 3 s.f.)

    (ii) The block does not hit the wall: it stops
when it has moved 0.680 m from its
starting position, i.e. when it is 0.320 m
from the wall.

4 (a)

  (b) $T_1 \sin\theta = 0.6g$
$\Rightarrow 0.8T_1 = 0.6g$
$\Rightarrow T_1 = 7.35\,\text{N}$

  (c) 0.2λ N   **(d)** 67.95 N

5 (a) $20 \times 9.8 = \frac{\lambda \times (2.7 - 2)}{2}$
$\Rightarrow \lambda = \frac{2 \times 20 \times 9.8}{0.7} = 560$

(b) (i) At maximum length, speed = 0

Gain in k.e. = 0

Loss in g.p.e. = $20 \times 9.8L = 196L$

Gain in e.p.e. = $\dfrac{560 \times (L-2)^2}{2 \times 2} = 140(L-2)^2$

Energy is conserved,

so gain in e.p.e. = loss in g.p.e.

so $140(L-2)^2 = 196L$

$\Rightarrow 140L^2 - 560L + 560 - 196L = 0$

$\Rightarrow 5L^2 - 27L + 20 = 0$

(ii) 4.51 m (to 3 s.f.)

Test yourself (p 127)

1 $40 = \dfrac{\lambda(1.3 - 0.8)}{0.8}$

$\Rightarrow \lambda = \dfrac{40 \times 0.8}{0.5} = 64\,\text{N}$

2 Initially, k.e. = 0, e.p.e. = $\dfrac{40 \times (2.5 - 2)^2}{2 \times 2} = 2.5$

When the string is slack, e.p.e. = 0,

k.e. = $\frac{1}{2} \times 0.8 \times v^2 = 0.4v^2$

Energy is conserved, so $2.5 = 0.4v^2$

$\Rightarrow v = 2.5\,\text{m s}^{-1}$

3 (a) $AB = BC = 13\,\text{m}$,

so extension = $2 \times 13 - 12 = 14$

e.p.e. = $\dfrac{1500 \times 14^2}{2 \times 12} = 12\,250\,\text{J}$

(b) 7.28 m s^{-1} (to 3 s.f.)

(c) 14.7 m (to 3 s.f.)

4 (a) (i) 78.4 J　　　　　**(ii)** 8.85 m s^{-1} (to 3 s.f.)

(b) (i) At maximum extension, speed = 0

k.e. gained = 0

g.p.e. lost = $2 \times 9.8 \times (4 + x) = 78.4 + 19.6x$

e.p.e. gained = $\dfrac{80 \times x^2}{2 \times 4} = 10x^2$

Energy is conserved,

so g.p.e. lost = e.p.e. gained

so $78.4 + 19.6x = 10x^2$

$\Rightarrow 10x^2 - 19.6x - 78.4 = 0$

(ii) 7.95 m

(c) Any of the following: no air resistance, light rope, elastic limit not reached

8 Motion in a vertical circle

Answers are given to three significant figures where appropriate.

A Circular motion with variable speed (p 128)

A1 (a) The conker's weight and the tension in the string

(b) There is a component of acceleration acting towards the centre of the circle resulting from the change in direction of the velocity. There is a component acting along a tangent to the circle resulting from the change in speed.

(c) As the conker moves towards its highest point, its p.e. increases and then it decreases again as it returns to the lowest point.

(d) The k.e. decreases as the conker moves up to the highest point and increases again as it returns to the lowest point. The speed decreases to a minimum at the highest point and increases again to a maximum at the lowest point.

A2 (a) (i) p.e. = $0.1 \times 9.8 \times 0.5 = 0.49\,\text{J}$

(ii) Energy is conserved, so

$0.49 + \frac{1}{2} \times 0.1v_B^2 = 3.2 \Rightarrow v_B = 7.36\,\text{m s}^{-1}$

(b) (i) p.e. = $0.1 \times 9.8 \times 1 = 0.98\,\text{J}$

(ii) Energy is conserved, so

$0.98 + \frac{1}{2} \times 0.1v_C^2 = 3.2 \Rightarrow v_C = 6.66\,\text{m s}^{-1}$

A3 (a) Height of D above $A = 0.5 - 0.5\cos\theta$

p.e. at $D = 0.1 \times 9.8 \times 0.5(1 - \cos\theta)$

$= 0.49(1 - \cos\theta)$

(b) Energy is conserved, so

$0.49(1 - \cos\theta) + \frac{1}{2} \times 0.1v^2 = 3.2$

$\Rightarrow 0.05v^2 = 2.71 + 0.49\cos\theta$

$\Rightarrow v^2 = 54.2 + 9.8\cos\theta$

(c) When the particle is at A, $\theta = 0°$ and $\cos\theta = 1$, its maximum value, hence the speed is maximum.

When the particle is at C, $\theta = 180°$ and $\cos\theta = -1$, its minimum value, hence the speed is minimum.

A4 (a) Acceleration = $\dfrac{v^2}{r} = \dfrac{7.36^2}{0.5} = 108\,\text{m s}^{-2}$ (to 3 s.f.)

(b) $T = ma = 0.1 \times 108 = 10.8\,\text{N}$ (to 3 s.f.)

(c) **(i)** $0.98\,\text{N}$ vertically downwards

    (ii) $9.8\,\text{m s}^{-2}$

A5 **(a)**

$0.1g\,\nabla\nabla T$

(b) $T + 0.98$

(c) $T + 0.98 = \dfrac{0.1 \times 6.66^2}{0.5} \Rightarrow T = 7.89\,\text{N}$

(d) **(i)** $0\,\text{N}$

    (ii) Towards the centre of the circle

A6 **(a)**

$T\,\nwarrow$

$0.1g \sin\theta\,\triangle\!\cdots\!\cdot$ $\,\lhd 0.1g \cos\theta$

$0.1g\,\nabla$

(b) $T - 0.1g\cos\theta = \dfrac{0.1v^2}{0.5}$

$\Rightarrow T - 0.98\cos\theta = 0.2(54.2 + 9.8\cos\theta)$

$\Rightarrow T = 10.84 + 1.96\cos\theta + 0.98\cos\theta$

$\Rightarrow T = 10.84 + 2.94\cos\theta$

(c) The value of $\cos\theta$ varies between 1, when the particle is at A, and -1, when the particle is at C. The tension is maximum when the particle is at A and it reduces as the particle moves round the circle to a minimum at C, and then it increases again.

A7 The normal reaction of the wire on the bead

A8 **(a)** $\frac{1}{2}mu^2 + 2mgr$

(b) $\frac{1}{2}mv_L^2 + mgr$

(c) Energy is conserved, so

$\frac{1}{2}mv_L^2 + mgr = \frac{1}{2}mu^2 + 2mgr$

$\Rightarrow \frac{1}{2}mv_L^2 = \frac{1}{2}mu^2 + mgr$

$\Rightarrow v_L^2 = u^2 + 2gr$

(d) $R\,\lhd\!\!-\!\!\bullet$

∇mg

(e) R, the normal reaction of the wire on the bead

(f) $R = \dfrac{mv_L^2}{r} \Rightarrow R = \dfrac{m(u^2 + 2gr)}{r}$

A9 **(a)** Energy is conserved, so

$\frac{1}{2}mv_M^2 = \frac{1}{2}mu^2 + 2mgr \Rightarrow v_M = \sqrt{u^2 + 4gr}$

(b)

∇mg

(c) $R - mg$

(d) $R - mg = \dfrac{mv_M^2}{r} \Rightarrow R = \dfrac{m(u^2 + 4gr)}{r} + mg$

$\Rightarrow R = \dfrac{mu^2}{r} + 5mg$

A10 The bead is the same height above M at both N and L, so its p.e. is the same at these points. As the total energy of the bead is constant its k.e., and hence its speed, must also be the same.

Exercise A (p 133)

1 $4.05\,\text{m s}^{-1}$

2 $5.95\,\text{m s}^{-1}$

3 **(a)** $6.97\,\text{m s}^{-1}$

(b)

$\nabla 0.2g$

(c) $18.1\,\text{N}$

4 **(a)** $\sqrt{u^2 - 4gr}$

(b)

$mg\,\nabla\nabla R$

(c) $\dfrac{mu^2}{r} - 5mg$

5 **(a)** **(i)** $0°$ **(ii)** $4.79\,\text{m s}^{-1}$ **(iii)** $777\,\text{N}$

(b) **(i)** $3.53\,\text{m s}^{-1}$ **(ii)** $580\,\text{N}$

(c) The boy can be modelled as a particle. The rope is light and inextensible. Air resistance can be ignored.

6 **(a)** Total energy at A = total energy at B

$mgl = \frac{1}{2}mv^2 \Rightarrow v^2 = 2gl$

Apply N2L at B: $T - mg = \dfrac{mv^2}{l}$

$\Rightarrow T = \dfrac{2mgl}{l} + mg = 3mg$

(b) $3mg\cos\theta$

7 **(a)** **(i)** $3.44\,\text{m s}^{-1}$ **(ii)** $7.4\,\text{N}$

(b) **(i)** $4.44\,\text{m s}^{-1}$ **(ii)** $14.75\,\text{N}$

(c) (i) Total energy of the bead at A
$$= \tfrac{1}{2} \times 0.25 \times 2^2 + 0.25 \times 9.8 \times 0.8 = 2.46\,\text{J}$$
Total energy of the bead at D
$$= \tfrac{1}{2} \times 0.25 v^2 + 0.25 \times 9.8 \times 0.4(1 - \cos\theta)$$
$$= 0.125 v^2 + 0.98 - 0.98 \cos\theta$$
The total energy is constant so
$$0.125 v^2 + 0.98 - 0.98 \cos\theta = 2.46$$
$$\Rightarrow v^2 = 11.84 + 7.84 \cos\theta$$

(ii) $7.4 + 7.35 \cos\theta$

8 (a) $3.73\,\text{m s}^{-1}$ (b) $0.327\,\text{N}$

9 (a) $\sqrt{\dfrac{4ga}{3}}$ (b) $\dfrac{mg}{3}$ (c) $\dfrac{19mg}{3}$

B Completing the circle (p 134)

B1 (a) The bead will fall back towards A, and oscillate about A.

(b) The bead will come to rest at the top, and remain there in unstable equilibrium. It would start moving again if displaced.

(c) The bead will move in a complete circle.

B2 (a) (i) Total energy at A = total energy at B
$$\tfrac{1}{2} \times 0.02 \times 6^2 = \tfrac{1}{2} \times 0.02 v^2 + 0.02 \times 9.8 \times 0.8$$
$$\Rightarrow v = 4.51\,\text{m s}^{-1}$$

(ii) The bead will move in a complete circle.

(b) (i) Total energy at A = total energy at B
$$\tfrac{1}{2} \times 0.02 \times 3^2 = \tfrac{1}{2} \times 0.02 v^2 + 0.02 \times 9.8 \times 0.8$$
$$\Rightarrow v^2 = -6.68$$

(ii) v^2 is negative, which cannot happen; this means that the speed of the bead has reduced to zero before it reaches B.

(iii) The bead oscillates about A.

(c) (i) The speed of the bead must be greater than zero at B.

(ii) $\tfrac{1}{2} \times 0.02 u^2 = 0.02 \times 9.8 \times 0.8$
$$\Rightarrow u = 3.96\,\text{m s}^{-1}$$

B3 (a) $\tfrac{1}{2} m u^2$ (b) $\tfrac{1}{2} m v^2 + 2mgr$ (c) $v^2 > 0$

(d) Energy is conserved, so $\tfrac{1}{2} m v^2 + 2mgr = \tfrac{1}{2} m u^2$ but $v^2 > 0$, so $u^2 - 4gr > 0 \Rightarrow u^2 > 4gr$

B4 (a) The speed of the conker reduces from its maximum value at A to its minimum value at C, and then increases again as it returns to A.

(b) The tension is maximum when the conker is at A, and reduces to its minimum at C, and increases again as it returns to A.

(c) If the tension reduces to zero, the string becomes slack and the conker will no longer move in a circle, but will move as a projectile until the string becomes taut again.

(d) If the speed becomes zero before the conker reaches B, the conker will oscillate about A.

B5 (a) (i) Total energy at A = total energy at B
$$\tfrac{1}{2} \times 0.02 \times 7^2 = \tfrac{1}{2} \times 0.02 v^2 + 0.02 \times 9.8 \times 1.2$$
$$\Rightarrow v = 5.05\,\text{m s}^{-1}$$

(ii) $T + 0.02 \times 9.8 = \dfrac{0.02 \times 5.05^2}{0.6}$
$$\Rightarrow T = 0.653\,\text{N}$$

(iii) The conker moves in a complete circle.

(b) (i) Total energy at A = total energy at B
$$\tfrac{1}{2} \times 0.02 \times 5^2 = \tfrac{1}{2} \times 0.02 v^2 + 0.02 \times 9.8 \times 1.2$$
$$\Rightarrow v = 1.22\,\text{m s}^{-1}$$

(ii) $T + 0.02 \times 9.8 = \dfrac{0.02 \times 1.22^2}{0.6}$
$$\Rightarrow T = -0.147\,\text{N}$$
The tension is negative, which means that the tension reached zero before the conker got to B, so it has not actually moved that far around the circle.

(iii) The conker moves in part of a circle until the string becomes slack at which instant it begins to move as a projectile.

B6 (a) $\tfrac{1}{2} m u^2$

(b) $\tfrac{1}{2} m v^2 + 2mgl$

(c) $T \geq 0$

(d) Energy is conserved, so $\tfrac{1}{2} m v^2 + 2mgl = \tfrac{1}{2} m u^2$
$$\Rightarrow v^2 = u^2 - 4gl$$
Apply N2L at B: $T + mg = \dfrac{m(u^2 - 4gl)}{l}$
$$\Rightarrow T = \dfrac{mu^2}{l} - 5mg$$
But $T \geq 0 \Rightarrow \dfrac{mu^2}{l} - 5mg \geq 0$
$$\Rightarrow u^2 \geq 5gl$$

B7 (a) The normal reaction of the cylinder on the marble

(b) The normal reaction at the highest point must be greater than or equal to zero.

(c) If the normal reaction reduces zero before the marble reaches the highest point, the marble will lose contact with the cylinder and move as a projectile. If the speed reduces to zero before the marble reaches the level of the centre of the cylinder, it will oscillate about the lowest point of the cylinder.

B8 (a) $\frac{1}{2} \times 0.2 \times 4^2 = 1.6\,\text{J}$

(b) $\frac{1}{2} \times 0.2 v^2 + 0.2 \times 9.8 \times 0.5(1 + \cos\theta)$
$= 0.1v^2 + 0.98(1 + \cos\theta)$

(c) Energy is conserved,
so $0.1v^2 + 0.98(1 + \cos\theta) = 1.6$
$\Rightarrow v^2 = 6.2 - 9.8\cos\theta$

(d)

(e) $R + 0.2 \times 9.8\cos\theta = \dfrac{0.2v^2}{0.5}$
$\Rightarrow R = 0.4(6.2 - 9.8\cos\theta) - 1.96\cos\theta$
$\Rightarrow R = 2.48 - 5.88\cos\theta$

(f) At B, $\theta = 0$, so $\cos\theta = 1$ leading to $R = -3.4$. R must be greater than 0 at B, so the ball cannot move in a complete circle.

(g) The ball loses contact when $R = 0$.
$2.48 - 5.88\cos\theta = 0 \Rightarrow \theta = 65.1°$

B9 (a) Total energy at A = total energy at X
$\frac{1}{2}mu^2 = \frac{1}{2}mv^2 + mgr(1 - \cos\theta)$
$\Rightarrow v^2 = u^2 - 2gr(1 - \cos\theta)$

(b) If v reaches zero when $\theta \leq 90°$, the ball will stay in contact with the surface of the cylinder and oscillate about O. If $\theta > 90°$, then the ball loses contact with the surface before v reaches zero.

(c) When $v = 0$, $u^2 - 2gr(1 - \cos\theta) = 0$
$\Rightarrow u^2 = 2gr(1 - \cos\theta) \Rightarrow \cos\theta = 1 - \dfrac{u^2}{2gr}$

But if $\theta \leq 90°$, $\cos\theta \geq 0 \Rightarrow 1 - \dfrac{u^2}{2gr} \geq 0$
$\Rightarrow u^2 \leq 2gr$

Exercise B (p 139)

1 (a) The speed at the highest point, $v > 0$

(b) The total energy is constant.
$\frac{1}{2} \times 0.4 \times 6^2 = \frac{1}{2} \times 0.4v^2 + 0.4 \times 9.8 \times 1.2$
$\Rightarrow v^2 = 12.48$
$v > 0$, so the ball moves in a complete circle

2 (a) The normal reaction at A, $R \geq 0$

(b) $6.36\,\text{m s}^{-1}$ **(c)** $11.5\,\text{N}$

3 (a) The total energy is constant.
$\frac{1}{2} \times 0.2 \times 4^2 = \frac{1}{2} \times 0.2v^2 + 0.2 \times 9.8 \times 1$
$\Rightarrow v^2 = -3.6$, which is impossible so the bead doesn't reach the highest point and doesn't move in a complete circle.

(b) Total energy at A = total energy at B
$1.6 = 0.2 \times 9.8 \times 0.5(1 + \cos\theta)$
$\Rightarrow \cos\theta = 0.6326...$
$\Rightarrow \theta = 51°$ to the nearest degree

4 (a) (i) $1815\,\text{N}$ **(ii)** $1320\,\text{N}$

(b) $14\,\text{m s}^{-1}$

5 (a) $3.13\,\text{m s}^{-1}$

(b) (i) $63.6°$ **(ii)** $1.14\,\text{m s}^{-1}$

6 Let the speed of the particle when the string makes an angle θ with the vertical be v.
The total energy is constant.
$\frac{1}{2} \times 0.5u^2 = \frac{1}{2} \times 0.5v^2 + 0.5 \times 9.8 \times 2(1 - \cos\theta)$
$\Rightarrow u^2 = v^2 + 39.2(1 - \cos\theta)$
When $v = 0$, $u^2 = 39.2(1 - \cos\theta)$
$\Rightarrow \cos\theta = 1 - \dfrac{u^2}{39.2}$
The particle oscillates if $v = 0$ when $\theta \leq 90°$.
$\Rightarrow 1 - \dfrac{u^2}{39.2} \geq 0 \Rightarrow u^2 \leq 39.2$

7 (a) $1.72\,\text{m s}^{-1}$ **(b)** $0.0192\,\text{N}$ **(c)** $43°$

8 (a) When the string becomes slack, $T = 0$,
so resultant force towards centre $= mg\sin 30°$
$= \dfrac{mg}{2}$
Apply N2L: $\dfrac{mg}{2} = \dfrac{mv^2}{l}$
$\Rightarrow v^2 = \dfrac{gl}{2} \Rightarrow v = \sqrt{\dfrac{gl}{2}}$

(b) $\sqrt{\dfrac{3gl}{2}}$

9 (a) Total energy is constant.
$\frac{1}{2}mu^2 = \frac{1}{2}mv^2 + mgl(1 - \cos\theta)$
$\Rightarrow v^2 = u^2 - 2gl(1 - \cos\theta)$

(b) Apply N2L: $T - mg\cos\theta = \dfrac{mv^2}{l}$
$\Rightarrow T = \dfrac{m}{l}(u^2 - 2gl(1 - \cos\theta)) + mg\cos\theta$
$\Rightarrow T = mg(3\cos\theta - 2) + \dfrac{mu^2}{l}$

(c) When $\theta = 180°$, $T = -5mg + \dfrac{mu^2}{l}$

The particle makes complete revolutions if $T \geq 0$ at this point.

$\Rightarrow -5mg + \dfrac{mu^2}{l} \geq 0 \Rightarrow u^2 \geq 5gl$

10 (a) Total energy at B = total energy at A

$\frac{1}{2}mv^2 - mgr(1 - \cos\theta) = 0$

$\Rightarrow v^2 = 2gr(1 - \cos\theta)$

Apply N2L at B: $mg\cos\theta - R = \dfrac{mv^2}{r}$

$\Rightarrow R = mg\cos\theta - \dfrac{mv^2}{r}$

$\Rightarrow R = mg\cos\theta - 2mg(1 - \cos\theta)$

$\Rightarrow R = mg(3\cos\theta - 2)$

(b) The ball loses contact when $R = 0$.

$mg(3\cos\theta - 2) = 0 \Rightarrow \cos\theta = \frac{2}{3}$

Vertical distance travelled = $r(1 - \cos\theta) = \dfrac{r}{3}$

Mixed questions (p 143)

1 (a) $u^2 = 2gr$

(b) (i) Total energy at P = total energy at B

$\frac{1}{2}mv^2 - mgr\sin\theta = \frac{1}{2}mu^2$

$\Rightarrow \frac{1}{2}v^2 - gr\sin\theta = \frac{1}{2} \times 2gr$

$\Rightarrow v^2 = 2gr(1 + \sin\theta)$

(ii)

(iii) $R = mg(2 + 3\sin\theta)$

(c) At C, $\theta = 90° \Rightarrow R = 5mg$.

When Steve is moving along CD, the motion is no longer circular, so $R = mg$.

The magnitude of the normal reaction has reduced by $4mg$.

(d) $\dfrac{g}{2}$

2 (a) (i) Gain in k.e. at S = loss in p.e. at S

$\frac{1}{2} \times 70v^2 = 70 \times 9.8 \times 5\cos 30°$

$\Rightarrow v = 9.21\,\mathrm{m\,s^{-1}}$

(ii) $1780\,\mathrm{N}$

(b) The man now moves as a projectile, so consider the vertical component of his motion.

Vertically, $u = 9.21\sin 30°$, $v = 0$,

$a = -9.8$, $s = d$

$v^2 = u^2 + 2as$: $0 = (9.21\sin 30°)^2 - 2 \times 9.8d$

$\Rightarrow d = 1.08$

He rises approximately 1 m.

(c) The height of the man is large compared with the length of the rope and the distances travelled. Air resistance would reduce the speed. Hence modelling him as a particle may produce significant errors.

3 (a) Apply N2L at C: $mg + R = \dfrac{mv^2}{r}$

But car only just stays in contact, so $R = 0$.

Hence $mg = \dfrac{mv^2}{r} \Rightarrow v^2 = rg$

(b) $u^2 = 5rg$

(c) Total energy at A = total energy at B

$mgh = \frac{1}{2}mu^2 \Rightarrow gh = \dfrac{5rg}{2} \Rightarrow h = \dfrac{5r}{2}$

(d) Consider friction.

4 (a) $\sqrt{10ga}$

(b) (i) Total energy at C = total energy at Q

$\frac{1}{2}m \times 10ga = \frac{1}{2}mv^2 + 2mgd$

$\Rightarrow v^2 = 10ga - 4gd \Rightarrow v^2 = 2g(5a - 2d)$

(ii) $5mg\left(\dfrac{2a}{d} - 1\right)$

(iii) The ball reaches Q if $T > 0$ at Q.

$\Rightarrow 5mg\left(\dfrac{2a}{d} - 1\right) > 0 \Rightarrow d < 2a$

(c) Any of the following:

air resistance can be ignored;

the ball is modelled as a particle;

there is no energy lost when the string hits P.

Test yourself (p 145)

1 (a) $\sqrt{\dfrac{4gr}{15}}$ **(b)** $\dfrac{79mg}{15}$

2 (a) Energy is conserved so

$\frac{1}{2}mu^2 = \frac{1}{2}mv^2 + mga(1 + \cos\theta)$

$\Rightarrow v^2 = u^2 - 2ga(1 + \cos\theta)$

Apply N2L at P: $R + mg\cos\theta = \dfrac{mv^2}{a}$

$\Rightarrow R = \dfrac{mu^2}{a} - 2mg(1 + \cos\theta) - mg\cos\theta$

$\Rightarrow R = \dfrac{mu^2}{a} - 3mg\cos\theta - 2mg$

(b) If the ball completes the circle, $R \geq 0$ at the top.

$\dfrac{mu^2}{a} - 3mg\cos 0 - 2mg \geq 0$

$\Rightarrow \dfrac{mu^2}{a} \geq 5mg$

$\Rightarrow u \geq \sqrt{5ga}$

3 (a) Maximum speed is at lowest point of arc.
Energy is conserved, so
$\frac{1}{2} \times 35 \times 2^2 + 35 \times 9.8 \times 4(1 - \cos 45°) = \frac{1}{2} \times 35 v^2$
$\Rightarrow v = 5.2 \, \text{m s}^{-1}$ (to 2 s.f.)

(b) 49°

(c) Any of the following:
the girl can be modelled as a particle;
the rope is light and inextensible;
air resistance can be ignored

4 (a) Energy is conserved, so
$\frac{1}{2} m \left(\frac{1}{2} \sqrt{rg} \right)^2 + mgr = \frac{1}{2} mv^2 + mgr \cos \theta$

$\Rightarrow \frac{1}{4} rg + 2rg = v^2 + 2rg \cos \theta$

$\Rightarrow v^2 = \frac{1}{4} rg (9 - 8 \cos \theta)$

(b) (i) $3mg \cos \theta - \dfrac{9mg}{4}$

(ii) When $\cos \theta = \frac{4}{5}$, $R = \dfrac{3mg}{20} > 0$, so it is still in contact.

(iii) $\cos \theta = \frac{3}{4}$

(iv) When $\cos \theta = \frac{3}{4}$, $v^2 = \dfrac{3rg}{4}$

$\Rightarrow v = \frac{1}{2} \sqrt{3rg}$

Index